OCLC Record

Diversity Consciousness

Opening Our Minds to People, Cultures, and Opportunities

SECOND EDITION

Richard D. Bucher

Baltimore City Community College

With contributions from
Patricia L. Bucher

PEARSON
Prentice Hall

Upper Saddle River, New Jersey
Columbus, Ohio

Library of Congress Cataloging-in-Publication Data

Bucher, Richard D.
    Diversity consciousness : opening our minds to people, cultures, and opportunities /
Richard D. Bucher ; with contributions from Patricia L. Bucher.—2nd ed.
        p. cm.
    Includes bibliographical references and index.
    ISBN 0-13-049111-X
    1. Diversity in the workplace. 2. Multiculturalism. I. Bucher, Patricia L. II. Title.
HF5549.5.M5 B83 2004
331.13'3—dc21   2002044390

Vice President and Executive Publisher: Jeffery W. Johnston
Senior Acquisitions Editor: Sande Johnson
Assistant Editor: Cecilia Johnson
Production Editor: Amy Gehl, Carlisle Publishers Services
Design Coordinator: Diane C. Lorenzo
Cover Designer: Jason Moore
Cover Art: Corbis
Production Manager: Pamela D. Bennett
Director of Marketing: Ann Castel Davis
Marketing Manager: Christina Quadhamer

This book was set in Garamond by Carlisle Communications, Ltd. It was printed and bound by
R. R. Donnelley & Sons Company. The cover was printed by Phoenix Color Corp.

Pearson Education Ltd.   Pearson Education Australia Pty. Limited
Pearson Education Singapore Pte. Ltd.   Pearson Education North Asia Ltd.
Pearson Education Canada, Ltd.   Pearson Educación de Mexico, S.A. de C.V.
Pearson Education—Japan   Pearson Education Malaysia Pte. Ltd.

10 9 8 7 6 5 4 3 2 1
ISBN: 0-13-049111-X

Foreword

By the year 2050, almost 50 percent of the population will be minorities and 50 percent will be women. These U.S. Bureau of Labor Statistics paint a very clear and convincing picture of why diversity must be viewed for what it truly is: a core corporate strategic initiative that directly affects the bottom line, not the latest human resources initiative or fad.

In order to compete in today's highly competitive labor market for skilled, creative, dedicated employees, leaders must achieve a diverse workforce at all levels of their organization. They must also create a corporate culture that will effectively utilize and retain the diverse talents they bring into their organizations.

At Fannie Mae, we made a serious long-term commitment to "look like America." We have discovered that when you broaden your employee base, then utilize that expanded pool of talent, experience, and insight, you let loose in your business a tremendous force for the creation of innovation and change. Our experience is that this leads to competitive advantages. In essence, diversity becomes a powerful tool you can use to create a positive impact on your markets and better capitalize on business opportunities. We know that our unwavering commitment to diversity is one of the key elements that has made it possible for Fannie Mae to achieve 12 consecutive years of double-digit earnings.

The cornerstone of any successful diversity initiative must establish and create a core culture and environment in which:

- employees are treated fairly
- employees are recognized and rewarded based on ability and merit for their contributions
- employees have equal access to opportunity for growth and advancement
- employees respect each other and are free from harassment, discrimination, and intolerance
- the diversity of American society is represented at all levels throughout the company
- the management and development of employees is viewed as crucial to the success of the business

On an individual level, developing a high level of diversity consciousness is an absolutely essential part of a student's preparation for entering the workplace. Students who hone these skills will find they have a distinct advantage when they look for jobs or seek advancement.

The single most essential element necessary to creating an environment in which diversity will thrive is the unwavering commitment and active, visible involvement of senior management, starting from the very top of the organization. Like any successful corporate initiative that affects the profitability and survival of an organization, diversity must be interwoven into every aspect of the organization. Results cannot be achieved overnight. There is no quick fix or panacea. It is hard work that pays big dividends.

The way America will be able to excel in the increasingly competitive world market of the twenty-first century is to utilize the incredible wealth of untapped, diverse talent in this country. Those companies that maximize their utilization of our greatest natural resource will be the ones who emerge as the global leaders of the next millennium. Diversity is an essential fact of life for everyone, every day in America. It is an issue that will never go away.

Richard Bucher's work makes a major contribution to a clearer understanding of how and why diversity is crucial to the basic prosperity and future survival of our country.

Franklin D. Raines
Chairman and CEO, Fannie Mae

Franklin D. Raines is Chairman and Chief Executive Officer of Fannie Mae, a New York Stock Exchange company and the largest non-bank financial services company in the world. Fannie Mae is the nation's largest source of financing for home mortgages. He became Chairman and Chief Executive Officer on January 1, 1999. He is the first African-American to head a Fortune 500 firm.

Under Raines' leadership, Fannie Mae was recently honored by *Fortune* magazine as one of the 50 best companies for Blacks, Asians, and Hispanics. *Working Mother's* magazine included Fannie Mae in their "Top Ten List" of family-friendly firms.

Raines serves as a member of the congressionally mandated Commission on Roles and Missions of the Armed Forces. He has also served on a number of federal and state public policy advisory groups regarding tax equity, education, poverty, and welfare reform.

Raines was elected a Fellow of the American Academy of Social Insurance, and the Council on Foreign Relations.

Raines graduated magna cum laude with a B.A. degree from Harvard College. He graduated cum laude with a J.D. from Harvard Law School. He also attended Magdalen College, Oxford University as a Rhodes Scholar.

Preface

Not long ago, I happened to pick up a magazine that featured this advertisement: "Life without technology isn't an option." As we begin the twenty-first century, it is becoming increasingly apparent that life without diversity is not an option either. Our personal worlds are expanding as people and cultures throughout the world become more and more interconnected. Human diversity, in its many shapes, forms, and colors, is an integral part of our everyday life. As a result, each of us desperately needs to develop our *diversity consciousness:* our awareness, understanding, and skills in the area of diversity.

Diversity consciousness is important for a number of reasons. It allows us to appreciate and enjoy the infinite variety of people and lifestyles that are part of our expanding social world. More specifically, we will increase our knowledge and stretch our thinking. By learning to interpret events through different cultural lenses, we will be able to think critically and adapt to a large variety of situations. Because of our ability to communicate and team with different kinds of people, we will be more successful at work, school, and in other realms of life.

This book is an outgrowth of my personal and professional experiences during the past 35 years. From the beginning, I have wrestled with the subject of diversity intellectually and emotionally. I attended Howard University, a historically black institution, to pursue my studies in the area of race and ethnic relations and earn my doctorate degree. As a white male, this experience radically altered my thinking about diversity. My experiences as a college professor have also been invaluable. For the past 28 years, I have taught students from a rich variety of cultures and backgrounds at Baltimore City Community College (BCCC). More than anything, this experience has taught me the importance of listening carefully to my students and appreciating their diversity. It has also made me look inward, into my own thoughts, feelings, and behavior. In addition to my teaching, I served as the first Director of BCCC's Institute for InterCultural Understanding (IIU). Nationally recognized for its work in diversity education, the IIU nourishes an inclusive, international learning community of students, faculty, staff, and community members. On a more personal level, my work with the IIU makes me more aware of the difficulty and importance of making students as well as educators more conscious of diversity and its central place in a high-quality education.

Another extremely important dimension of my own diversity is my family life. I am the father of a son who has a disability called autism. My son, as well as the rest of my family, provides me with daily reminders of the joys and challenges of diversity.

Jimmy has enriched our lives and brought our family closer together. Because of Jimmy, my family and I see and experience life differently. My daughter Katie, who is a recent college graduate, was asked to write about someone who has had a profound influence on her life. She wrote about Jimmy. "Growing up with my autistic brother, I have discovered more and more about myself and other people. He has shown me that not everything wonderful seems wonderful at first sight. When you have someone so different that is so close to you, you develop an uncommon compassion for others."

The aim of this book is two-dimensional. First, it examines the relationship between a person's success and his or her ability to understand, respect, and value diversity. Success, as defined in this book, means to achieve your goals. A second aim is to explore how people can develop diversity consciousness. Subjects such as teamwork, conflict management, communication, and flexible thinking are discussed in a style that promotes self-reflection and dialogue. A wide variety of real-life student experiences and perspectives appear throughout.

Diversity Consciousness introduces a perspective that is largely absent in college courses. Many of these courses avoid diversity issues or treat them as an afterthought. For example, it is a common assumption that students share the same perspectives and life experiences. Some instructors assume that students will learn about diversity "on the side" or "on their own." Unfortunately, students may interpret this to mean that diversity is not central to their education or their success. This interpretation is not borne out by numerous studies in the fields of education and business. These studies, cited throughout the book, reveal that a wide range of diversity skills, such as teaming, communication, and conflict resolution, are directly related to success in college and beyond.

Throughout the book, I have used different terminology to refer to certain groups of people. For instance, I use the term Black as well as African-American, and Latino as well as Hispanic. Using a variety of terms is one way of acknowledging that we do not all agree regarding the labels we attach to human differences.

Diversity Consciousness: Opening Our Minds to People, Cultures, and Opportunities possesses five key features that make it relevant and meaningful to students. This book is:

1. *Student-Oriented.* It is infused with genuine anecdotes and perspectives from a very diverse population of students. Too often, educators do not really listen to students when we teach and write. We do not actively collaborate with students in the process of learning and sharing. This book provides a sounding board for a large number of college students from a wide variety of educational, social, and ethnic backgrounds. One distinguishing feature is the integration of real-life "student perspectives" throughout each chapter. They provide a wealth of insight that we need to digest and share. As you read this book, you will recognize everyday struggles, stories, and achievements.

2. *Success-Oriented.* More and more employers are realizing that diversity awareness and skills are crucial because they result in greater teamwork, creativity, productivity, and profit. Students who have a solid grounding in the area of di-

versity have more to offer their employers. Research shows that diversity is not some feel-good issue. Only now are we beginning to realize that education in the area of diversity relates strongly to success.

3. *Focused on Personal Growth and Empowerment.* The book emphasizes the importance of educating oneself in the area of diversity. The process begins with one's own background and culture and then extends to others. In addition, the book views diversity education as an ongoing process rather than an event—a process that requires self-reflection and evaluation, patience, and commitment. Although education of this nature is hard work, it pays off regardless of who you are or where you come from.

4. *Grounded in Research.* A growing number of studies have examined the impact of education or training in the area of diversity. For example, research indicates that college students who are exposed to diversity issues are more apt to be culturally sensitive and satisfied with college life. Similarly, a number of companies report that diversity education programs are making a measurable difference in worker creativity and productivity. These kinds of studies are important because they move us beyond anecdotal evidence. Research can help us evaluate the impact of educational strategies and plan for the future.

5. *Oriented Toward the Value of Diversity.* Throughout our lives, we have been taught that diversity is a problem rather than a valuable resource. Traditionally, the focus has been on minimizing or denying differences rather than rethinking how we approach differences. To be successful we need to develop a new kind of thinking that enables us to appreciate diversity and use it to benefit ourselves and others.

The second edition of *Diversity Consciousness* has been revised extensively. New features include:

Case Studies. "Running" case studies appear at the end of each chapter. Three individuals are followed throughout the book. After reading about their personal experiences dealing with complex issues and situations involving diversity, you are asked to assess each specific case study.

Diversity Links. A number of excellent Web sites are listed, including an Internet address and a short description of the information available.

Instructor's Manual. This manual provides teachers with concrete suggestions related to pedagogy. Included are possible test questions, teaching resources, and guidance regarding subjects such as difficult dialogues and classroom climate.

In addition, there is a new section on diversity education in the workplace. Numerous issues, such as globalization, the Internet, and U.S. population trends and their implications, are discussed in more detail.

Throughout each chapter, an abundance of information has been updated. Numerous new research studies and relevant information from Census 2000 are cited. The events of September 11, 2001, have been integrated into a number of chapters. A variety of issues that relate to the social ramifications of the terrorist attacks—such as religious identity, harassment and profiling, cross-cultural communication, and globalization—are addressed in this new edition.

As you read the book, remember that it is designed to help you do more than just learn about diversity. Regardless of your feelings about diversity, try to approach the book with an open mind. Rather than simply taking in what you read, get involved and stretch yourself intellectually and emotionally. One way to do this is to respond to journal questions. Whenever you see ✎ or any time you feel a need to record something in writing, place an entry in your journal. Writing in a journal reinforces your learning, provides you with a record of your thoughts, and provides a basis for further reflection.

Try to open your thinking to different points of view. Take time to reflect on what you read and how it relates to you. Imagine how the world might be viewed by people who do not look, think, and act like you. Wrestle with the subject matter. If what you read makes you feel uncomfortable, that is OK. It is an inevitable part of the learning process. Finally, share your thoughts and feelings *and* learn to listen carefully and respectfully to others—even when it is difficult.

I welcome feedback from students, faculty, employees and employers, or anyone else who might read this book. You may e-mail your comments to me at rdbucher@aol.com; or write me at Baltimore City Community College, 2901 Liberty Heights Avenue, Baltimore, MD 21215. Furthermore, you may access my Web site at diversityconsciousness.com.

ABOUT THE STUDENT EDITORS

Lisa Richards is a native of Trinidad and Tobago, where she resided for 25 years before emigrating to the United States. She is a graduate of Baltimore City Community College (BCCC). At BCCC, she was president of the International Students' Club as well as president of the Student Governance Board. Lisa is currently enrolled at the University of Maryland Baltimore County (UMBC), where she is studying political science with a minor in International Relations. Lisa says, "I am most passionate about equality, social justice, and bridging the gap that exists among us as individuals, communities, and nations. This is an area in which I see myself being most effective in the future, because from my perspective it is not simply a profession, but a divine destiny. It is a cause to which I foresee devoting my entire life." Upon completion of her B.A. degree in Political Science, Lisa plans to enroll in a joint degree program in law and diplomacy or international affairs. Her goal is to become a U.S. diplomat.

Lauren Storms recently graduated magna cum laude from James Madison University (JMU) with a bachelor's degree in Social Work. She completed an undergraduate honor thesis at JMU entitled "An Invisible Population: Fairfax County Homeless Families." In the course of this study, she examined barriers that homeless families in Fairfax County, Virginia, encounter in accessing services. Lauren is currently working toward her master's degree in Social Work at Virginia Commonwealth University (VCU). Lauren's past experiences include work with the mentally ill, the mentally retarded, homeless families, pregnant teenagers, the elderly, health clinics, and schools. To quote Lauren, "The social work profession gives me an opportunity to work with individuals whom I never would have worked with or met otherwise. I truly believe that even a very small improvement to a person's life, such as making them smile or helping them learn a skill, leaves a lasting effect; it is important in some way in the entire scheme of things."

Patrick Henderson is currently a student at Baltimore City Community College (BCCC). Among his many activities at BCCC are serving as student representative to the Board of Trustees and president of the Student Governance Board. He is a member of Phi Theta Kappa International Honor Society. Returning to school at age 51, he says, was a little scary. Prior to attending BCCC, Patrick pursued his love of music, which he describes as the common language for all people. Besides being nominated for four Grammy Awards, he has earned a number of gold and platinum records. He has written music for the Doobie Brothers, Michael Bolton, and Aretha Franklin; played piano with the Edwin Hawkins Singers for the pope; and has gone on world tours with Leon Russell and Nils Lofgren. According to Patrick, he is driven by the belief that "those of us who have gained much are required to pass it on, so that others might know they can reach their dreams and ambitions; they have only to believe, work hard, and stay focused."

ABOUT THE CONTRIBUTOR

Patricia L. Bucher is a graduate of Skidmore College and received her master's degree in Mathematics Education at Western Maryland College. She has over 60 additional hours of graduate work in the areas of learning differences and behavior management. She currently works for Montgomery County Public Schools (MCPS) as a teacher, curriculum writer, and trainer. The student population of MCPS, located in suburban Washington, D.C., is one of the most racially and ethnically diverse in the nation. MCPS serves approximately 137,000 students who speak over 120 different languages.

Pat is an experienced, highly innovative educator. She regularly presents workshops on *Teaching Mathematics to Diverse Learners*. She has also received local and national recognition for her teaching excellence.

After graduating from Skidmore, Pat had a brief career as a music teacher, which included teaching children with severe emotional and behavioral problems. She soon found out that those years would prove invaluable to her after giving birth to her first child, Jimmy, who has autism and mild cerebral palsy. The next 14 years she spent at home teaching her own son whom many labeled as unteachable. Jimmy can now read a newspaper, watch over his finances, and hold a job. Pat says, "Those years of trying to reach and teach my son taught me more about flexible thinking and creative pedagogy than any other experience of my life."

During that time she also became a passionate advocate for children with developmental disabilities. She created a camp in Carroll County, Maryland, where none existed for children like her son, started a parent support group, and lobbied locally as well as nationally for better educational opportunities for children with disabilities. She was the recipient of the "Carnation Volunteer of the Year for Central Maryland."

▣ IN APPRECIATION

This book has been a true team effort, from its inception to the final product. I am indebted to so many people.

First, I want to thank all the students from many different colleges and universities who have taught me so much and are such a big part of this book. In particular, I would like to acknowledge the valuable contributions of students I have taught at Baltimore City Community College (BCCC) for the past 28 years. I would be remiss if I did not mention my three wonderful student editors, Lisa Richards of the University of Maryland Baltimore County (UMBC), Lauren Storms of Virginia Commonwealth University (VCU), and Patrick Henderson of Baltimore City Community College (BCCC).

In addition, the help of my colleagues has been invaluable. These people include numerous colleagues at BCCC. Particularly, I am indebted to former Board of Trustees member Sara Taylor, as well as a number of faculty and staff: Walter Dean, Karen McClaskey, Schuzan Yang, Sukuntella Dhanesar, Meintje Westerbeek, and Betsy Mackey.

My job has been made that much easier by an extremely strong, supportive team at Prentice Hall. While I cannot name everyone, there are a number of people to whom I am deeply indebted. They are Sande Johnson, Acquisitions Editor; Cecilia Johnson, Assistant Editor; and Amy Gehl, production coordinator at Carlisle Publishers Services. Each member of this team has given me the encouragement and guidance I needed, but also the freedom to explore and create. For that, I am extremely appreciative.

As a writer, I have had the luxury of working with a very diverse and knowledgeable group of reviewers. They have put in countless hours and their input has been invaluable. The reviewers include

Ted Atkinson
Eastern Oregon University

Elizabeth L. Harris
University of Houston-Downtown

G. Maxine Beatty
Thomas Nelson Community College

Bahaudin Mujtaba
University of Phoenix—Tampa Campus

Glenda A. Belote
Florida International University

T. Y. Okosun
Northeastern Illinois University

Charles R. Frederick
Indiana University-Bloomington

Laura Riolli-Saltzman
California State University, Sacramento

Jean Gordon
St. Thomas University

John A. Rushing
Barry University

A number of other people have also made significant contributions. Regina Bryan, an accomplished photographer, provided advice and contributed one of her photographs. Kathy Calderazzi, a lawyer based in Virginia, has shared her expertise regarding a number of questions dealing with diversity and its relation to conflict resolution and the law. Additionally, I have corresponded with a large number of educators and businesspersons throughout the country. Their insight was extremely helpful, and in some cases their comments appear in the book.

I would like to express my deep gratitude to members of my family. Every day they teach me something new and different about diversity. My son, Jimmy, and my daughters, Katie and Suzy, help me laugh at myself and keep my priorities in order. My mother, who is living in the San Diego area, and my late father, a teacher as well as a prolific writer, provided me with my first lessons in valuing diversity.

Finally, my wife, Pat, has been the person who has supported me the most. While writing this book I have continually asked questions of her. Somehow she always found the time to help, whether it was providing another perspective, helping me with a computer question, or pushing me to probe deeper. Without Pat's help, this book would never have been written.

Richard D. Bucher

To my mother and my father

Contents

CHAPTER **3**

Personal and Social Barriers to Success   69

CHAPTER **4**

Developing Diversity Consciousness   109

CHAPTER **5**

Communicating in a Diverse World   144

CHAPTER **6**

Teamwork   179

CHAPTER **7**

Conclusion   216

Note: Every effort has been made to provide accurate and current Internet information in this book. However, the Internet and information posted on it are constantly changing, so it is inevitable that some of the Internet addresses listed in this textbook will change.

Diversity: An Overview

Chapter Objectives

Upon completion of this chapter, you will be able to:

- Define diversity.
- Explain what is meant by our *changing cultural landscape*.
- Describe and give examples of demographic, social, and cultural changes that are responsible for the growing importance of diversity.
- Contrast assimilation and pluralism and give an example of each.
- List and explain three dimensions of diversity.
- List and explain five diversity myths.
- Define diversity consciousness.
- Define diversity education.

> Many cultures contribute to the richness of our world community. Just as every culture has time honored traditions that make its heritage unique, each of us has individual qualities and characteristics that make us special. Let us learn more of one another . . . in knowledge there is understanding; in understanding there is respect; and where there is respect, growth is possible.[1]

Diversity is defined in the dictionary as "a state of unlikeness" or "the condition of being different." Diversity can be viewed and defined in many different ways. In this book, **diversity** refers to *all* of the ways in which people are different. This includes individual, group, and cultural differences.

Today, diversity is getting a great deal of attention. We don't have to look far to see why. Imagine a group of employees at work or a class of students at college. Then imagine how that same group might have looked, thought, and acted differently two or three decades ago. Now picture how this same group might change by the year 2050.

▣ OUR CHANGING CULTURAL LANDSCAPE

Traditionally, the concept of diversity is most often used in relation to culture. **Culture** refers to our way of life, including everything that is learned, shared, and transmitted from one generation to the next. Language, values, rules, beliefs, and even the material things we create are all part of one's culture. *Landscape* means a scene or a setting. When we talk about **cultural landscape,** we are referring to the different lifestyles, traditions, and perspectives that can be found in the United States and throughout the world. Our cultural landscape is changing constantly.

Demographic Changes in the United States

Diversity is not a new phenomenon. If we look back at the first U.S. Census in 1790, we see some interesting differences and similarities with today's society (see Fig. 1.1). The first U.S. Census revealed our rural character. Only 3 percent of the population lived in settlements of 8,000 or more.[2] In 1790, almost one of five residents (about 19 percent) was African-American. It is interesting to note the cultural diversity among Whites at that time. About 75 percent of the White population were white Anglo-Saxon Protestant (English, Scots, Scots-Irish); 25 percent were mainly Dutch, French, German, Irish, and Swedish.[3] These statistics show that early inhabitants of this country were not monocultural. In other words, they were not all culturally alike.

Since 1790, the cultural landscape of the United States has continued to change. We are no longer a rural society. Approximately 75 percent of our population lives in

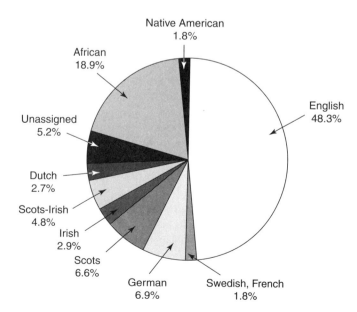

FIGURE 1.1 Total U.S. population distribution in 1790. *(From the U.S. Bureau of the Census,* Historical Statistics of the United States, *Part II, Series Z 20-132, U.S. Government Printing Office, 1976.)*

Native American 1.8%
African 18.9%
Unassigned 5.2%
Dutch 2.7%
Scots-Irish 4.8%
Irish 2.9%
Scots 6.6%
German 6.9%
Swedish, French 1.8%
English 48.3%

TABLE **1.1**   Population by Race and Hispanic Origin for the United States: 2000

Race and Hispanic or Latino	Number	Percent of Total Population
RACE		
Total population	**281,421,906**	**100.0**
One race	274,595,678	97.6
White	211,460,626	75.1
Black or African-American	34,658,190	12.3
American Indian and Alaska Native	2,475,956	0.9
Asian	10,242,998	3.6
Native Hawaiian and Other Pacific Islander	398,835	0.1
Some other race	15,359,073	5.5
Two or more races	6,826,228	2.4
HISPANIC OR LATINO		
Total population	**281,421,906**	**100.0**
Hispanic or Latino	35,305,818	12.5
Not Hispanic or Latino	246,116,088	87.5

Source: U.S. Census Bureau, Census 2000 Redistricting (Public Law 94-171) Summary File, Tables PL1 and PL2.

urban areas.[4] Our racial and ethnic mix has a different look as well (see Table 1.1). The percentage of African-Americans has declined from approximately 19 percent in 1790 to slightly more than 12 percent today. Asians and Pacific Islanders have steadily increased in numbers, since they were first counted in the 1860 Census. Census 2000 data show that Asians and Pacific Islanders as well as Hispanics are the two fastest-growing minority populations in the United States. During the 1990s, the size of these populations surged. Although data for Census 1990 and Census 2000 are not directly comparable because the question on race was modified, it is clear that the rapid growth in these populations is being fueled by immigration. The impact of immigration, according to essayist Richard Rodriguez, can be seen in the number of people who come to this country speaking a language other than English. For example, he observes, "Because of the massive migration of Latin Americans northward, the United States has become the fifth-largest Spanish-speaking country in the world, after Mexico, Spain, Argentina, and Colombia."[5] In comparison to Asians and Hispanics, the growth rate among Whites was significantly less during the 1990s. This continues a trend. Whites, who made up approximately 90 percent of the U.S. population in 1940, now constitute roughly 75 percent. Based on Census estimates for the year 2050, shown in Chapter 7, the percentage of Whites who are not Hispanic (Hispanics can be of any race) will shrink noticeably to just over 50 percent.

Census data must be interpreted cautiously. Different groupings have been used since the first Census. In 1870, for instance, the terms *quadroon* (one-fourth Black, or having one black grandparent) and *octoroon* (one-eighth Black, or having one black great-grandparent) were used to indicate the exact amount of a person's black heritage.

In recent years, racial categories have been added and an increasing number of people have chosen to identify themselves as "other." Many people do not feel that they belong in a single category, and others do not want to be categorized at all. One student, who refuses to select any category, explains, "I'm not White, I'm not Black, and I sure don't want to be an *other*."

A number of authors have written autobiographical accounts describing experiences in which they cope and adjust to fitting no single racial category. Examples include *Life on the Color Line: The True Story of a White Boy Who Discovered He Was Black* by Gregory Howard Williams (1995), *Notes of a White Black Woman* by Judy Scales-Trent (2001), *The Color of Water: A Black Man's Tribute to His White Mother* by James McBride (1996), *Caucasia* by Danny Senna (1999), *Divided to the Vein: A Journey Into Family and Race* by Scott Minerbook (1996), and *Black, White, and Jewish: Autobiography of a Shifting Self* by Rebecca Walker (2002). In *What Are You? Voices of Mixed-Race Young People* (1999), Pearl Fuyo Gaskins shares poetry, essays, and portions of interviews of some 45 mixed-race youth. She organizes her chapters around a variety of themes such as "The Color of My Skin Is Not the Color of My Heart," "Roots: Random Thoughts on Random Hair," and "Are You Dating Me or My Hair?" (see Suggested Readings).

Don't Box Me In

An increasing number of people are resisting the pressure to be boxed in by color. Tiger Woods, for example, has made it known that he objects to being called African-American. Rather he prefers "Cablinasian" a term he made up that combines his Caucasian, Black, Indian, and Asian ancestry. Other well-known people who have affirmed their mixed ancestry are Keanu Reeves (Hawaiian, Chinese, Caucasian), Mariah Carey (Black, Venezuelan, Caucasian), and Johnny Depp (Cherokee, Caucasian). Groups such as Wesleyan University's Interracial Students Organization are becoming more common on college campuses. This trend will probably continue as interracial marriages become more common and society becomes more comfortable with different and new ways of defining one's heritage.

The racial options of the 2000 Census were modified to accommodate those who want to express their multiracial heritage (see Fig. 1.2). For the first time, respondents could identify themselves as members of more than one racial category. Other major changes were:

- A separate question about ethnicity appears before race. Respondents are now given the choice of Hispanic or Latino rather than just Hispanic. This change is based on research showing that Latino is a more popular term in the western United States.
- Black now reads "Black, African-American, or Negro."

FIGURE 1.2 Racial options of the 2000 Census.

- The American Indian and Alaska Native categories are combined. In 1990, there were separate categories for American Indian, Eskimo, and Aleut.
- The 1990 category "Asian or Pacific Islander" is now split into Asian and Native Hawaiian and other Pacific Islander.

Detailed information concerning the new racial categories is available on the U.S. Census Bureau Web site (http://www.census.gov).

Nearly 7 million Americans, or about 2.4 percent, identified themselves as members of more than one race in the 2000 U.S. Census. Many demographers expect this figure to increase dramatically by 2050. Evidence for this can be found in the responses of young people. Among those younger than 18, 4.2 percent were multiracial. According to U.S. Census officials, the major reason for this response is the significant increase in the number of interracial couples.[6]

Latinos, who can be of any race, often find it difficult to relate to rigid racial categories. In the 2000 Census, more than 40 percent of Latinos rejected the racial categories listed and selected "other race."[7] Clara Rodríguez, author of *Changing Race: Latinos, the Census, and the History of Ethnicity in the United States*, points out that analysts often misinterpret what this means. Analysts mistakenly assume Latinos are confused, says the author, when in fact they see themselves as stretching across racial lines.

I was born in 1959 and I was "Black." I did not challenge forms when I was younger, because I did not realize then how important the information those forms requested would become to me. If the form asked me to check "Negro," I did. I don't remember there being racial categories other than Black/Negro or White.

As I grew older and learned through family conversation that there was another culture that was part of me, I began a hesitant journey of uncovering who I am as a complete person. This began with acknowledgment that my Native American heritage is as important to me as being Black. My first acknowledgment of my racial completeness was to check "other." Checking "other" was one of the most difficult things I have ever done. With that act came extreme guilt at the thought of abandoning my given culture and race.

I soon discovered that the guilt came from a sense of having banished myself to neutrality. "Other" meant recognizing no race at all. I went back to checking "Black," which once again made me comfortable but incomplete. I have now settled on checking both "Native American" and "Black."

—Another perspective

THINKING THROUGH DIVERSITY

Would you describe yourself as multiracial, or do you see yourself as belonging to a single race? Why?

It is clear that our nation's schools and workforce will feel the effects of growing diversity for some time. Demographic data indicate that

- Women, minorities, and people with disabilities will continue to account for the vast majority of new entries in the workforce. As more women are added to the labor force, their share will approach that of men. Employment projections for 2008 show that women will make up approximately 48 percent of the U.S. labor force.[8] According to the Bureau of Labor Statistics, women and minorities will represent roughly 70 percent of new entrants in the workforce by 2008.[9] Finally, the percentage of workers with disabilities is expected to increase due to a number of factors. The workplace is becoming more accessible due to the removal of both attitudinal and physical barriers and the protection of the Americans with Disabilities Act. New figures from the 2000 Census point to continued growth in the number of people with disabilities.
- Students at all levels of education will continue to grow increasingly diverse. One indication of this trend is the recent change in the percentage of K–12 pub-

lic school students who are members of racial and ethnic minorities. The percentage has climbed steadily, from approximately 30 percent in 1986 to 38 percent in 2000.[10] Likewise, the number of ESL (English as a Second Language) students has increased dramatically over this same period.[11] Census projections indicate that these are long-term trends. Data from the U.S. Department of Education reveals a similar pattern among college students, who have become increasingly diversified in terms of their race, ethnicity, gender, and age.[12]

- The international student population in the United States is growing. The Institute of International Education estimates that there are 450,000 international students in the United States.[13] Most of these students come from Asian and Latin American countries.

America's Schoolchildren: A Look at the Future

What if the entire population of elementary and secondary schools in the United States were shrunk into one class of 30 students? What would it look like? According to the National Center for Research on Cultural Diversity and Second Language Learning, 10 of the 30 students would come from racial or ethnic minority groups. Of these 10, six would come from homes in which languages other than English are spoken, and two would be from immigrant families. Of the six students who spoke another language, four would speak Spanish as their native language, one would speak an Asian language, and the other student would speak any one of more than 100 languages. Ten students, one-third of the class, would be poor.[14]

Technological and Social Changes

A number of social and technological changes have also altered the cultural landscape in recent years.

Globalization and Technology

People and cultures throughout the world meet each day. Several forces make this possible, one being the growing interdependence of economies in various countries. Another is the speed and ease of modern transportation. Technological advances have transformed our social world into what Marshall McLuhan termed a *global village*.[15] In other words, increasingly we need to think of the entire world when we talk about our social environment. Computers, satellites, and communication technology have brought the world closer together and made cross-cultural encounters an everyday occurrence.

The emergence of the global economy, a recent surge in immigration, and the growing diversity of the U.S. population are transforming the business arena. For example, U.S. companies are creating more multilingual Web sites to expand their market, improve sales, and remain competitive. Dress codes are being revised to include headwear and other articles of clothing required by various religions. Companies are providing consumers with a greater array of products that reflect their diverse lifestyles and tastes. With an increase in white-collar service jobs, companies are paying more attention to cross-cultural interaction among workers and between workers and customers.

The impact of globalization has been particularly noticeable in the hotel and restaurant business. A case in point is a Hilton hotel in Washington, D. C., where workers speak 36 languages and some speak no English at all. To communicate with his staff, the hotel's general manager has memos translated into five different languages and read aloud to workers. During meetings, supervisors rely heavily on gesturing, tone of voice, and the written word to clarify complex thoughts to non-English speaking workers. And language is only one of the many challenges. According to the hotel's assistant director of housekeeping, a growing segment of the hotel's workforce is Muslim women. During the Islamic holy month of Ramadan, these women fast from sunup to sundown. However, they were reluctant to take their normal lunch break during Ramadan because they were surrounded by the smell of food in the employee cafeteria. When the Muslim women asked if they could work through the lunch hour and leave earlier, the assistant director agreed. However, she later heard from fellow managers who were concerned that other employees might take advantage of the situation.

The attacks of September 11, 2001, as well as the economic and political efforts to respond effectively to them, underscore the growing importance of developing a **global perspective,** meaning a view of the world and our place in it. For example, the government is stepping up its efforts to address current and projected shortages of employees with foreign language skills. Agencies such as the Army, the FBI, the State Department, and the Commerce Department are in dire need of language specialists with expertise in Arabic, Mandarin and Cantonese Chinese, Indonesian, Japanese, Korean, Farsi, Russian, Turkish, and other languages.

For each of us, developing a clearer, more encompassing view of the world around us is absolutely necessary. By doing so, we:

1. Develop greater insight into our interconnectedness. Electronic technology, commerce across national borders, and immigration and emigration have linked the United States with the rest of the world like never before. The loss of human life on September 11 was not just an American tragedy; it was felt worldwide. People from more than 60 countries were victims of the World Trade Center disaster. Figures provided by individual governments, or the U.S. Department of State, show the number of victims from countries such as Pakistan (200), India (250), Australia (55), El Salvador (71), Austria (15), and Nigeria (94 reported missing by Nigerian press, no official number).[16]

2. Expand our awareness of different perspectives. Before September 11, profiling or targeting certain populations was seen primarily as a criminal justice issue involving Blacks and Whites. Now, profiling has taken on a new and more inclusive meaning.

3. Enhance our self-awareness. For example, by becoming more aware of the tenets of Islam, we can become more aware of our own faith.

I am a citizen, not of Athens or Greece, but of the world.

—Socrates

Expanding our global perspective is not easy. Thirty minutes of world news each night does not begin to fill the void. A college president recently told the story of a visiting professor from Australia who spent a semester in the United States. During that time, he did not see a single story or commentary about *his* country, except for a shootout with a madman.[17]

Heightened Awareness of Diversity

Stories about diversity appear in the news each day. These stories deal with such issues as affirmative action, discrimination, social conflict, global education, and religious as well as language differences. On September 11, many of these issues captured the public's attention in an instant. People in the United States suddenly became much more aware of their own vulnerability and cultural isolation, as well as the growing importance of world economies, world geography, communications networks, migration, cultural values and traditions, and religious diversity.

In the immediate aftermath of September 11, many felt a need to isolate themselves psychologically and socially. Reaction throughout the United States ran the gamut from hope to hostility, impulsive behavior to reflection, a reordering of priorities to mundane concerns, and violence and threats of violence to community support and random acts of kindness. Public reaction to Muslims, or people thought to be Muslim, was varied as well. A poll taken by *The Washington Post* shortly after the attacks asked, "Do you think the attacks this week will make you personally more suspicious of people who you think are of Arab descent, or not?" Forty-three percent said "yes" and 56 percent said "no."[18] Nearly six months later, findings from a *USA Today*–CNN–Gallup poll show that a significant percentage of people (42 percent) in the United States say Muslim immigration should be reduced. Sixteen percent say it should be ended completely.[19] For some, the attacks implicate all foreigners. As we were discussing the events of September 11 in my sociology class the next day, one of my students remarked, "Right now I want to just hate all people who look Middle-Eastern, but I know that's not right. I feel we can't trust foreigners now."

Corporate leaders have responded to the attacks of September 11 by heightening security, denouncing discrimination and promoting tolerance, and providing support and counseling. Many workers across the country point to at least one positive repercussion; closer relationships and a more communal atmosphere in the workplace. A crisis such as this can bring people together and change their perspective on working, personal relationships, and life itself.

Scholarship on the subject of diversity has mushroomed in recent years. Diversity itself has become a thriving industry. Books, Web sites, diversity consultants, courses, workshops, and conferences have proliferated as more and more money is spent in this area. Pride in our cultural roots is championed by popular music, movies, ethnic festivals, and cultural exhibits. As diversity has become more visible in everyday life, it is more apt to become an issue that we address, discuss, and debate publicly and privately.

Continued Cultural Separation in the Midst of Diversity

Although some parts of our cultural landscape are becoming more diverse, other parts show little of this change. Sociologists refer to this as **cultural lag,** a condition in which one part of a culture is not keeping pace with another part. This lag or gap

Global Marketing on the Internet

Nowhere in business today is the value of the global market more apparent than on the Internet. Data from a recent report, "Web Globalization: Write Once, Deploy Worldwide," show that a growing majority of the online population is non-English speaking.[20]

Web buyers are more likely to select products and services if the supplier's Web site is culturally relevant and if it is available in their native language, according to the report. If U.S.-based companies want to extend their market reach and remain competitive, they will have to create multicultural, multilingual Web sites. Already, many companies have globalized their Web sites, including:

- General Electric—links allow the user to access G.E. home pages in 40 different countries. Each site is in the native language of that country.

- Mazda—home page links to sites in over 20 different languages. If you visit the site, you will be asked to download a font set for receiving information in Japanese (if you don't already have it).
- Houseseeker4u—local California real estate company offers translations of their site in any of eight different languages, including Portuguese and Chinese.
- Google.com—widely used Web browser offers an interface in more than 80 different languages. By clicking on Google's "language tools," the user can enter any URL (Internet address) and have each page translated in any one of six different languages—English, Spanish, French, German, Portuguese, and Italian. For instance, the user can access a Web page in Portuguese and have it translated to English, or vice versa.

is becoming increasingly evident when we look at where we live, worship, go to school, and work. Consider the following examples.

1. Many residents of the United States continue to live in neighborhoods that are separated along racial, ethnic, and economic lines. The upper, middle, and lower social classes gravitate to separate communities. Hispanic barrios, Little Japans, Little Italys, and Chinatowns are commonplace. So too are "chocolate cities and vanilla suburbs," a phrase used by musical artist George Clinton. William Frey, in his analysis of recent population estimates from the Census Bureau, concludes that most communities in the United States lack significant racial and ethnic diversity.[21] Data from the 2000 Census reveal high segregation levels in large urban areas where racial groups have a history of living in separate neighborhoods. For Hispanics, increasing segregation is largely related to a significant influx of immigrants. This change is especially apparent in the South.[22]

2. According to the U.S. Labor Department's Federal Glass Ceiling Commission, the upper levels of big business remain mostly white and mostly male.[23] The Commission found that the **glass ceiling**—attitudes and actions that block the promotion of minorities and women into top management positions—is still very much in place. These barriers may exist because of individ-

THINKING THROUGH DIVERSITY

Have you or any member of your family ever encountered a glass ceiling or a glass wall?

ual prejudices and discrimination, or they may be rooted in the policies, procedures, and culture of a business. Other barriers, referred to as *glass walls,* make
it difficult to move from one position to another at the same level. For example,
minority employees may be pigeonholed into certain departments that are more
oriented to human relations and minority affairs, such as community relations
and public affairs. As others with a background in finance or marketing move
into upper-level management, minorities may find themselves trapped by positions that eventually limit their upward mobility.

3. Martin Luther King once called our time of worship the most segregated hour of
the week. Despite a trend toward more integrated neighborhoods, especially in
some suburbs, racial segregation remains firmly in place at many religious services, as evidenced by recent data from a nationwide poll by *The New York Times.*
Ninety percent of Whites who attend religious services at least once a month said
that none or only a few of their fellow congregants were Black. Similarly, 73 percent of Blacks said that almost all of their fellow congregants were Black.[24]

4. While the percentage of students of color is increasing significantly, racial diversification among teachers has not kept pace. Data show that while racial minorities constitute approximately 35 percent of public school students, the vast
majority of teachers are White (87 percent).[25]

5. In recent years, there has been a resurgence of intergroup hostility and intolerance. This is not simply the work of a select few. When we think of intolerance,
how many of us visualize a member of the Ku Klux Klan (KKK) or a skinhead?
Unfortunately, intolerance can also come dressed in a three-piece suit, a military uniform, or more casual wear. Schools, places of worship, and job sites
throughout the country have recently witnessed an upsurge in hate crimes. Hate
literature, graffiti, threatening e-mail and telephone calls, property damage, and
physical violence point to a continuing cultural lag between the diversity we encounter and our ability to respect or at least tolerate that diversity.

Cyberhate

A former student at the University of
California–Irvine was the first person in the
United States to be charged and convicted of
committing a hate crime over the Internet. In
1996, he sent out an e-mail threat to 59 students,
most of whom were Asian. The message read, in
part: I personally will make it my life's work to
find and kill every one of you personally. OK?
That's how determined I am. Do you hear me?[26]

Hate speech on the Internet has grown
rapidly in recent years. Web sites, e-mail, bulletin
boards, and chat rooms may target, among other
things, a person or group's race, creed, sexual
orientation, religion, disability, or national origin.
A number of universities have enacted policies to
punish students who post hate messages on the
World Wide Web. Other universities see this type
of regulation as a violation of the First
Amendment right to free speech. They maintain
that suppressing hate speech is far more
dangerous than permitting it.

People react differently to the changes that continue to transform our cultural land-scape. Some adapt, others resist or remain oblivious. In a way, it is a lot like the growing importance of computer technology. We may adjust and learn more because

The real voyage of discovery consists not in seeking new landscapes but in having new eyes.

—Marcel Proust

we know that if we do not become computer literate, our chances for success will be severely limited. The same holds true for diversity. Whether we realize it or not, diversity touches each of us on a daily basis. If we are not in a position to capitalize on diversity, we will be at a disadvantage socially and economically. In Chapter 2 we focus on the relationship between diversity and success.

VIEWS OF DIVERSITY: ASSIMILATION AND PLURALISM

Throughout our nation's history, our diversity has been described as a *melting pot, tossed salad, rainbow, quilt,* and *kaleidoscope*. These images illustrate the fact that we are different. Our differences, and the way we view them, change constantly.

In the early twentieth century, a Jewish immigrant named Israel Zangwill of-fered this description of the United States in his book *The Melting Pot:* "There she lies, the great melting pot—listen! Can't you hear the roaring and the bubbling? There gapes her mouth—the harbour where a thousand mammoth feeders come from the ends of the world to pour in their human freight. Ah, what a stirring and a seething—Celt and Latin, Slav and Teuton, Greek and Syrian, Black and Yellow . . . Jew and Gentile."[27]

According to Zangwill, European immigrants would gradually lose their tra-ditional ways of life and blend together. A new mixed culture would emerge from this process. This is commonly referred to as **assimilation,** the process in which people lose their cultural differences and blend into the wider society. In-ternational students as well as those born and raised in the United States some-times sense their culture slipping away. They have many ways to deal with the pressure to assimilate. Some see it as inevitable and desirable. Others see it as something to avoid at all costs. Still others find themselves assimilating, but not completely. As one of my students put it, "I do it up to a point, as long as it does not rob me of my identity."

It took 22 years for me to develop my own personality and goals despite the struggles I have and the struggles my race still has. By assimilating—that is like saying Dr. Martin Luther King died for nothing. That Malcolm X and all of the other people who gave their lives so that I would have a chance died for nothing. To me, assimilation is another word for slavery.

Work is a perfect example of how I assimilate my identity so that I feel comfortable. If changing the way I dress and act makes me feel more accepted on the job, then that's what I want to do.

⌘

My personal background provides me with a very strong belief that I am to be who I am. I think my Jewish background as well as my mother's influence help me deal with assimilation. I know who I am, as far as race, culture, and personality. And I know that I'm not changing for anyone. Therefore, when the idea of assimilation is presented in any way to me, I instinctively decline.

⌘

In America, everyone at some point and time will be forced to assimilate themselves with another culture or group. Being a young black male, assimilation is probably the most frequently used pattern of interaction in my life. In my neighborhood, especially with my circle of friends, it is a cardinal sin to assimilate with the white culture. We see ourselves as the shunned group. At every possible opportunity, we thumb our collective noses at white society. By learning the "rules of the game" a long time ago, I know that assimilating with the majority society is a must. When forced to assimilate, I just separate my two worlds. I'm always going to be Black with black sentiments and I'll never compromise that for anything. However, I will play by the rules dictated, at least to an extent, to further myself and my people.

—Other perspectives

Assimilation may have negative as well as positive consequences for immigrants or society in general. For instance, it can mean learning good or bad habits or values. Research has shown that sometimes students who work the hardest and show the most respect tend to be the most recent immigrants. To some immigrants, negative influences are a constant concern. They see their children taking on negative values that create tensions within families. One 32-year-old mother from Mexico worries about her children, "In the Hispanic tradition, the family comes first, not money. It's important for our children not to be influenced too much by the 'gueros,'" a term she uses to refer to "blondies" or Americans.[28]

Other studies have found that some immigrants consciously choose when and where to assimilate. In *Accommodation Without Assimilation*, anthropologist Margaret Gibson shared findings from her study of Asian-Indian students in a city in the Sacramento Valley of California. She discovered that the students did well in school, often outperforming their Euro-American peers, by following the advice of their immigrant parents. The Asian-Indian students were told to follow rules and regulations at school and adopt only "desirable" aspects of Euro-American behavior rather than assimilate completely.[29]

What Is an American?

How would you define the term *American?* For some, the term applies solely to those living in the United States. Others maintain that those who inhabit any of the countries in North, Central, or South America are Americans. Still others feel that the term has a racial connotation. Toni Morrison, in her book *Playing in the Dark*, observes "deep within the word 'American' is its association with race . . . American means white."[30] A student of color sums up her feelings this way: "Being an American is a phrase way down on my list of descriptive words. America has caused me to describe myself in a lot of ways—Black, woman, minority. The word *American* is not part of that list. I wish I could feel a part of this country. But everyday I am quickly reminded that I am not an American but a nuisance."

Do you feel that you are an American? What does *American* mean to you? What does an American look like? In his book *A Different Mirror: A History of Multicultural America*, Ronald

Takaki describes a personal experience while riding in a taxi in Norfolk, Virginia. The driver, who looked to be in his 40s, asked him how long he had been in the United States. Takaki replied that he had been born in the United States. He further explained that his family came here from Japan more than 100 years ago. The driver's assumption was that he didn't really look "American."[31]

Why do we make this kind of assumption? According to Takaki, schools have to accept at least part of the blame. He argues that from kindergarten to college, teachers and textbooks have cultivated a narrow view of U.S. history. Typically, the experiences of African-Americans, Hispanics, Native-Americans, and Asian-Americans have been ignored. In addition to schools, our upbringing can influence our thinking. A college student elaborates: "The way I was brought up was to think that everybody who was the same as me were 'Americans,' and the other people were of 'such and such descent'."[32]

Many now question whether the model of the melting pot fits our society. They argue that people want to be accepted for who they are. A growing number of people are unwilling to give up what makes them distinctive, even if it is only for a certain period of time each day. When they go to work or school, they do not want to leave their culture at home. They feel that like the ingredients in a salad or the colors of a rainbow, differences can coexist and complement each other (see Fig. 1.3).

Pluralism is a process through which cultural differences are acknowledged and preserved. By way of illustration, advocates of multicultural education argue that the study of U.S. history should be more pluralistic. History should reflect the distinctive cultural experiences of all people. According to this perspective, courses in history often ignore the experiences, perspectives, and contributions of women or people of color. Those who share this opinion argue that if history courses were truly inclusive, there would be no need for a Black History Month or a Women's History Month.

Whether pluralism is positive is subject to debate. Those who oppose pluralism argue that it promotes tension and conflict at a time when we need to ignore our differences and come together as one, much as we did in the aftermath of the events

FIGURE 1.3 "People call us a melting pot, but we never have been. What we really represent is a quilt of different colors, different textures, all held together by a common thread." —Kweisi Mfume, President of the NAACP. Self portrait blocks created by children from the Ellicott City Head Start Program and visiting artist Maria Theresa Fernandes. *(Courtesy of Howard County Arts Council, Inc.)*

of September 11. Proponents of pluralism maintain that cultural diversity is a national resource that we should preserve. Furthermore, they maintain that when people preserve their cultural identity, including language, religion, and customs, it can be a source of pride and motivation.

> *I think it is important to hold onto one's culture; it is a means of guidance. For instance, my great grand-dad was born in Cameroon in a place called Doula. In Doula, the people were said to be very wise. The story went on to say a bird used to fly around them trying to get their knowledge; and this bird actually was a human being. So they used to hide their knowledge by wearing a hat. I still do this. For me, it's fun, but it reminds me of where I am from. It reminds me I am supposed to be a wise man.*
>
> —Another perspective

DIMENSIONS OF DIVERSITY

Dimensions of diversity refer to specific traits viewed as distinguishing one person or group from another. Race, gender, and ethnicity are three examples. **Race** refers to a category of people who are *perceived* as physically distinctive on the basis of certain traits, such as skin color, hair texture, and facial features. Notice that what makes this group distinctive is our perception of differences. The concept of race is discussed later in more detail.

Whereas race relates to physical differences, ethnicity focuses on cultural distinctiveness. **Ethnicity** is defined as the consciousness of a cultural heritage shared with other people. **Gender** has to do with the cultural differences that distinguish males from females. For instance, in any given culture, people raise males and females to act certain ways. Do not confuse the term *gender* with *sex*. Sex refers to biological differences, such as hormones and anatomy.

Social Class Differences in the United States

Social class refers to one's status in society. In the United States, status is usually determined by a variety of social and economic criteria, including wealth, power, and prestige. Even though social class influences where we work, live, and go to school, its importance is addressed infrequently. Perhaps class distinctions are downplayed or ignored because we are uncomfortable, psychologically speaking, acknowledging the tremendous inequality that exists in this society. Moreover, the concept of social class is "fuzzy" and inconsistent. For example, how would we classify other students in our class? *Lower, middle,* and *upper class* mean different things to different people.

A groundbreaking study of social class was recently undertaken by Barbara Ehrenreich, a well-known author who has written extensively about women and poverty. She decided to assume a secret identity as a waitress in order to research the ramifications of changing her social class. In *Nickel and Dimed: On (Not) Getting By in America,* Ehrenreich discusses her life as a waitress, working 10-hour shifts for $2.43 an hour plus tips. She worked in Florida,

Maine, and Minnesota. With her Rent-A-Wreck car and a laptop, her goal was to earn enough money for basic necessities and to pay rent. She soon discovered that she needed additional income to keep her afloat, so she took second jobs as a motel housekeeper, professional maid, nursing home dietary aide, and Wal-Mart employee. To Ehrenreich, the experience was mentally as well as physically challenging. She says, "I wasn't prepared for how mentally challenging this was going to be. I mean intellectually challenging. I knew I was going to have to work hard and I was afraid it was physically maybe too much for me. Actually, I did fine physically—though I don't know how fine it would have been after many months. But here I am with a Ph.D. in biology and I was struggling to master all these things that were being thrown at me."[33] Ehrenreich recounts how her coworkers roomed together in hotels, slept in cars, and medicated themselves because they had no money for doctor visits. As a result of her research, she became much more aware of the separate, distinct worlds of the haves and have-nots in U.S. society.

When we talk about the dimensions of diversity, social class, sexual orientation, religion, personality, learning style, communication style, and family background are invariably ignored. Some people may perceive these and other dimensions to be more important than race or gender. When students are asked what makes them unique, their answers reflect a very inclusive view of diversity (see Diversity Box: Who Am I?)

The meaning of the term *diversity* is expanding continually. Roosevelt Thomas, a leading expert on managing diversity in the workplace, makes this point

Who Am I?

Students in a college success class were asked to write down five things that describe each of them. Then they wrote all of their descriptors on the board as follows:

Jewish   African-American   born-again Christian

American   student

baby boomer   fifty plus   family oriented

religious   flexible

member of intergenerational household

good mother   proud

sincere   female

young   poor   Muslim

male

warmhearted

intelligent   young at heart

Indo-Guyanese   White

short   fat

open-minded   WHO AM I?   outspoken

independent   artist

strong-willed   single parent

hardworking   half Black/half Jewish woman

Roman Catholic

Blackfoot-Native   child of two loving parents

product of interracial marriage   recovering alcoholic

caring   truthful

descendant of slaveholders

vegetarian   right-handed

southwesterner   family man

Polish

agnostic   mother of a special child

American of German and Irish descent

middle-aged menopausal

baby of the family

in his book *Beyond Race and Gender*. He defines diversity in a way that includes everyone. According to Thomas, workforce diversity is not something that is simply defined by race or gender. Rather, it encompasses a variety of other dimensions, such as age, personal and corporate background, education, job function and position, geographic origin, lifestyle, sexual orientation, and personality.[34] To this list we can add ancestry, national origin, creed, religion, economic class, leadership style, personality, family background, marital status, military background, and disability. The list goes on and on. In short, it includes whatever we think distinguishes us.

As you read about diversity and, in particular, various dimensions of diversity, keep these points in mind.

1. *Dimensions of diversity may be hidden or visible.* Diversity is not only skin deep. According to one theory, diversity is like a cultural iceberg. Only about 10 percent of it is visible. Most dimensions mentioned by students (see Diversity Box: Who Am I?) would be invisible in the classroom. For example, we would not know that a classmate was a descendant of slaveholders, a vegetarian, or a born-again Christian unless the person chose to share this with us.

2. *Dimensions of diversity are found within groups as well as within individuals.* People possess varied personalities and talents as well as different learning and communication styles. Similarly, everyone within a group is not the same. Differences within a group are often ignored when we distinguish between groups. Diversity within groups is addressed later in the chapter.

3. *Dimensions of diversity are in a constant state of flux.* In different situations, we see ourselves and are seen by others differently. In some situations a student might want to be seen as a Muslim female. In another situation, she might simply want to be viewed as a student.

4. *Dimensions of diversity are not always clear-cut or easily defined.* Diversity means different things to different people. A good example is the term *race*. Even though we talk about race as if it can be biologically defined, there is no easy way to distinguish people based solely on their skin color, hair texture, shape or color of their eyes, or any other physical trait. Racial mixing has blurred the boundaries between races. Skin color, for example, is a common but unreliable indicator of race. There are Whites who are more dark-skinned than some Blacks. Many Hispanics have dark skin but do not consider themselves Black. Anthropologist Ashley Montagu addressed this issue in his book *Man's Most Dangerous Myth: The Fallacy of Race*. According to Montagu, the term *race* has no scientific basis and cannot be applied to real life.[35] There is almost total agreement among scientists today that race is arbitrarily and socially defined. Yet it is important because we make it important, and we model its importance for children (see Fig. 1.4).

In summary, diversity is multidimensional. Various dimensions may be hidden or visible. Moreover, they may or may not have anything to do with race or gender.

Master Status

People are often identified and distinguished by their **master statuses;** positions that stand out in the eyes of society and hide one's individuality. Ask yourself what is the first thing that people see when they look at you? Is it your race, gender, disability, or some other master status?

In his autobiography, Malcolm X discusses his experiences as a student in Mason, Michigan, a town just outside Lansing. He was one of the top students in his class and excelled in English. He vividly remembers talking with Mr. Ostrowski, his English teacher, about his plans for a career.

"'Malcolm, you ought to be thinking about a career,' said Mr. Ostrowski. 'Have you been giving it thought?' The truth is, I hadn't. I never have figured out why I told him. 'Well, yes, sir, I've been thinking I'd like to be a lawyer.' Lansing certainly had no Negro lawyers—or doctors either—in those days, to hold up an image I might have aspired to. All I really knew for certain was that a lawyer didn't wash dishes, as I was doing.

Mr. Ostrowski looked surprised, I remember, and leaned back in his chair and clasped his hands behind his head.

He kind of half-smiled and said, 'Malcolm, one of life's first needs is for us to be realistic. Don't misunderstand me, now. We all here like you, you know that. But you've gotto be realistic about being a nigger. A lawyer—that's no realistic goal for a nigger. You need to think about something you *can* be. You're good with your hands—making things. Everybody admires your carpentry work. Why don't you plan on carpentry? People like you as a person—you'll get all kinds of work.'

The more I thought afterwards about what he said, the more uneasy it made me. It just kept treading around in my mind."[36]

It is clear from this excerpt that race was a master status during this period of Malcolm X's life. Although Mr. Ostrowski knew that Malcolm X was intelligent, he also understood the social norms that were in place at this time. From Mr. Ostrowski's point of view, it did not matter that Malcolm X was smart. He had to learn that aspiring to be a lawyer was at odds with the "place" reserved for him in the wider society.

FIGURE 1.4   Race is socially defined. *(By permission from Copley News Service.)*

◉ DIVERSITY BETWEEN AND WITHIN GROUPS

The United States is home to one of the most culturally diverse populations in the world. Nevertheless, we often ignore or gloss over these differences. When we focus our attention on race, we think in terms of Blacks and Whites or sometimes Latinos and Whites. Our society, and even our communities, are described as biracial rather than multiracial. This can be particularly uncomfortable and offensive to those who are constantly stereotyped or left out of the picture. An Iranian student describes how she has struggled with this dilemma: "I am an Iranian woman, one who can't pass as white because I'm too dark, but certainly can't pass as black because I have Middle-Eastern features . . . . When I date black men, I receive animosity from those who feel that black men belong with black women. When I date white men, I've been accused of selling out and trying to be white. Iranian men who expect me to fit within a certain mold find me strange. I also seem to have this peculiar power to make people at airports and train stations visibly uncomfortable." She describes her feelings when she was informed she would not be allowed to join the BLSA—the Black Law Students Association—at her college. "My first impulse had been to argue with the man sitting behind the table with the introductory flyers. He looked me in the eye and said, 'Look, if you're not black, then as far as I'm concerned, you're white." She goes on to say: "What was I to do, start an 'ILSA' of which I would be the sole member?"[37]

We may paint diversity with such a broad brush that we fail to capture the differences that exist within groups as well as between them. Indeed, the differences within groups are often greater. For instance, we tend to get caught up with how men and women differ from each other. We forget or ignore the significant differences that can be found when we simply look at a group of men or a group of women. Women can be assertive or passive, dependent or independent, and supporters or opponents of feminism. Similar differences exist among men.

Differences exist among the largest ethnic groups in this country. These groups include African-Americans, Latinos, Asian-Americans, and Native-Americans. For this reason, we cannot talk about the Latino family any more than we can talk about the white family. Discussing *the* Asian-American or *the* Latino experience in this country ignores the diversity that exists within groups and individuals from these populations. Asian-Americans include Chinese, Japanese, Filipinos, Vietnamese, Laotians, Cambodians, Hmong, Koreans, Samoans, and others. Latinos are also distinguished by a wide range of skin colors, ethnic or cultural lifestyles, religions, and languages. Many object to the term *Latino* or *Hispanic* because it masks the uniqueness of the particular culture. *Mexican, Puerto Rican, Cuban,* or some other term identifying one's nationality may be preferred.

Sociologist Douglas Massey reminds us of the vastly different histories shared by Latinos and the salience of their social class backgrounds. "They may be fifth-generation Americans or new immigrants just stepping off the jetway. Depending on when and how they got to the United States, they may also know a long history of discrimination and repression or they may see the United States as a land of opportunity where origins do not matter. They may be affluent and well educated or poor and unschooled; they may have no personal experience of prejudice or discrimination, or they may harbor stinging resentment at being called a 'spic' or being passed over for promotion because of their accent."[38]

DIVERSITY MYTHS

Diversity is a concept that means many things to many people. It can trigger a wide range of positive and negative feelings. Unfortunately, what we learn about this subject is often incomplete and inaccurate. Some of the more common misconceptions that surround diversity follow.

Myth 1: Diversity = Women + Minorities.   Diversity includes everyone. All of us, for example, bring different talents and perspectives to school and work. This includes white males.

Myth 2: Diversity Is a New Phenomenon.   There has always been diversity, but now it is receiving more attention. Some changes are not as new as we might believe. As an example, statistics indicate that more women are entering the job market than ever before. This masks the fact that a large percentage of women of color have always worked.

Myth 3: Diversity = Deficiency.   This myth is based on the premise that diversity results in standards being lowered. Today, professionals increasingly view diversity as a resource rather than a deficit. Big businesses such as IBM, Xerox, and Digital Equipment approach diversity as good business for a number of reasons. It makes companies more attuned to markets at home and abroad, it expands their talent pool, and it contributes to the creativity that fosters the development of new, innovative products.

An advertisement by Atlantic Richfield Company (ARCO) illustrates the bottom-line implications of diversity. The top of the ad reads, "The value of diversity is priceless." Underneath the ad is a picture of foreign currency and these words: "As a multinational corporation, ARCO is committed to filling the needs of our customers at home and around the world. Diversity in our staff and in our business relationships help enhance our effectiveness in the global marketplace. It's a win–win situation, because diversity increases opportunity for others and strengthens our own organization. Diversity makes sense. And pounds, francs, yen . . . ."

Myth 4: Diversity = Divisiveness.   Many assume that our society is divided because of our differences. Does the problem lie with our differences or our inability to respect and learn from these differences? Being exposed to diversity can bring people together.

In *What Matters in College?* Alexander Astin discusses findings from his research on 217 colleges and universities.[39] He found that a student's diversity experiences in college can be a potent way of bridging the gap between various groups and easing tensions. These experiences might take the form of a workshop or a course on diversity. Equally important was the frequency with which students interacted socially with persons from different racial and ethnic groups.

Myth 5: Diversity Is to Be Feared.   By focusing exclusively on our differences and ignoring our similarities, we create fear. Fear is cultivated by our ignorance of differences and similarities. Fear is compounded by our inability to communicate effectively with people who disagree with us about difficult issues. People often shy away from talking about diversity because it is so emotionally charged. As one student put it, "All it takes is one slip of the tongue." How we approach diversity can make all the difference. If we approach it with a sense of humility and a sincere desire to learn more about others and ourselves, it need not be something to fear or avoid. In a video entitled *The Color of Fear,* a group of men of varying racial and ethnic backgrounds attend a retreat and "open up" to each other about the issue of race. After a few days, it appears the racial divisions among the men are almost insurmountable. Their fear and mistrust almost make it impossible for them to communicate effectively. Toward the end of the retreat, they begin to connect with each other by confronting their fears, sharing intimate feelings, and really listening. They become more aware of some of the feelings they have in common.

> *Differences aren't necessarily a burden but a blessing.*
>
> —Another perspective

The kind of dialogue that unfolds in this video is rare because it is genuinely open and honest. Consequently, it can be very painful at times. Toward the end of the video, one of the participants comments on the anger and hurt that surfaces during the group's discussions. "Sometimes," he says, "the cure for the pain is in the pain."[40]

WHAT IS DIVERSITY CONSCIOUSNESS?

THINKING THROUGH DIVERSITY

Should we always treat everybody the same and ignore differences? Are there any situations in which we should treat people differently?

The definition of *consciousness* in the dictionary is being fully aware or sensitive to something. Another way of defining it is the full activity of the mind or senses. This state of mind is necessary to develop **diversity consciousness:** understanding, awareness, and skills in the area of diversity.

Diversity consciousness is not simple and straightforward. It cannot be manufactured during a one-hour TV talk show or a day-long training session. Try to keep the following points in mind as you read about diversity consciousness.

Diversity Consciousness Is Not

■ *Simply common sense*—Common sense is not sufficient. We need to educate ourselves and each other. Adam's Mark, a large hotel chain that recently settled a racial discrimination suit filed by the National Association for the Advancement of Colored People (NAACP), incorporates real-life scenarios as part of its training for all 11,000 of its employees, including senior executives. A scenario might target something as simple as exchanging money with a customer, a common interaction in the hotel industry that many people do not even give a second thought. For example, some minorities are aware that some people will not put money directly in their hands; rather, they will lay the money on the counter. This may create the impression that an employee does not want to touch the hands of certain people because of their race, disability, or for some other reason. If employees are not taught this, many will not be sensitive to it.

- *The result of good intentions*—I have heard people say, "If my heart is in the right place, that is enough." Trying extra hard to be fair and respectful of others or having the best of intentions is a good start, but only a start. It is possible to show insensitivity and ignorance even though you mean well. People who talk to adults with disabilities in a childlike manner may think that they are being kind. People who tell you to forget our differences and just "be human" may think they are offering helpful advice. Leonard Pitts, a columnist for the *Miami Herald,* writes, "I've lost count of the times well-meaning white people have advised me to quit being black and 'just be a person.'"[41]

- *The result of some simple formula or strategy*—This is a reflection of what George Ritzer terms the "McDonaldization" of our society.[42] Sociologists use this phrase to describe our preoccupation with doing things quickly and efficiently, much like McDonald's restaurants. However, diversity consciousness requires lifelong soul searching, self-reflection, and active learning.

- *Important for just some of us*—Are events held during African-American History Month more apt to attract African-Americans? How many men are in attendance at Women's History Month events? All of us need to be culturally literate and responsive to survive and succeed in the twenty-first century. According to Dr. Benjamin Carson, one of the world's most renowned surgeons, it is a mistake to think that it's not my problem or it doesn't affect me. "All of our ancestors came to this country in different boats. But we're all in the same boat now. And if part of the boat sinks, eventually the rest of it goes down too."[43]

- *Simply ignoring differences and treating everybody the same*—It is necessary to distinguish between sameness and equal opportunity. Should an instructor, for example, always treat everybody the same? On one hand, she should have high expectations for all of her students regardless of who they are. That same instructor, however, will have to distinguish among students in determining how she can teach the material most effectively and how she can help individual students succeed.

- *Some "feel good" activity*—Diversity consciousness is not a matter of merely feeling good about ourselves and others. It goes deeper. Superficial acceptance is replaced by a deeper and more critical understanding.

- *A passing fad*—Diversity has always been with us, and responding to it with ease and competence will become more and more important. A good example is our increasing life span. Census predictions point to a much grayer population by the year 2050 because we are living longer. America's "baby boomers" will begin to reach age 65 in the year 2010. By 2020, nearly one-fifth of the U.S. population will be 65 years of age or older.[44] People are not only living longer, but they are also healthier and retiring at a later age. Therefore, the older population will be a growing part of the diversity that surrounds us daily.

▣ DIVERSITY EDUCATION

Diversity has always been a powerful, even a necessary, catalyst for intellectual progress.

—David H. Porter, President Emeritus, Skidmore College

Diversity education refers to all the strategies that enable us to develop diversity consciousness. Through diversity education, we develop awareness, understanding, and a variety of skills in the area of diversity. Throughout the book, these skills are referred to as **diversity skills.** Among these are flexible thinking, communication, teamwork, and leadership skills, as well as the ability to overcome personal and social barriers.

Diversity education takes many forms. It is something we can initiate and control, such as reading a book, attending a workshop, and exchanging ideas about diversity issues with thousands of people over the Internet. One form of diversity education, which has proliferated throughout the country in recent years, is study circles. Anyone can form a study circle.

The Circle of Learning

The idea behind study circles is to involve communities in ongoing dialogues on diversity. Anyone or any group can initiate a study circle. In many communities, organizations such as churches, businesses, schools, and clubs sponsor study circles. Support from the Study Circles Resource Center (SCRC) is also available at no charge. SCRC provides free discussion materials and assistance (http://www.studycircles.org).[45]

People who join study circles agree to meet regularly over an extended period of time. This long-term proactive approach to dialogue allows study circle participants to get to know one another and begin to share their innermost feelings. Everyone is given a "home" in the conversation. By participating in study circles, everyday people gain ownership of issues that relate to diversity. Typically, the discussion focuses initially on personal experiences and perspectives. Participants then examine how personal and community issues interrelate and what action needs to be taken. Unlike many other forms of diversity education, which do not go beyond dialogue, study circles combine talk with action.

The experiences of study circles throughout the country show promise. In some cases, hundreds and even thousands of people participate in community-wide dialogues. Roughly 500 people and 30 organizations in Minneapolis/St. Paul are involved in study circles on the challenge of racial segregation in housing and education. A statewide program in Oklahoma helped initiate sweeping changes in the corrections system. In Miami, Florida, the "Many Voices, One Community" project is addressing a number of diversity issues, including immigration and education, race relations, language differences, and job opportunities.

Typically, long-term relationships form out of circles. I have a best friend that I met in a study circle. Often, there is a need for a second level of the same circle that further narrows the focus. If the first circle was good, the participants are reluctant to leave. There is a bonding that takes place that transcends culture and race. This makes us simply human beings who have gained a wiser understanding of one another and the need to know more.

—Another perspective

Although much of the literature uses the terms *diversity education* and *diversity training* interchangeably, there are important differences. Unlike training, diversity education is a lifelong process. The term *education* refers to a complex and unpredictable process that is both cognitive and affective. Training, however, tends to be more straightforward, standardized, and descriptive. Education, as opposed to training, is more apt to entail questioning, disagreement, and reflection. In essence, diversity training may constitute one component of diversity education.

Much of the dialogue in recent years regarding diversity equates diversity with diversity education. They are not the same. Diversity simply refers to our individual and collective differences. Without education, diversity is simply untapped potential.

Unlike many other forms of learning, true diversity consciousness requires continual, fundamental change. Change of this nature, what best-selling author Stephen Covey terms *real change,* takes place "from the inside out." In *The Seven Habits of Highly Successful People,* Covey elaborates. Real change "doesn't come from hacking at the leaves of attitude and behavior with quick fix personality ethic techniques. It comes from striking at the root—the fabric of our thought, the fundamental essential paradigms which give definition to our character and create the lens through which we see the world."[46] In other words, fundamental changes involve growing as a person, both intellectually and emotionally. Although change of this nature is not easy, the rewards are worth it.

In summary, the cultural landscape in the United States is changing due to the influence of demographic, technological, and social changes. The term *diversity* has gained new meaning; it is not limited to racial, ethnic, and gender differences. Despite the attention diversity receives, our views and understanding of diversity are often influenced by myths about diversity and the role it plays in our lives. Diversity education enables us to move beyond these myths and develop our diversity consciousness.

In the next chapter, we focus on skills that enable us to capitalize on diversity. We examine how diversity consciousness makes us more successful at school and on the job. Additionally, we explore the numerous ways in which organizations benefit from the diversity consciousness of their employees.

CASE STUDIES

The following three case studies follow three individuals (Ligua, Mary, and Michael) through each chapter. Even though the stories are rooted in real-life experiences, the characters are fictitious. You will learn about each of the three—their backgrounds, day-to-day challenges that revolve around diversity, and how they attempt to resolve certain complex issues addressed in each chapter. This chapter simply introduces each individual. In Chapters 2 through 6, you will learn more about Ligua, Mary, and Michael. After reading each case study, you will be asked a series of questions that will challenge your diversity consciousness. The final chapter brings each case study to a close.

Case Study One

Name: Ligua Querling

Education: High school diploma

Marital Status: Married

Children: Kenneth, 3 years; Lisa, 6 years; Michael, 8 years

Hometown: Albuquerque, New Mexico

Current Residence: Northern California

Ligua aspires to be a high school math teacher. Like many of her friends, she somehow manages to find the time to be a mother, an employee, and a part-time student. She is taking courses at a predominantly white, suburban community college that is a short commute from her two-bedroom apartment. Ligua works a full 40-hour workweek as a salesperson at a nearby car dealership.

As a working mom, Ligua's biggest challenges are giving 100 percent on her job, 100 percent at school, and most importantly, 100 percent to her family. Given all there is to do in the course of a day, she tries to make every minute count. Often, Ligua's needs are an afterthought. *Role conflict* (interference among the duties associated with the multiple positions held by an individual), stemming from her multiple statuses as a mother, wife, student, and employee, consume her at times. For financial reasons, she needs her job. But she wants her job too. Her husband, a building contractor who works long hours, helps out when he can. Ligua feels there's nothing balanced about her life at home and at work. Sometimes, she feels like she neglects her family because she is playing "catch-up" at work and school. At other times, the scale shifts much more toward her family, with family illnesses, running errands, and just "being there" when her children and husband need her.

Case Study Two

Name: Mary Stuart

Education: College senior

Marital Status: Single

Children: None

Hometown: Rushville, Illinois

Current Residence: Chicago, Illinois

Mary is a 21-year-old white female attending an undergraduate university in a large city. Mary's family, whom she describes as upper-middle class, resides in a rural area of the same state in which she attends college. Going to school in a large city enables Mary to experience new ideas and cultures. Mary is currently in her fourth year of the university's social work program. She is completing two practicums, one at a children's mental hospital and one at a private, nonprofit agency that provides both outpatient services and in-home family preservation counseling services. After graduating with her bachelor's degree in social work, Mary wants to pursue a master's degree in social work and become a licensed clinical social worker. The majority of Mary's friends are white females with similar backgrounds.

Mary is a descendant of highlander Scots originating in four different regions of Europe. During the last few years, Mary has taken a much greater interest in her cultural heritage. She enjoys celebrating her cultural heritage by taking part in Scottish games and Celtic festivals. The atmosphere is very sociable, especially with the "clan" gatherings. Clans are groups of families or households, the heads of which claim descent from a common ancestor. Music is a big part of the festivals. Also, clan gatherings provide a time to reflect on more traditional times when community values seemed to hold more importance. Now things seem more impersonal to her.

Case Study Three

Name: Michael Butler

Education: College degree in computer engineering

Marital Status: Divorced, won custody of only child

Children: Aaron, 11 years

Hometown: Greensboro, North Carolina

Current Residence: Atlanta, Georgia

Michael describes himself as multiracial. His mother identifies herself as part Cherokee Indian, part African-American. His father refers to himself as Black, although his ancestry is mixed (African-American, Caucasian, Asian). With so many different racial groups running through his bloodline, Michael rejects any attempt to categorize himself into one race. If he did, he says that he would be depriving himself of much of his heritage.

Michael works as a senior manager for a small consulting firm. The job requires quite a bit of travel and a great deal of networking. Over the years, the firm's workforce has become more diverse, especially in terms of race, ethnicity, and age. With regard to gender, however, few women can be found at the management and decision-making levels. Overall, Michael's evaluations have been excellent. He enjoys the long hours his job requires.

When life gets difficult, Michael takes comfort in his strong spiritual background. He was brought up as a Baptist and is an active member of his church. According to Michael, his religious and ethnic background gives him peace, and helps him get through the day. Michael is intent on passing on his strong religious beliefs to his son.

 EXERCISES

In-Class

Exercise 1: Dear Gabriella

Directions for Instructor

1. Ask students to write a "Dear Gabriella" letter. Gabriella is a graduate student with a dual major in psychology and social work. She provides an ear and an answer to those students struggling with a wide variety of diversity issues on campus. Her "Dear Gabriella" column is a regular feature in the student-run newspaper.
2. In writing the letter, tell students to describe a personal struggle that deals with diversity in some way. It can be real or fictitious. Then students should ask Gabriella for her advice. At the bottom of the letter, students write their names.
3. Instruct students to pass letters to another student. Next, students should take the role of "Gabriella" and answer the letter in front of them. In writing their response, they should explain the diversity issue, suggest how this person might deal with this issue, and sign Gabriella's name at the bottom.
4. Instruct students to pass the letter on to still another student. Students should write an analysis of both the letter and response, and sign their name.
5. Finally, ask students to return the letter to the original writer.

Please note: This exercise can be done using computers. If computers are used, follow the same set of instructions but have students type their letters so they appear on the computer screen. Have students switch seats rather than pass letters.

Exercise 2: What Is an American?

Directions for Instructor

1. Provide each student with a sheet of poster paper and magic markers.
2. Ask students, "What does it mean to be an American?" Students should respond by drawing pictures or images on the poster paper (*no* writing).
3. Have students display their pictures. If possible, tape them to the wall of the classroom or somewhere else where they can all be seen at once.
4. Ask each student to explain her or his drawing. Then ask the entire class to analyze their responses. What patterns emerge? Who is included and excluded in their visual representations?

Out-of-Class

Exercise 1: What Is Diversity?

1. Ask 10 students not in this class to complete the sentence:
Diversity is _____.
Record their responses.
2. Write a paragraph describing the similarities and differences in the responses of
the 10 students. Do any of their responses reflect diversity myths? Explain.

Exercise 2: Thinking Through My Cultural Diversity

Describe, in a reasonable amount of detail, your background in terms of the following dimensions of cultural diversity.

- Your early environment: the kind(s) of community(ies) in which you grew up
  (large city, suburb, small town, rural area)
- Your social class as you grew up, the jobs and levels of education of those who
  raised you, and the social class levels of your neighbors
- Your social heritage—specifically, your racial, ethnic (cultural), and religious background (you may not necessarily identify with all three)—and its importance to you
- The culture other than your own that has had the greatest impact on you, and why

Exercise 3: What's in a Name?

1. What is your full name? How do you feel about your name? Why?
2. Find out as much as you can about your name. For example, what is the history
and significance of your name? What is the meaning of your name?

INTERNET ASSIGNMENT

1. Go to a search engine site such as www.yahoo.com or www.hotbot.com. Do a
search on "diversity education" (put the two words inside quotes so that the
search is for that exact term).
2. Read the selection of links you receive and choose one that interests you. Go to
that site and print either the home page or an article of interest.
3. Write a two-paragraph summary of what you learned from visiting this Web site
and any links that you visited.

NOTES

[1] "Inclusion," *Book and Video Catalog* (Manhattan, KS: The MASTER Teacher, 1999), 5A.

[2] Vincent N. Parillo, *Diversity in America* (Thousand Oaks, CA: Pine Forge Press, 1996), 65.

[3] U.S. Bureau of the Census, *Historical Statistics of the United States, Part II,* Series Z 20-132
(Washington, DC: U.S. Government Printing Office, 1976).

[4] U.S. Bureau of the Census, *Statistical Abstract of the United States 1997,* 117th ed. (Washington, DC,: U.S. Government Printing Office, 1997), 44.

[5] Richard Rodriguez, "Se Habla Espanol." Online, May 9, 2000. Available: http://www.pbs.org/newshour/essays/may00/rodriguez_5-9.htmlrl.

[6] D'Vera Cohn and Darryl Fears, "Multiracial Growth Seen in Census," *The Washington Post,* March 13, 2001, A1.

[7] Clara Rodríguez, "Latina America," *Latina,* July 2001, 87.

[8] Labor Force, "Occupational Outlook Quarterly," Winter 1999/2000.

[9] Bureau of Labor Statistics, *Projections from Current Population Survey,* 1988–1998.

[10] *Digest of Education Statistics,* U.S. Department of Education, National Center for Education Statistics, 2000.

[11] Northeast and Islands Regional Educational Laboratory at Brown University, *Student Voices: English Language Learners,* 2000.

[12] "The Nation: Students," *The Chronicle of Higher Education Almanac,* Sept. 1, 2000, 24+.

[13] Barbara Fraser, "U.S. Colleges Step Up Recruiting in Latin America," *Chronicle of Higher Education,* XLIV(10), Oct. 31, 1997, A58–A59.

[14] Barry McLaughlin and Beverly McLeod, "Educating All Our Students: Improving Education for Children from Culturally and Linguistically Diverse Backgrounds." Online. World Wide Web. June 1966. Available: http://www.ncbe.gwu.edu/miscpubs/ncrcdsll/edall.htm.

[15] Marshall McLuhan, *The Mechanical Bride: Folklore of Industrial Man* (Boston: Beacon Press, 1967).

[16] Reuters, "Victims by Country." Online, Sept. 20, 2001. Available: http://www.cnn.com/SPECIALS/2001/trade.center/interactive/victims.map/mpa.exclude.htmlrlUntitled.

[17] Jane Pinchin, "Let Them Go—Because 60 Seconds of World News Is Not Enough," *The Colgate Scene,* March 2002.

[18] Thomas B. Edsall, "Anti-Muslim Violence Assailed," *The Washington Post,* Sept. 15, 2001, A9.

[19] Gannett News Service, "Muslim Nations, U.S. Have Opposite Views," *Carroll County Times,* March 5, 2002, A11.

[20] Lori Enos, "Report: English-Only A Mistake for U.S. Sites," *E-Commerce Times.* Online, May 17, 2001. Available: http://www.ecomercetimes.com/perl/story/9812.html.

[21] William Frey, "The Diversity Myth," *American Demographics,* June 1998, 38–43.

[22] Sarah Cohen and D'Vera Cohn, "Racial Integration's Shifting Patterns," *The Washington Post,* Feb. 1, 2001, A1.

[23] Federal Glass Ceiling Commission, *A Solid Investment: Making Full Use of the Nation's Human Capital* (Washington, DC: U.S. Department of Labor, 1995), 6.

[24] Kevin Sack with Janet Elder, "Poll Finds Optimistic Outlook but Enduring Racial Division." Online, July 14, 2000. Available: http://www.nytimes.com/library/national/race/071100sack-poll.html.

[25] T. Snyder, (ed.), *Digest of Education Statistics, 1998;* U.S. Department of Education National Center for Education Statistics, 1998; American Association of Colleges of Teacher Education, *Teacher Education Pipeline IV: Schools, Colleges, and Department of Education,* Washington, DC: AACTE, 1999.

[26] Southern Poverty Law Center, "E-mail on Trial," *Intelligence Report,* Winter 1988, 5.

[27] Israel Zangwill, *The Melting Pot* (New York: The Jewish Publication Society of America, 1909), 198–199.

[28] William Branigin, "Immigrants Question Idea of Assimilation," *The Washington Post,* May 25, 1998, A1.

[29] Timothy Fong and Larry Shinagawa, *Asian Americans: Experiences and Perspectives* (Upper Saddle River, NJ: Prentice Hall, 2000).

[30] Toni Morrison, *Playing in the Dark* (Cambridge, Mass.: Harvard University Press, 1992), 47.

[31] Ronald Takaki, *A Different Mirror. A History of Multicultural America* (Boston: Little, Brown, 1993).

[32] Ruth Frankenberg, *White Women, Race Matters: The Social Construction of Whiteness* (Minneapolis, MN: University of Minnesota Press, 1993), 198.

[33] Athima Chansanchai, "She Walks the Line of Poverty, Incognito," *The Sun,* Sept. 16, 2001, 1N+.

[34] Roosevelt Thomas, *Beyond Race and Gender: Unleashing the Power of Your Total Work Force by Managing Diversity* (New York: American Management Association, 1991).

[35] Ashley Montagu, *Man's Most Dangerous Myth: The Fallacy of Race* (Cleveland, OH: World Publishing, 1964).

[36] Malcolm X, *The Autobiography of Malcolm X* (New York: Ballantine Books, 1965), 36, reprinted by permisson of Random House, New York.

[37] Amanda Enayati, "Not Black, Not White," *The Washington Post,* July 13, 1997, C1.

[38] Douglas Massey, "Latino Poverty Research: An Agenda for the 1990s," *Social Science Research Council Newsletter,* 47, March 1993, 7–8.

[39] Alexander Astin, *What Matters in College? Four Critical Years Revisited* (San Francisco: Jossey-Bass, 1993).

[40] *The Color of Fear* (video) (Oakland, CA: Stir Fry Productions, 1994).

[41] Leonard Pitts, Jr., "Watching Whites Struggle to Understand Their Whiteness," *The Sun,* Apr. 21, 1997, 9A.

[42] George Ritzer, *The McDonaldization of Society* (Thousand Oaks, CA: Pine Forge Press, 2000).

[43] Benjamin Carson, "Carson Philosophy Is 'Think Big,'" *The Sun,* Aug. 24, 1997, 6H.

[44] Richard W. Judy and Carol D'Amico, *Workforce 2020: Executive Summary* (Indianapolis, IN: Hudson Institute, 1997), 3.

[45] For more information, contact Study Circles Resource Center, P.O. Box 203, 697 Pomfret Street, Pomfret, CT 06258; tel: 203-928-2616; fax: 203-928-3713.

[46] Stephen Covey, *The Seven Habits of Highly Effective People* (New York: Simon & Schuster, 1989).

2

Diversity Consciousness and Success

Chapter Objectives

Upon completion of this chapter, you will be able to:

- Explain sociocultural theory.
- List and discuss diversity skills that promote success at school.
- List and discuss diversity skills that promote success at work.
- List and discuss the ways in which organizations benefit from the diversity consciousness of its employees.
- Describe diversity education and discuss examples.
- Explain why a lack of diversity consciousness is costly to individuals and organizations.

To be a black man in this society is hard, but not that hard that I shouldn't push to make my goals come true. Now I'm your average brother who plays basketball. Beside worrying about the white man trying to knock me down, there are people that I love doing the same thing (putting a brother down).

It all started when I found out I was going to a college in New Jersey to play ball. I got that chance to get an education while doing something I loved. Everyone was proud of their son, as well as their boy for taking the chance to better his self in today's cruel world. Besides the man using me to win him a championship in basketball, everyone I knew wanted me to get them out of my neck of the wood. Of course I'm going to help my boys that I grew up with. This was my boys, we did everything together since we could walk. If you think about it, they were the ones who got my game to where it needed to be to get me in school anywhere. So I owe them a lot, and I know this.

A small problem arised when I came home after the first year ended. Everything I said or did, I was acting White or I was lunchin. Everything I would say was wrong, because they said that I was trying to be better than them. All of a sudden jealousy rose between my click and I. The situation was getting in my mind because I could not understand why my peoples were faking on me because I was in school. In class one day, we were talking about how if you are trying to make it in today's world, no matter what the race, there is always someone trying to bring you down. That helped me understand what I was going through but that is today's society. You got to live with it or kill yourself. I know that I got things to achieve for my two sons and I, so don't look for my funeral arrangements yet. For my boys, I rubbed off on a couple. They are in school trying to get their GED. For the others we still have love for one another.

—Another perspective

DEFINITIONS OF SUCCESS

We define *success* in a variety of ways. One meaning, according to the dictionary, is the attainment of wealth, honors, and position. Another is simply to achieve what you want to achieve. In this book, success is the process of achieving our goals. Continual growth and learning are an integral part of this process—whether the goal is getting a good job, earning a degree, or simply doing one's best.

How do students define success? Often, the emphasis is on achieving a personal goal: getting through another day or earning a certain grade. Other definitions tend to focus more

THINKING THROUGH DIVERSITY

How do you define success?

on helping others: being a good role model or learning to work with others. Sometimes, students equate success with certain personal qualities such as character, self-awareness, or peace of mind. The following definitions reflect some of the markedly different ways in which students view success.

Success means establishing goals for yourself, and then not allowing anything to stand in your way.

⌘

Success is reaching a goal that seemed out of view. It is something you feel when you graduate after many years of schooling.

⌘

Success is having the bills paid, food in the fridge, a place to live, a car to drive, and the opportunity to live just one more day.

⌘

Success is not only materialistic. It is having a spiritual belief that values every person as your brother.

⌘

Success is what I believe it is. Success cannot be defined by anyone other than me.

⌘

Success is striving to be a better person by learning all that I can from numerous sources. Success for me is being able to learn something from a 2-year-old to the drug addict on the corner. It is being grounded enough to be able to communicate to people on their level and accept them for who they are.

⌘

Success is being aware of oneself. It is learning and growing from new experiences, being able to examine your strengths and weaknesses honestly, and having the courage to change if needed.

—Other perspectives

When I ask my students whom they consider to be highly successful, many list big-name entertainers, sports stars, and well-known political and business leaders. Interestingly, many more students include the names of people whom they know on a personal basis, including parents, friends, teachers, and others. Once in a while they mention themselves. In many of these cases, success is not the result of a single accomplishment. It is a work in progress; the culmination of many events: some positive, some negative.

One person who is at the top of my success list is my mother. Before dying, she changed her life of prostitution and drugs after 20 and some odd years. My aunt is also on my list because she just bought a car, something she'd been waiting for forever, but never seemed to have the money because of more important factors like her children.

⌘

My father, and for one reason only. Because he is now a part of my life. When I really, really need him now; he is there. It wasn't always so simple.

⌘

My brother, who is now 21 years old. He struggled with his asthma, and the fact that our father was never really around. He stayed in a depressed state for a couple of years. He overcame his depression with a lot of love from my mother and me. At 22, he started working and moved into his own apartment. Now, he holds a manager's position at a local shoe store.

—Other perspectives

Too often, we sell ourselves short. We fail to appreciate just how much we have to offer and all that we have accomplished. One of the things I do at the end of each semester is ask students to bring something to class that makes them feel special and successful. I tell them it should be something they feel comfortable sharing with their classmates. It is one of my favorite class sessions because it brings out a wonderful mix of success stories.

It is impossible to predict what students will choose to "show and tell." For instance, in one class, a student brought a picture of her family. Her pain was etched in her face as she recounted how she was abused as a child and how she has coped. A few brought in pictures of their children, each child described with such pride and love. One older student showed the high school diploma he earned in 1993. He explained that he was supposed to graduate in 1961 but dropped out of school during his senior year. "I was never satisfied until I got it," he said. A middle-aged male passed around a 50-cent coin that he had found as a little boy. As he described it, the coin had a picture of Booker T. Washington's face on one side and a slave cabin on the other. "My father," he explained, "preached to me that the only thing out there for black men is to be laborers. As long as I held on to that coin, I felt I could do more." With each student, a success is revealed and acknowledged. Even though their successes are markedly different, they unite through feelings of accomplishment and pride in themselves and each other.

> *When I listen to society's definition of success, I have to keep reminding myself that even though I am a part of society, I don't have to fit their mold. Success is contentment and it is something that is learned. It does not matter whether I have a lot or very little, because it will not change who I am. My success is achieved through a peaceful heart, a calm spirit, and a content state of being.*
>
> —Another perspective

Success stories are all around us and within us. They come in a wonderfully diverse assortment of shapes, sizes, and colors. Some are more obvious than others. As one of my students suggests, they can be found by looking for beauty in the ugliest of circumstances. At times, only we can appreciate the grandiose nature of what we accomplish.

What constitutes success and the paths to success vary from person to person. Consequently, there are an infinite variety of success stories. Too often, we hear only the success stories that make the news and involve the "rich and famous." It is of utmost importance to remember that success is relative. It depends on where we start, how far we come, and the obstacles we encounter along the way.

> *I have learned that success is to be measured not so much by the position that one has reached in life as by the obstacles which he has overcome while trying to succeed.*
>
> —Booker T. Washington

SOCIOCULTURAL THEORY AND SUCCESS

Social workers assess and evaluate clients by using a model they refer to as PIE, person in the environment. Using an *ecomap*, a drawing that illustrates the interdependence between an individual and his or her social environment, social workers determine the relationships among various systems in a client's life. A circle in the middle of a piece of paper represents a client. Other circles that are drawn around the client may be family, friends, and community organizations. Working together, the client and the social worker identify and explain the strengths and possible strains of each relationship. For example, strains found between a client and other systems are often due to diversity issues in the workplace, school, and/or healthcare system. This same model can help you discover interrelationships which impact on your successes.

Although any attempt to make sense of your success must focus on you, you are only part of the picture. The bigger picture includes your social environment, both past and present. This explanation of success is closely tied to **sociocultural theory,** a perspective that focuses on the social and cultural context of one's thoughts and actions.

According to sociocultural theory, we do not live in a vacuum. Interaction with **social forces,** or those omnipresent social influences that surround us, goes a long way toward explaining our attitudes, character, knowledge, and other individual attributes. Social forces even shape the way we view success and the explanations we offer for success. A study by Olson (1988) found that women and men explained their successes and failures differently during a mock interview. In comparison to men, women were more likely to see their successes resulting from luck. Olson concludes that this viewpoint may stem from social relationships that teach women to appear modest and avoid self-serving explanations.[1]

Each of us has a choice in how we react to situations, people, and events. *Every* response to *every* situation is something we can choose and ultimately control. Although our life experiences may *influence* who we are, they do not *determine* who we are. In *Sermons from the Black Pulpit,* Samuel Proctor says: "It does not matter where we were born, what kind of rearing we had, who our friends were, what kind of trouble we got into, how low we sank, or how far behind we fell. When we add it all up, we still have some options left, we still have some choices we can make."[2]

> *I'm 27. I live in a homeless shelter with other women. Living in that homeless shelter and coming to college is hard. When I'm at the shelter, I don't really get into what I'm doing that much because there is the envy and the jealousy among the other women and the counselors. I do a lot of downplaying. I keep it real low key. It can be very stressful. It's not that I feel I'm trying to be better than them. I feel there is enough for everybody. I always stress that you can do what I am doing if you really want it.*
>
> *I have to build my self-esteem. That's a daily thing. I think what helps me is my will, my determination. I am strong willed. I've been down. I want to be a power of example to the best of my ability. I want to be able to say "Look at me. I did it. You can."*
>
> —Another perspective

Too often, we arrive at simplistic explanations of success by failing to look at an array of individual and external influences and the interrelationships among them.

The idea that "no one is going to hire me because of the way I look" ignores the importance of motivation and hard work. These and other individual traits can help us overcome such barriers if indeed they exist. Equally naive is the thinking that "I don't need anyone" and "I can make it on my own."

Maureen, a college student, offers a more inclusive and empowering perspective. She acknowledges the origin of her values: "My mother instilled good values in me just like her mother did for her. She always told me I could get anything I want out of life if I work hard enough." Furthermore, Maureen is aware that her ethnic background shapes her goals and influences the way some people view her. In Maureen's case, this awareness becomes a motivator. "I feel as though some people view Latinos as lazy people who don't want to better themselves. They think all Latinos want a free ride, or welfare, which is not true because I go to college and I also work at night. It is this perception of Latinos that has motivated me to work hard at making life better for my daughter."

THINKING THROUGH DIVERSITY

One way of relating sociocultural theory to your life is to think of the bridges you have crossed to get where you are. People, both past and present, can be bridges in that their efforts make it possible for you to do the things you do. Oprah Winfrey talks about the bridges in her life: Sojourner Truth, Harriet Tubman, Fannie Lou Hamer, and others. What people have been bridges for you?

By relating sociocultural theory to our own lives, we will be better able to understand the importance of diversity skills. For example, my son Jimmy has autism. Autism is a severely incapacitating, lifelong disability. People with autism have a difficult time relating to others and dealing with change. They frequently act in a way people find strange and unacceptable. These autistic behaviors, which may be continual and almost impossible to control, seriously limit the person's ability to be independent.

As Jimmy's father, I become more empowered in many different realms as I realize I need the help of my wife and family, friends, social agencies, support groups, teachers, and therapists. For a long time, I was tempted to try to isolate myself from the rest of society. However, to get through each day and find the support and services Jimmy and I need, I have to develop my teamwork and interpersonal skills. I am more sensitive to others who may encounter the looks, ignorance, and insensitive comments that continue to be part of my daily life. Because I chose not to remain isolated, I developed diversity skills I would not have otherwise. Being aware of sociocultural influences helps us make the connection between our own lives and the resources that surround us.

WHY DIVERSITY SKILLS ARE IMPORTANT

An integral part of developing diversity consciousness is developing **diversity skills;** those competencies that allow people to interact with others in a way that respects and values differences. Diversity skills such as communication, teamwork,

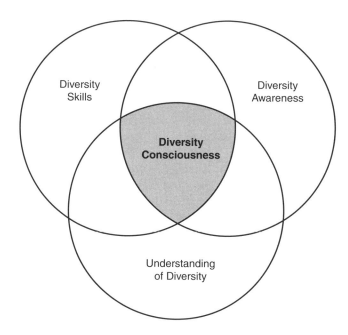

FIGURE 2.1 Diversity consciousness consists of three interrelated components; diversity awareness, understanding of diversity, and diversity skills.

and self-evaluation are key components of diversity consciousness. As defined earlier, diversity consciousness is more than just being knowledgeable about or aware of differences. It is the awareness, understanding, *and* skills that allow us to think through and value human differences. As our awareness and understanding expand, so do our diversity skills. Similarly, developing and refining our diversity skills increases our awareness and understanding (see Fig. 2.1).

We often ignore or trivialize the relationship between diversity consciousness and success. This is due, in part, to our limited perception of diversity. Traditionally, the idea of diversity has revolved around some of the more obvious differences among people, such as race, ethnicity, and gender. In this chapter and throughout the book, we adopt the more current, inclusive view of diversity. Dimensions of diversity also include learning styles, multiple intelligences, personalities, personal expectations, and a wide variety of other differences that often remain hidden. By broadening our conceptualization of diversity, we are better able to develop an array of skills that can motivate and empower us. These skills are referred to throughout this book as diversity skills. A comprehensive list of these skills can be found in Chapter 4, page 114.

Success at School

If we develop our diversity consciousness, we can be more successful in the classroom. Research, case studies, and student experiences underscore the importance of diversity skills. As you read about five of these skills, examine yourself. Which are strengths of yours? Which need a little or a lot more work? What might you do to improve certain skills?

1. *Flexible thinking.*   This is the ability to understand and adapt to a variety of perspectives, depending on the situation. One good example of flexible thinking is being able to understand and respect **learning styles**, the way people learn. A good deal of research has identified numerous learning styles. For instance, some students find they learn best when they interact with others in small groups. Some prefer a highly structured lecture format. Whereas some are visual learners, others prefer listening. There are students who can learn from anybody, and those who find learning nearly impossible if they cannot relate to their instructor. Research has shown that we can change and expand our learning style. Developing this flexibility benefits us.

Involvement in Learning, a report by the Study Group on the Conditions of Excellence in American Higher Education, concludes that students can be more successful by taking control of their own education.[3] Being aware of your learning styles as well as becoming a more flexible learner can help you identify your strengths and avoid problematic situations. Begin by asking yourself: "How do I learn best?"

More than 30 learning style testing instruments have been developed to assess learning style preferences and strengths.[4] However, it is important to remember that no one assessment can definitively tell us what we can and cannot do when it comes to learning. It can, however, indicate possible tendencies and habits.

The concept of cultural learning styles suggests that cultural upbringing plays a critical role in determining a student's learning style. Cultural group's values may influence child-rearing practices and, in turn, the learning styles children develop. Numerous studies have attempted to identify learning style preferences among students from diverse cultural backgrounds. For example, in their review of research, Irvine and York (1995) found that Native American students tend to be *field-dependent.* Field-dependent students like to work with others to achieve a common goal and are more sensitive to the needs of others than *field-independent* students, who prefer to work independently and compete for individual recognition. Their study also revealed that Native American students tend to prefer learning in private rather than public, and prefer learning by watching and doing.[5]

In spite of research findings that point to cultural learning styles, there remains significant intracultural variability. For example, within any cultural group, ways of thinking and speaking vary with age, income, education, and class status. Hence, broad depictions of African-Americans, Native-Americans, or Latinos as having different learning styles are likely to be stereotypical and resented by members of these groups who are not accurately represented by these generalizations.

Once you have a better idea of how you learn, you are better able to monitor, adapt, and ultimately improve your learning. In a given class, you may determine that your learning style conflicts with your instructor's teaching style. Perhaps you learn best when *you* talk about something but your instructor is a straight lecturer. Knowing this, you might compensate by forming a study group and talking about the lecture after each class.

I have a physics instructor who speaks and pronounces words a lot differently than I do. These differences between her language and mine created a conflict at first because I kept telling myself I can't learn from this woman. But I began to pay closer attention and improve my listening skills. She also helped me learn I cannot depend on my instructors to teach me everything. I also have to use my textbooks and talk to others to get a full understanding of the subject at hand.

—Another perspective

Researchers have also examined different intellectual strengths or intelligences. These strengths may come into play during the learning process (see Diversity Box: Multiple Intelligences). A greater awareness of the variety of intelligences as well as learning styles can empower us and maximize our chances for success. Also, it can help us acknowledge and value the large variety of individual capabilities we will encounter. Consequently, we are better able to appreciate that an individual's lesser abilities in one intellectual area do *not* imply lesser abilities in all intellectual areas. Some of us may be artistic while others may show more promise in science or music. It is, however, important not to use our own differences in learning styles as an excuse.

When I am faced with a teacher whose strategies of teaching conflict with my learning style, I try to adapt instead of giving up. All teachers have different strengths and weaknesses. I think that in order to succeed in the classroom, you have to take the responsibility for adjusting to all kinds of teaching styles.

—Another perspective

Multiple Intelligences

In 1983, Harvard University professor Howard Gardner identified a number of different intelligences.[6] Currently Gardner theorizes that while each of us possesses at least eight intelligences some are more fully developed than others. This theory may help explain why we can pick up some things very easily and other tasks come much harder. It also sheds light on why a particular subject might be difficult for you but not for some other students in your class.

Gardner identifies the following eight intelligences: Verbal-linguistic, logical-mathematical, spatial, bodily-kinesthetic, interpersonal, intrapersonal, musical, and environmental. Throughout our school years, most of us are taught by teachers who use verbal-linguistic and logical-mathematical strategies. Our ability to understand them depends on our capacity to use language and understand logical reasoning and problem solving. Those of us with undeveloped skills in one or more of these areas may be at a disadvantage. In some other classes, however, we may encounter teachers who use alternative teaching methods that tap other types of intelligence.

Picture yourself in Professor B's math class. You are someone who has a long history of problems in math. However, your grades in this class are good for a change. You think it might have something to do with the way Professor B teaches: She seems to connect very well with students and employs a variety of teaching styles. One technique in particular seems almost funny at first but you find it helps. She creates raps out of different formulas and mathematical definitions. The class then does the rap together and some of the students really "get into it." The following is one example: it is a rap that helps you remember the steps to follow when graphing a line.

The Slope-Intercept Form Rap

$y = mx + b$
b's the y-intercept, so plot it first, ya' see?
m is the slope—rise over run.
So go up or down and to the right and then
   you're done.

According to Professor B, raps such as this make learning easier because they draw upon a number of different intelligences, including musical, interpersonal, and bodily-kinesthetic. The rhythmic nature of rap, for example, appeals to those students who have a well-developed capacity to hear and remember musical patterns. Bodily-kinesthetic intelligence, the capacity to use hands, arms, and other body parts to take in knowledge, feeds into the rhythmic feel of rap. Furthermore, the fact that it is an interpersonal activity utilizes still another type of intelligence.

What can we learn from this experience? It is not enough to view this one class as a positive unique experience and leave it at that. It might be helpful to seek out other teachers who teach this way. But realistically speaking, how many Professor B types are there? Maybe a better strategy is to realize how much this way of remembering helps you and use this technique in another class. In your next math class, you might try putting some of the new formulas to rhythm. Another idea is to get together with a group of other students from Professor B's class and try to create similar ways of remembering math or maybe another subject.

2. *Ability to appreciate and maintain pride in one's background and culture.* In her book *Affirming Diversity,* Sonja Nieto describes her research on a diverse group of "successful students." In this study, success meant that the students were still in school and planning to complete high school, or had recently graduated. They also have good grades, generally enjoy school, have plans for their future, and describe themselves as successful. Nieto concludes, "one of the most consistent, and least expected, outcomes to emerge from these case studies has been the resoluteness with which young people maintain pride and satisfaction in their culture and the strength they derive from it."[7] Furthermore, Nieto states that learning about one's culture, and how it informs and enriches us, is not easy. Chapter 4 elaborates on this important area of diversity consciousness.

I am an Orthodox Jew and it is very important for me to practice my religion. I cannot go out and act any old way. Two nights a week I go to Talmud classes and

I am not allowed to go to school or study on the Sabbath or Jewish holidays. When I am at school, I say a blessing before and after I eat lunch. I also pray three times a day. When I am studying with someone during the time I observe afternoon prayer, I simply tell that person I have to stop and pray for a few minutes. I understand that the world does not revolve around the Jewish calendar. Therefore, I have learned to focus on my religion no matter who is around or what the situation is. This has made me a stronger Jew and a stronger student. I take pride in my difference—in my strong family and religious background.

⌘

My grandparents were both from France. My grandfather served in the French calvary and lost his leg in World War I. Henriette, my grandmother, came to this country alone. Even though she only knew a few words in English, she somehow managed to find a job and save enough money to buy a house. Her husband and children then joined her. Henriette and I were very close. She made me proud of my French and American heritage. When things get stressful, especially at school, thinking of Henriette puts things in perspective, and gives me strength.

⌘

My relatives raised me to have self-esteem, to know of my history. We were taught that from the time we could read, when there weren't any black coloring books. My mother used to color the kids in the coloring books black. Jack and Jill were black. They might have been coal black but we understood where they were coming from.
    Later on, I went to a racially mixed high school and I never felt inferior to anybody. And it got me into trouble because I do not allow that kind of stuff to filter into my mindset. I was always arguing with the teachers because I refused to answer questions a certain way. I would say "look at Ethiopia, look at the pyramids, look at this, look at that."

—Other perspectives

THINKING THROUGH DIVERSITY

What is the best way for you to learn? What do you do when you find yourself in a learning environment that does not match your learning style?

3. *Ability to network and learn from everyone and anyone.* In his national study (1993) of undergraduates, Astin examines whether students' direct involvement in "diversity experiences" affects their academic progress. One of these experiences was the frequency with which students socialize with persons from diverse backgrounds. Astin found that interaction of this nature has a significant positive effect on practically all measures of students' academic development and satisfaction with college.[8] In other words, we increase our chances for success by expanding and diversifying our social network. In so doing, we learn more about who we are and our ability to relate to others. This, in turn, helps us develop our diversity consciousness. In Chapter 4 we elaborate on this.

4. *Ability to deal effectively with barriers.* Much research examines the relationship between expectations and success. In many cases, our own expectations or the expectations of others act as barriers. According to the concept of the self-fulfilling prophecy, students conform to the expectations of teachers. However, students' expectations of themselves are equally important. For example, there are teachers who say their course is hard and one-half of the class will drop by midsemester. While some students respond by mentally preparing themselves to drop the course, others react differently. They view expectations of this nature as a challenge and do everything in their power to complete this course "successfully." Barriers to success, and their relationship to diversity, are the focal point of Chapter 3.

The fact that I know everyone expects me to fail causes me to work very hard. I am on a mission to prove to everyone that I am capable. Every time I experience racism I tell myself that my ancestors experienced worse. I want to be an example of what my people are capable of; so I strive to accomplish the impossible.

⌘

From the time I was little, my parents taught me to believe in myself and what I could do. With great pride, they took me to museums and replicas of pioneer villages to show me what my culture has produced. When school gets overwhelming, I find myself thinking back on what I was taught. I believe I can get through anything if I work hard enough.

⌘

My cultural background has been an important factor in my success at school. Because of my major, I had to take biochemistry at the beginning of my sophomore year. The class I attended had only three African-American students. About three weeks into the course, we had our first test. All three of us failed. I remember feeling embarrassed and very intimidated. I felt like quitting, but I didn't want my classmates to think that all African-Americans are dumb plus quitters. I vowed that I would be in the top percent of my class. When the next test was announced, my instructor informed the other two students and myself that we needed to study because there was an academic standard that must be upheld at this school. I felt she had purposely singled us out because other students had failed and yet they didn't get the same kind of warning. At this point, it became a matter of principle to do well on the test. Initially I was going to do well just for my own pride. But after the teacher's remark it became something more. It seemed to me that if I didn't do well on this test, she would forever think that I and all other African-Americans were not capable of meeting the academic standards of the school. On that test, I made a 97, which was the second-highest grade in the class. I continued to study hard and made very good grades until I received my diploma.

—Other perspectives

Punjabi Student Expectations

The Punjabi families who reside in the California community of "Valleyside" are immigrants from India. They offer valuable insight into the relationship between expectations and success. Punjabi students are highly successful. Their families teach them that they are responsible for their own success. These students have high expectations of themselves. They know they must study hard and succeed in school for the honor of themselves, their families, and their community. If not they put themselves at risk for being withdrawn from school and sent back to work in the fields.[9]

5. *Ability to balance "fitting in" and "being yourself."* When students attend college, they may encounter a cultural setting that is unfamiliar and uncomfortable.

THINKING THROUGH DIVERSITY

If someone were to write your life history, what would we learn about the relationship between expectations and academic success?

As one example, due to their social class background, students might encounter an environment that makes it difficult to learn and succeed. Some students may feel they have to deny or cover up their social class in order to fit in with students from higher or lower socioeconomic backgrounds. Making this cultural adjustment on a daily basis can have profound implications. Like other diversity skills, the ability to make this kind of adjustment is connected with our diversity consciousness. More specifically, each of us can develop this ability as we learn to understand and value ourselves, individually and culturally.

Sometimes, certain ways of accommodating or fitting in are necessary. For example, some rules and expectations must be followed. Mastery of English or the language of instruction is critical. Some students resist talking standard English or even getting good grades because they equate it with "selling out." Willie Jolley, a motivational speaker who grew up in one of the poorer neighborhoods of Washington, DC, recounts how one of his friends took his books to and from school in a plastic bag because he did not want to appear too studious. Stacie, one of my students, describes how her own family criticizes the way she speaks. "A lot of times at home they would say, 'Why are you talking like you're White?'" Her response was, "I'm not talking like I'm White. I'm just trying to speak correct English."

Findings from research[10] point to the potential benefits of transculturation. **Transculturation** is the process by which a person adjusts to another cultural environment without sacrificing his or her own cultural identity. In analyzing the factors that affect the academic achievement of Native American and white students attending college in South Dakota, Huffman discovered fundamental differences. High school grade-point average and parental encouragement to attend college relate significantly to the academic success of Whites. Among Native Americans, the retention of traditional cultural heritage is the most important predictor of success.

A middle-aged woman talks about making the necessary adjustments at college without assimilating or losing her cultural distinctiveness. "When we go to school we live a non-Indian way but we still keep our values. . . . I could put my values aside just long enough to learn what it is I want to learn but that doesn't mean I'm going to forget them. I think that is how strong they are with me."[11] Although this study focuses on Native-Americans, transculturation can benefit all of us. We empower ourselves when we learn we can adjust to any situation without sacrificing or compromising our beliefs.

My culture is in my soul all the time.

—Another perspective

THINKING THROUGH DIVERSITY

When you find yourself in a cultural environment outside of your own, how do you know when to adjust and when to resist?

Success at Work

> With our workforce demographics rapidly changing, managing diversity has become a critical managerial skill for those desiring to succeed in corporate America. In healthcare and in particular at the Johns Hopkins Hospital, we have long served patients from around the world. Now, our employees increasingly come from a variety of backgrounds and experiences. The extent to which our caregivers understand differences and have respect for each other as well as our patients will be the extent to which we will be successful in delivering excellent patient care.
>
> —Ron Peterson, President, Johns Hopkins Hospital
> (ranked by *U.S. News and World Report* as the nation's #1 hospital)

> We believe that to survive and thrive in today's multicultural business environment, we must appreciate differences in education, backgrounds, experiences and perspectives. In doing so, we create a stronger team and a better workplace.
>
> —Max Messmer, Chairman and CEO, Office Team
> (the nation's leading staffing service, specializing in highly skilled office and administrative support professionals)

There is a mismatch today between the skills that college graduates bring to the workplace and what employers need (see Fig. 2.2). More and more employers need workers who can cooperate, collaborate, build trust and contribute to teams, negotiate disagreements, and constantly learn and adapt in any situation. Unfortunately, many employers complain about new hires as well as more experienced workers

FIGURE 2.2   Dilbert, by Scott Adams. *(By permission from United Media.)*

lacking these skills. Consequently, key interview questions often target how well one relates to and works with others. Some common examples follow:

- With what type of people do you have the most difficulty working? Why?
- Which of your skills would you rate higher—your "technical" or interpersonal skills? Why?
- What do you do when someone is critical of you and seems not to like you?
- If you sensed that your work group was not accepting you, what might you do?

According to a recent study by the American Management Association, new hires were found seriously lacking in a number of skills that employers consider crucial.[12] Each of these skills relate to diversity consciousness. Specifically, new hires were deficient in "speaking one-on-one," "relating to others," and "working as a team player" (see Fig. 2.3). Comments from leaders in business and education throughout this chapter provide further insight into the importance of key diversity skills.

Clearly, diversity conscious individuals are very much in demand. Employers value them. Thus, developing this consciousness enhances your chances of landing a job and becoming a highly valued, successful employee. With this in mind, ask yourself the following question: Given your background, knowledge, and experience, how well can you meet employers' needs in the following areas?

1. *Interpersonal skills.*   In subjects ranging from business management to healthcare to teacher education, it is not uncommon to see entire chapters in textbooks devoted to the subject of interpersonal skills. Increasingly, educators and employers are realizing that strong people skills are just as important as technical expertise. A study

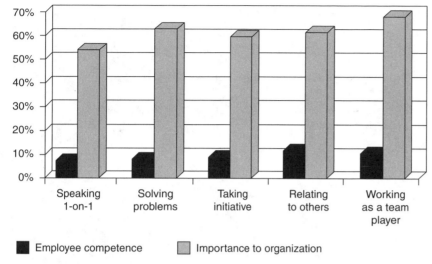

FIGURE 2.3 Workforce skills among new hires.
(Data from American Management Association, 1997.)

by Dowd and Liedtka, commissioned by the faculty at the University of Virginia's Darden Graduate School of Business, examined what corporations are seeking in the MBAs they hire. Analysis of interview questions by corporate recruiters nationwide revealed that one of the most desired capabilities is interpersonal skills. These skills include the ability to adapt to the feelings and concerns of others, motivate people, and deal effectively with adversity and conflict.[13] In another study, the Secretary of Labor's Commission on Achieving Necessary Skills determined interpersonal skills to be one of four critical competencies in today's workforce. More specifically, the commission concludes that employees need to function effectively on teams, teach others, serve customers, lead and negotiate, and work well with people from culturally diverse backgrounds.[14] Interpersonal skills are discussed at length in the chapters on communication (Chapter 5) and teamwork (Chapter 6).

Employees need to relate effectively to the customer at the point of encounter (see Fig. 2.4). This requires interpersonal skills that some businesspeople refer to as *emotional intelligence* (see Diversity Box: Emotional Intelligence). Profits in any service-oriented industry depend to a large degree on employees who greet and service the public. A well-trained receptionist with excellent interpersonal skills can make a customer feel valued. Conversely, a salesperson or security guard who lacks these skills and is insensitive to diversity can hurt business.

The importance of treating people with respect and sensitivity was evident in a recent incident involving Eddie Bauer, a large upscale clothing store chain. Alonzo Jackson, a young black male, was detained by store personnel as he was leaving an Eddie Bauer outlet in the Washington, DC metropolitan area. A security guard became suspicious when he noticed that Mr. Jackson's shirt looked new. It was. He had

FIGURE 2.4 In addition to being technically proficient, students need diversity skills. In the words of one dental hygiene instructor, "If one of my students leaves one small piece of plaque or calculus, that's not the most important thing. What is really important is whether that student connects with the patient. The patient should feel like she or he is the most important person in the world."

bought the shirt at the store the previous day. However, Mr. Jackson did not have the receipt in his possession so employees forced him to remove his shirt. When he returned to the store with a receipt the next day, they gave him back his shirt but did not apologize. Mr. Jackson later filed a suit against the company, accusing Eddie Bauer of "consumer racism." To the plaintiffs, the incident typified how black shoppers are targeted. Eddie Bauer's lawyers countered by arguing that the individual employees themselves, not the company, should be held responsible. Eddie Bauer lost the case and alienated many customers.

Emotional Intelligence

In his best-selling book *Working with Emotional Intelligence,* Daniel Goleman analyzes those skills that distinguish average performers from superstars.[15] On the basis of data collected from more than 150 business firms he concludes that emotional intelligence skills are the key.

Emotional intelligence is the ability to acknowledge, value, and manage feelings so that they are expressed appropriately and effectively, laying the groundwork for meaningful relationships and true teamwork.

Goleman goes on to say that it is not enough to be technically proficient and possess a high IQ. Although school smarts might get you into the office, your ability to handle emotions and relate to people effectively allows you to excel on the job.

As an example, Goleman points to a 1997 study cited in the *Journal of the American Medical Association.* This study reports physicians who lacked empathy got sued more often. However, physicians who never had a malpractice suit possessed better interpersonal skills. They were empathetic and took time to communicate at length with their patients. During this time, they told their patients what to expect from treatment, checked their understanding, and asked their opinion. They encouraged questions and even laughing and joking.[16]

2. *Flexible thinking skills and adaptability.* Perhaps you are a single parent who has struggled though difficult times. Maybe you have a military background that has given you the opportunity to live in numerous countries throughout the world. These kinds of experiences may help you think creatively and flexibly. Gene Polisseni, a vice president of marketing for a highly successful processing firm, is typical of many employers nowadays. He wants "people who are upbeat. . . who know life isn't always perfect and can go on when they hit a pothole."[17]

Flexible thinkers do not lock themselves into one mode of thought. Rather, they can adjust mentally to different situations. More and more employers need and want workers who are problem solvers, who can do more with less by examining both the familiar and unfamiliar from a variety of perspectives. This kind of thinking requires practice and a will to learn. In Chapter 4 we examine how flexible thinking enables us to increase our diversity consciousness.

Thinking Outside the Box

In the business world, flexible thinking is sometimes described as thinking outside the box. This kind of thinking is necessary to solve the following problem.

Directions: Draw four straight lines, without lifting your pencil, that touch all the dots. (*Note:* See the answer at the end of the chapter.)

In his book *A Kick in the Seat of the Pants,* Roger von Oech describes the flexibility of thought that characterizes creative thinkers. "Like race-car drivers who shift in and out of different gears depending on where they are on the course, creative people are able to shift in and out of different types of thinking depending on the needs of the situation at hand. Sometimes they're open and probing, at others they're playful and off-the-wall. At still other times, they're critical and fault-finding. And finally, they're doggedly persistent in striving to reach their goals."[18]

3. *Teamwork skills.*   More and more organizations are turning to teams to solve problems and create better products and services. Consequently, people need to prepare themselves to join and contribute to teams. According to Andrea Dolph, coauthor of *How to Hit the Ground Running in Your New Job,* new graduates are sometimes insensitive to the needs of other team members in the workplace. She recalls when she started her career. "I was ambitious and often insensitive to some of the issues and priorities other people at work had to deal with."[19] When working on any team, it is important to remember "you're working with people from a variety of age groups and with different events in their lives—people with elder care issues or children for example. Have respect for the differences among people in your workplace."[20] In Chapter 6 we focus entirely on the subject of teamwork.

4. *Cultural awareness and understanding.*   Awareness and understanding make it possible for you not only to recognize cultural differences and similarities, but also to grasp their meaning and significance. This learned skill is absolutely essential, at home or abroad, given a customer base that is becoming increasingly multinational and multicultural. As the buying power of minorities in the United States increases, businesses are directing more of their attention to minority marketing. Numerous advertising agencies now specialize in Asian-, African-, and Hispanic-American marketing. As the marketplace expands, a lack of cultural awareness and understanding is even more of a liability. It is clearly difficult to design and develop merchandise for markets you do not understand. Kentucky Fried Chicken found this out the hard way. Their advertising slogan "finger-lickin good" became "Eat your fingers off" when translated into Chinese.

5. *Self-evaluation.*   Stephen Covey, best-selling author and business consultant, says a common complaint of business leaders is that they cannot find workers who will take on the responsibility for making good things happen.[21] To do this requires continuous self-evaluation. This skill is particularly critical for managers. According to psychologist Daniel Goleman, research reveals that exceptional managers have faults like anyone else; however, "they are *aware* of their limits—and so they know where they need to improve, or they know to work with someone else who has a strength they lack."[22] By being open to feedback from others and monitoring yourself, you are more apt to realize why diversity consciousness is so important and what skills you may need to develop. Rather than simply relying on someone else to make this happen, you take the initiative. Self-evaluation, or what I term in later chapters "checking up on yourself," is a key area in the development of diversity consciousness.

In subsequent chapters, flexible thinking, cultural awareness and understanding, teamwork, communication, self-evaluation, and other basic diversity skills are discussed in more detail. Improving skills such as these allows us to develop our diversity consciousness. The benefits are numerous. We grow more aware of the value of human differences and the limitations imposed by close-mindedness. At the same time, we do not preoccupy ourselves with differences. This means that we can acknowledge, respect, *and* see beyond differences. In so doing, we relate to others more effectively and capitalize on human potential—our own as well as that of others.

▣ INDIVIDUAL/ORGANIZATIONAL BENEFITS

> *Understanding, celebrating and embracing differences provide a rich environment and taps into the best of everybody.*
>
> —Frank Blethen, CEO of the Seattle Times Company
> (winner of the 1997 Ida B. Wells Award for his leadership in hiring,
> training, and advancing minorities in media careers)

> *If businesses are going to succeed, regardless of their goals, they need to understand the business case for diversity. It will honestly determine their success.*
>
> —Carl Jefferson, Diversity Manager, Interstate Hotels Corporation
> (the largest hotel management firm in the United States)

> *In our rapidly changing business, high-technology companies need people who come from diverse backgrounds and who can contribute different talents and perspectives to problem solving. Diversity is key to problem solving and problem solving is key to technology. To be the best, we must utilize the talents of all segments of the population. I believe diversity and valuing individuals has helped Texas Instruments grow into a stronger and more competitive company.*
>
> —Tegwin Dyer Pulley, Vice President, Texas Instruments (the world's
> leading designer and supplier of digital signal processing solutions)

The Individual

Increasingly, "qualified" is synonymous with college educated *and* diversity conscious. And as companies compete for the best talent available, both in the United States and abroad, it is prospective employees' diversity consciousness that gives them a competitive edge (see Fig. 2.5). Take a look in the employment section of any major newspaper in the United States. What follows are some actual, typical ads for a variety of positions.

THINKING THROUGH DIVERSITY

Select one school you attend(ed). If you were to grade this school on its ability to capitalize on diversity, what grade would you give, and why?

- ■ "Great communicators wanted. Talk is cheap. Communicating is what really counts. After all, this is the Information Age. And if you don't have it, you won't be around very long." (communication specialist)

FIGURE 2.5 The ability to recognize the power and possibilities of diversity has increasingly become a requirement for success in today's competitive business environment. *(Photo by Regina Bryan.)*

- "Demonstrated ability to bring about constructive change using participatory processes and strong human relations skills." (college administrator)
- "We require excellent communication and customer service skills. Fluency in French or Spanish strongly desired." (sales and service representative)
- "Excellent interpersonal and communication skills. Communication experience on a global level a plus." (marketing/promotional writer)
- "Candidates must have strong computer programming and analytical skills, leadership potential, and the interpersonal skills needed to work effectively in a demanding team environment." (technical associate—information)
- "We are looking for a team-oriented professional to provide leadership, direction, and technical expertise to support the current reporting infrastructure across our global enterprise-wide organization." (program analyst)
- "The position requires an individual who is a quick learner of new technologies with proven qualities of leadership, effective teamwork, and communication . . . . Our people are diverse, and we capitalize on that diversity as we help each other grow and develop our talents in our areas of expertise." (Web application development and support)
- "Outstanding client relationship skills. Outstanding communication (written and verbal) skills. Strong self-starter, self-motivated, and willing to take on responsibility as an absolute team player." (computer assurance services)
- "We develop innovative programs and treatment modalities to meet the complex needs of an increasingly diverse population. . . need someone to help foster effective interaction with facility staff, patients, consumers, their families, and locally based providers to deliver a progressive continuum of mental health services." (mental health facility director)

One indication of the importance of diversity consciousness is the emergence of diversity training into a highly competitive and profitable industry. Schools, government agencies, and major companies such as Levi-Strauss, IBM, Dow, Digital, and Avon spend millions each year on training of this nature. In some cases, the evaluation of an employee's contributions in the area of workforce diversity is one of the performance criteria that determines his or her salary and bonuses. A more detailed discussion of diversity training and its role in diversity education appears later in this chapter.

The Organization

We are in an industry that historically has not been inclusive. To move forward we need to learn how to communicate effectively with people who are different. Diversity efforts are critical components of reaching our business objectives.

—Richard Gaskins, Vice-President, Diversity Resource Center, American Express Financial Advisors (one of the largest financial planning and money management companies in the United States)

Diversity has tremendous power. The work we do involves dealing with a few pieces of information. We make a decision based on that. With a diverse group of people, we can be more objective. In a diverse group, I get a more balanced view of a problem than if I was looking at the data myself.

—Jose Arreola, Vice President of Research and Development, Cypress Semiconductor (a $600 million international supplier of high-performance semiconductors for the computer, networking, and telecommunications industries)

Why is it important for you to understand why organizations attach so much importance to diversity consciousness? In the course of your lifetime, you will deal with many **organizations,** groupings of people organized to achieve one or a number of goals. Many organizations are employers, including businesses, government agencies, educational institutions, and charitable agencies. Examining how and why organizations operate the way they do will allow you to assess what skills are in demand. Also, you will be better able to understand how diversity consciousness affects the organization and its members. Why, for example, do people at all levels and in all positions need diversity skills? How do these skills affect productivity? Why do surveys consistently show that CEOs of large and growing companies believe diversity is essential to their ongoing success? Whatever your position and function, you need to develop a perspective that is organizational as well as individual.

At the organizational level, the advantages afforded by a diversity conscious workforce are numerous.

1. *More innovation and adaptability.*   Diversity consciousness generates a variety of innovative responses to challenges. In dealing with technological advances, international developments, and other social and economic changes, there is less reliance on tradition and more of a focus on creative problem solving. In the business world, the result is typically better products and better services, new customer/client populations, and the expansion of existing markets. For example, U.S. companies alter their marketing strategies as they grow more aware of the buying power of all types of minorities. American Telephone and Telegraph (AT&T) mailed brochures depicting three couples in affectionate poses: two women, two men, and a man and a woman. The slogan reads "Let Your True Voice Be Heard." Other companies, such as Saab, are now running their usual ads in gay publications.

2. *Better communication.*   It is not enough to have employees with diverse talents and backgrounds. In sports, this is why the team with superior talent may not always win. Teams with less talent, but better communication skills and a stronger commitment to the group, are able to maximize their collective talent. They put the team first and reach a consensus on their goals and roles.

The same thing holds true in the workplace. Without effective communication, teamwork suffers and talent is wasted. An example of this is **groupthink,** going along uncritically with the expectations of a group, which in turn limits understanding of an issue. Groupthink, a dynamic identified by Irving Janis (1972), is one of the great challenges of homogenous groups. When group members share similar backgrounds and beliefs, cohesion and conformity can become an end in itself. People fail to think independently as they quickly agree with what appears to be the consensus of the group.[23] For example, an employee might think of a radically different approach to a group problem. Reluctantly, she keeps it to herself because of the vibes she has gotten from other group members in the past. Her ideas are often dismissed as far-fetched and idealistic. Rather than take a chance, she ends up going along with the group because she doesn't want to "rock the boat." This scenario, which is very common in work teams, produces mediocre solutions to difficult problems.

3. *Recruitment and retention of the best employees.*   Those organizations with the best reputation for attracting and maintaining an inclusive and highly competent workforce will be at an advantage in terms of recruiting and keeping the best talent. The consequences of limiting the talent pool are obvious when we examine intercollegiate athletics. Formerly all-white southern colleges and universities did not recruit Blacks and other students of color. Consequently, they denied themselves some of the best athletic talent available at that time.

4. *Less likelihood of incurring the costs of discrimination.*   Discrimination is very expensive. It creates conflict, siphons off people's talents and energies, and leads to the underutilization of human potential. A fact-finding report by the Glass Ceiling Commission states that "barriers persist," slowing down the advancement of women and minorities and depriving companies of the talent and diversity they need to compete globally.[24]

5. *Greater productivity.*   If you feel valued, you are going to be more productive. This is the rationale behind "managing diversity." **Managing diversity** does *not* imply control or manipulation; rather, it means creating an environment that enables everyone to contribute their full potential.

People who develop their diversity consciousness are more valued employees. They can help members of any organization work together to improve the quality of their product or service. This, in turn, will increase profits. Therefore, the importance of diversity consciousness is not some "feel good" issue. It relates directly to the "bottom line"—productivity and profit.

> *Unless we recognize and appreciate diversity—I don't mean tolerate but appreciate— we are doing more harm than good. By adding accountability for diversity in annual performance summary for managers, we make sure people are really getting it. They're not just getting what diversity means, but doing something about it.*
>
> —Debbie A. Smith, Senior Vice President and Director of Diversity, Allfirst Financial, Inc.

> *Valuing and creating a work environment that is diverse is a priority at Xerox. If it's a priority, then it needs to be tracked and rewarded. If objectives are not met, then there needs to be a consequence.*
>
> —Pat Elizondo, Vice President and General Manager, Xerox Corporation (Xerox is the winner of the first award given by the Federal Glass Ceiling Commission for commitment to diversity)

DIVERSITY EDUCATION IN THE WORKPLACE

Given the challenges of creating a diversity conscious workforce, many employers in business, government, healthcare, education, and numerous other fields have begun to offer and even require diversity education. Spurred on by demographic data that point to a continually shrinking percentage of white males in the workforce, many human resource departments now send workers to lectures and workshops to help them work with colleagues and relate to customers in a multicultural, multiracial environment. Recently, there has been a proliferation of videos, seminars, books, and journals on managing and valuing diversity. "Diversity managers" are now commonplace in Fortune 500 companies.

In many organizations, diversity education is a multifaceted, comprehensive program to attract, educate, and retain a more diversified workforce (see Fig. 2.6). For example, International Business Machines (IBM), a corporate leader in embracing

The American Business Collaboration
Child and Elder Care Resource and Referral Service
Community Contributions
Community Outreach:
    Community Service Assignment
    Diversity Campus Executive Program
    Faculty Loan Program
    Technical Academic Career Program
Diversity Councils
Diversity Network Groups
Diversity Training:
    Global
    Employee
    Manager
Executive Task Forces/Shared Leadership Teams
Fund for Community Service
K-12 Initiatives
LifeWorks
Mentoring
Minority/Women/People with Disabilities Business
Development Program
People of Color/People with Disabilities Technology
Committee
Recruiting:
    Diversity-Experienced Professionals
    Entry Point (AAAS)
    Project View
Women's Initiatives
    Global
    Multicultural Women
    Technical

FIGURE 2.6 IBM diversity education programs. *(Source: IBM "Directory of Diversity Programs," http://www3.ibm.com/employment/us/diverse/programs_ibm.shtml, accessed 8/28/02. Reprinted by permission of IBM.)*

and valuing differences, organizes its diversity programs on three platforms—Equal Opportunity, Affirmative Action, and Work/Life. In their "Directory of Diversity Programs," IBM characterizes each platform as follows:

> *Equal Opportunity* means opening doors of every level of the company. It includes nondiscrimination and nonharassment.
>
> *Affirmative Action* includes taking the steps to ensure that everyone is allowed to compete on an equal basis. It provides practical assistance to people in groups historically excluded from participating in our economic system. Our intent is not to provide advantage, but to eliminate disadvantage.
>
> *Work/Life* programs help employees to balance the needs of the office and home. They are designed to allow employees to be productive and serve our cus-

tomers at the same time, while also fulfilling the responsibilities of their personal lives.[25]

Diversity education usually refers to a variety of initiatives that ideally reflect an ongoing, organization-wide commitment to continuous learning. Among these initiatives are mentoring; learning centers with books, videos, and other learning materials; and training in areas such as leadership, team-building, and customer service. Increasingly, organizations measure the outcomes of diversity education.

Specific objectives of diversity education include understanding the challenges and benefits of diversity, identifying assumptions that interfere with teamwork, and developing specific diversity skills. Initiatives may target change in an individual's awareness, attitudes, and behaviors, or change in the culture of an organization, meaning its programs and policies, chain of command, and generally the way it conducts business.

Interactive Drama at Xerox Corporation

At Xerox Corporation, managers are evaluated on their ability to deal with diversity issues. Managers attend special interactive theater productions around the country as part of their training. These dramas represent a joint effort by the Theater Department at Cornell University and Xerox. Actors portray a variety of scenarios in which managers interact with employees who may look, think, and act differently. After each short play, the actors stay in character and respond to questions. Managers evaluate the choices made and offer suggestions. The productions' aim is to make managers more aware of discrimination and give them the tools to deal with it.

An increasingly important focus of diversity education is **ethics,** people's morals or standards regarding the rightness and wrongness of certain human actions in light of specific circumstances. Most people associate ethics with values or moral principles that help us determine what is fair and honorable. In a diverse marketplace and workplace, deciding what is right is increasingly difficult. Because of cultural differences, there is often a difference of opinion and therefore ethical conflicts can arise. For instance, until recently it was generally believed that physicians knew what was in their patients' best interests. Therefore, they took it upon themselves to make medical decisions regarding treatment, diet, disclosure and truth telling in cases involving the terminally ill, and end-of-life decision making. Now, many patients and their families want to be involved, and their values and priorities may generate ethical dilemmas. Constantly changing ethical issues in the field of healthcare influence a variety of professionals, including physicians, nurses and other healthcare providers, social workers, lawyers, and chaplains.

The success of diversity training has been mixed. One of the biggest challenges for trainers is the mindset of the audience. Typically it ranges from reverence and approval to indifference to disapproval, confusion, and possibly outright hostility.

This is especially true if upper management has not identified education diversity as a priority. Moreover, expectations are often unrealistic. Exploring diversity issues and developing diversity consciousness takes a lifetime, yet the goals of many programs do not reflect this.

For example, participants in a daylong workshop may at best be taught to recognize certain biases they possess and, with additional work and commitment, suppress those biases, and even begin to unlearn them. Nevertheless, it is not uncommon to see unrealistic goals that target massive individual and organizational changes in a short span of time. Attitudes and behaviors evolve over years and are reinforced repeatedly. Rather than changing those attitudes in the span of a few hours, it is more fruitful to think in terms of identifying and recognizing the need for personal growth and development in this area. With a strong sense of commitment and clear, achievable goals, each training session becomes one more opportunity to do just that.

Examples of ill-conceived educational initiatives abound. In one diversity training session, teachers decided to create a poster for each classroom in a school system. The poster, which read "In this classroom, all people are treated with respect," was distributed to all teachers. Unfortunately, there was no systematic effort to ensure that people knew what concerns gave rise to this initiative and how students and teachers from various social backgrounds might define respect differently. And there was no follow-up to make sure that teachers were taking this statement seriously. What began as a promising idea became, in the eyes of some, a shallow and meaningless publicity effort.

Diversity training programs are held up for criticism because in some instances they are combative and guilt-driven, and therefore end up alienating and offending employees. One such example took place at the Federal Aviation Administration. During one session, men were told to walk through a "gauntlet" of women. After touching and looking over the men, who were clothed, the women rated each one's masculinity on a scale of one to ten.[26] In another example, a Chicago company instructed employees to repeatedly watch a film that showed Whites lynching Blacks. Employees were then asked questions designed to assess their racial attitudes, including whether they agreed with a number of insulting statements about African-Americans and Puerto Ricans. A black employee later sued the company, claiming that this attempt to highlight differences in people's attitudes created a hostile workplace.[27]

Other initiatives have produced better results. Many of these are proactive, ongoing, and more focused in terms of what they seek to achieve. Police in a large urban area, in response to complaints from the hearing impaired, have begun teaching sign language to selected members of the force. Police have interpreters on call and TTY telephones in a number of stations. Although more workshops are needed, police have set up training for officers, especially in the area of communication. Many complaints stemmed from the reluctance of certain officers to communicate in writing when requested, or the tendency of police to draw guns when deaf drivers reach for something to write on after being stopped.

A sizable number of research studies in recent years have provided medical schools with the impetus to focus more of their coursework on helping healthcare providers become culturally competent.[28] **Cultural competence** refers to a set of attitudes and skills that make it possible for organizations and staff to not only ac-knowledge cultural differences but also incorporate these differences in working with people from various cultures. The term *cultural competence* is similar to *diversity consciousness;* however, the latter term emphasizes that competencies of this nature need to be more holistic and transformational. In the process of learning to be diversity conscious, providers undergo profound personal change.

A diversity conscious healthcare provider must be sensitive to patients' language preferences and religious beliefs, in addition to beliefs about sickness, death, and bereavement; the role of the family in healthcare; diet; and norms regarding modesty. One program, piloted at the University of Michigan, seeks to provide first-year medical students with a variety of integrated learning experiences. These include discussions that require students to examine their own value systems, their perspectives on caring for patients from different cultures, and specific methods of care that involve the patients' families, members of the healthcare team, and the wider community. The students listen to fourth-year medical students' personal stories about treating diverse patients and working with diverse colleagues. Another component of the program asks students to critique a videotape in which patients recount their experiences with cultural insensitivity in the healthcare system.[29]

▣ THE COSTS OF INADEQUATE DIVERSITY CONSCIOUSNESS

People with business backgrounds need to have strong interaction skills and EI (emotional intelligence). There's such a big learning curve when new employees walk through the door. Often, they are not ready to produce.

—Carl Jefferson, Diversity Manager, Interstate Hotels Corporation

Imagine that you are a doctor. You have been asked, along with a large number of other doctors, to participate in an experiment designed by a team headed up by Dr. Schulman of the Georgetown University Medical Center in Washington, DC. You agree, and make the necessary arrangements. Once you arrive at the site of the experiment, you are taken to a private room where you are shown a video. You observe a patient describing heart pain, and recommend what you consider to be appropriate treatment. You are told the results will be published, but that your individual response will be kept confidential.

Later that same year, the results of this study are made public in *The New England Journal of Medicine.* Evidently, you were one of 720 doctors who watched videos with actors as patients. Actors wearing plain white hospital gowns read identical scripts describing heart pain. The actors included Blacks and Whites, males and females. Findings revealed that the doctors who participated in the study were generally much less likely to recommend appropriate treatment for the Black and female patients. After subjecting data to statistical tests to ensure reliability and validity, the study's authors conclude that the disparity in what are potentially life-and-death decisions with regard to medical care is most likely due to the doctors' unconscious biases about gender and race.

As a professional, you find this very hard to believe. As far as you are concerned, you do not have a prejudiced "bone in your body." Not only do you see yourself as highly educated and open-minded, but you also think you relate extremely well to other professionals at the hospital where you work. After thinking back to the study, you begin to wonder if the patient's race or gender did make a difference. This may be the first time that you have ever even entertained this notion. It is something you begin to struggle with, at least momentarily.

The aforementioned study by Dr. Schulman[30] is part of a growing body of research that has brought to light significant gaps in the quality of healthcare due to race, gender, and social class. The consequences of inadequate healthcare affect one's quality of life and, in some cases, mean the difference between life and death. In 2002, findings from a report entitled "Unequal Treatment" were released. Upon reviewing more than 100 studies, a 15-member committee of the Institute of Medicine concluded that racial minorities in the United States receive worse healthcare than Whites, even when the minorities had the same income and health insurance as Whites. The biggest discrepancies in the quality of healthcare were found in the areas of cardiovascular disease, HIV/AIDS, cancer, and diabetes. Researchers identified a number of reasons for inferior treatment. Among these are language barriers, patients' mistrust of healthcare providers, bias among doctors and nurses, and a lack of awareness among doctors and nurses regarding cultural beliefs that can affect health.[31]

Regardless of your education or career plans, your failure to develop diversity consciousness will, in all likelihood, have far-reaching and serious consequences. As a student, you may find it difficult to learn from instructors and other students who do not share your background, personality, values, or learning style. Lacking the skills to be a "team player" may make it difficult for you to work with others in study groups. Beyond resulting in alienation and emotional stress, poor communication skills can make it difficult for you to find the help you need in and out of class. At work, you may not know how to interpret and respond to both verbal and nonverbal cues. When you interact with someone who does not share your point of view, you may find it difficult to listen actively and think flexibly. As a result, you may unconsciously alienate others and sabotage future opportunities in the process.

Organizationally speaking, people who lack diversity consciousness will strain interpersonal relationships, threaten team spirit, and waste time. Costly lawsuits are more likely. Ultimately, the reputation of an organization may be undermined.

With each of the following real-life examples, the individual and organizational costs are significant.

1. Tom interviews for a high school teaching position. He meets a team of six people, only one of whom is female. Tom is highly qualified for the position and answers all the questions flawlessly. However, when it is time to rank the candidates, the lone female on the search committee observes that Tom addressed the male interviewers' questions more fully. In addition, she is the only person with whom he did not establish eye contact. The committee decides that he is not worth the risk and does not offer him the job.

2. American Telephone and Telegraph (AT&T), widely acknowledged as a corporate leader in managing diversity, experienced a public relations nightmare as a result of a cartoon published in its employee magazine. It shows customers on various continents making a telephone call. Four customers in different parts of the world are represented as people: a white man in North America, a white woman in South America, and a white man and woman in Eastern and Western Europe. The caller in Africa is a gorilla. After a flood of complaints from angry customers, employees, civil rights groups, and politicians, AT&T management apologized for the "racist" illustration.

3. In 1994, Denny's restaurants paid $45 million to settle class-action suits. African-American customers charged that they were treated differently by the chain's waiters and managers.

4. In 1996, a suit filed against Texaco alleged racial and religious discrimination. A secret recording of Texaco executives making disparaging remarks about African-Americans and Jews added to the evidence. Texaco paid out $176 million in damages. As part of the settlement, the company agreed to spend millions on programs designed to "wipe out" discrimination.

5. Mitsubishi Motors agreed to pay $34 million in 1998 to settle a sexual-harassment lawsuit. The settlement will be shared by 350 women who worked at the Mitsubishi auto plant in Illinois. The suit stemmed from complaints about male coworkers and supervisors kissing and fondling women, calling them "whores" and "bitches," posting pornographic drawings of the female workers, demanding sexual favors, and retaliating against women who refused. Furthermore, it was alleged that company managers did little to stop the mistreatment. Twenty Mitsubishi employees have been fired as a result of the case.

6. Coca-Cola paid $193 million in 2000 to settle a racial discrimination lawsuit brought by black workers. The settlement went beyond monetary compensation. Coke agreed to make significant changes in the way it manages, promotes, and treats its minority employees, and to set a "gold standard" in diversity among Fortune 500 companies.

7. Houston-based American General Corporation, the third-largest life insurer in the United States, agreed to pay $206 million to 9 million black and poor Americans in 2000. The settlement was in response to accusations of overcharging for life insurance policies.

8. The federal government paid the largest award ever in an employment discrimination case. In 2000, roughly 1,100 women were awarded $508 million. The women said they were denied jobs and promotions at the U.S. Information Agency and Voice of America. These women, who sought work as international radio broadcasters, technicians, writers, and production specialists, were relegated to jobs as hostesses or were denied jobs in favor of less qualified men.

According to one highly respected economist, "the labor force of the early 21st century is a potential powder keg for discrimination suits."[32] The reasons are numerous.

In addition to becoming a larger part of the U.S. workforce, a sizable percentage of minorities maintains that chances for getting ahead in today's society are not yet equal.[33] Some analysts argue that upper-level management at many companies has been reactive rather than proactive. They have been slow to acknowledge the existence of discrimination. Others say that when companies have programs to guard against bias, it can be difficult for executives to ensure that managers and workers fully commit to them.

The relationship between diversity consciousness and success has been examined throughout this chapter. Numerous research findings, personal anecdotes, and perspectives and comments from CEOs and other leaders attest to the critical importance of specific diversity skills. Through education, and constant practice of these skills, you have the power to improve your diversity consciousness. This will enhance your chances for success. By developing these skills, you will become a better student and a more valued employee. Conversely, ignoring these skills will be very costly.

Subsequent chapters focus on these and other diversity skills, and their relationship to diversity consciousness. A number of questions are addressed. For example, how do we develop and refine diversity skills? How do these skills enable us to overcome barriers to success? Finally, why will diversity consciousness become even more important in the future?

CASE STUDIES

Case Study One

Ligua is a car salesperson who works on a commission basis. On Ligua's job, everybody seems to be "out for themselves." With the emphasis on individual accomplishments and evaluations, competition is the norm. Ligua is much more comfortable helping others. But if she tries to be nurturing, people think she is weird or they see it as a weakness. They don't see that she's doing this on purpose so that the entire staff can do the job more efficiently.

A few months ago, she discussed this situation with a friend. Her friend, Katina, could readily identify with her situation. Katina, who was raised to help people in need, said, "If I see you struggling, I will stop and offer help." But where Katina works, it's not that way either. When she reaches out to a coworker, her supervisors want to know, "Why are you concerning yourself with someone else's problems?" Trying to fit in has been a constant source of stress for Katina as well as Ligua.

Questions:

1. If Ligua wants to be successful, does she have to buy into a work culture that values independence and individual accomplishments? Explain.
2. How could the work setting be changed to accommodate individuals who may feel more comfortable in a group-oriented atmosphere?
3. What diversity skills might Ligua work on developing to help her with these conflicts? Explain.

Case Study Two

Mary is taking a class from a professor who is of a different nationality than she. Although the professor has lived in the United States for several years, he has a very pronounced accent and she finds his English difficult to understand. Mary feels that this particular professor is very knowledgeable and has a lot of relevant personal experiences to share with the class. The class is a lecture class, with the professor talking for the majority of the time. Because the material is new and somewhat difficult to understand, the language barrier can make it more difficult at times.

Mary actively listens and follows along in the book. She raises her hand when she does not understand what the professor is saying. He is always more than happy to explain further. Also, he is aware that at times students may find it difficult to understand him, and he is not embarrassed to ask for help from the class. Mary has discovered that she is actually learning more from the class because she is following in the book and attending more closely to the professor's words than she would otherwise.

During class, it is easy to hear mumbling about the professor from some of her classmates. After class, these same students openly share their feelings within earshot of the professor, saying he is not a good teacher and does not know his subject matter. Mary is upset by the students' comments, which she attributes to their inability to understand what he is saying.

Questions:

1. If you were in Mary's situation, how would you view the class and the professor?
2. If you were in Mary's situation, what would you say to your classmates who you feel are being unfair to the professor?
3. Which diversity skills do Mary's classmates need to develop in order to be more successful in this class? Explain.

Case Study Three

Dennis, a new employee who reports to Michael at work, is a native of Brazil. Dennis asked Michael to approve his request for personal leave. Dennis wants to take paid leave to attend the funeral of his "compadre"—a close, personal friend. Company policy grants five days of paid, excused absence from work for "Death in the Family." Because his friend's funeral is in Brazil, he needs to take a full week off. Nothing in the company's leave policy covers this situation. Dennis feels a deep commitment to the family of his compadre. According to Dennis, a compadre is far more than a friend; a compadre is like family. In his request, he points out that there is no direct English translation for the word *compadre*. Michael is not sure how he feels about this. While he sympathizes with his friend, he thinks that agreeing to Dennis's request establishes a bad precedent.

Questions:

1. Do you think Michael should approve Dennis's request? Can this request be justified given company policy?

2. If Dennis is allowed to do this, should the company treat all other employees who have a very close friend the same?

3. Dealing with Dennis's request will require Michael to use a number of diversity skills. In this situation, which of Michael's diversity skills do you think will be the most critical? Why?

EXERCISES

In-Class

Exercise 1: The Meanings of Success

Directions for Instructor

1. Seat students in pairs.
2. Have each student read each of the following questions, writing down his or her individual responses.
   - How do you define success?
   - How have your life experiences shaped your attitudes regarding what constitutes success?
   - What three names are at the top of your list of successful people? For each person, explain why you included her or him.
3. Have students share their responses with their partners.
4. As a class, ask all students to examine their lists of successful people. Are there any traits or talents that seem to distinguish most or all of the people on their lists? If so, what are they? Record these traits on the board.

Exercise 2: A Picture of Success

Directions for Instructor

1. Give each student a large sheet of paper and make available colored markers and pencils.
2. Ask them to think of childhood experiences that have contributed to their success.
3. Instruct students to draw one of these experiences on the sheet of paper. They should not use words in their drawings. If possible, display the drawings where everyone can see them.
4. Ask each student to describe what her or his drawing represents and how it relates to success.

Out-of-Class

Exercise 1: Social Class and Success

1. Has your social class background shaped your definition of success in any way? Explain.

2. What advantages and disadvantages have you experienced due to your social class background?

3. Imagine that you wake up tomorrow and discover that you have a lottery ticket worth $100 million. How do you think this money will change your definition of success? Will your educational and career goals change? Explain.

Exercise 2: Learning and Teaching Styles

Below are some sample student evaluations of two different instructors.

Instructor A:

Taneka: "I feel I learn a lot in this class, and I think I will get a good final grade. I really like the way the instructor uses examples from everyday life and lets us work in groups so much. It makes it easier to understand and more interesting. I usually do not participate much in discussions. But this class is different. I think the instructor has a lot to do with this. She is very friendly and informal."

Luis: "I have a hard time understanding why I have to take this course. I find the course to be pretty boring. I am always listening to students. I am taking this class to find out what the instructor knows about the subject. After all, that is what we're going to be tested on."

Michael: "This class is always interesting and I like the instructor, but I don't think I'll get a decent grade. I have a hard time figuring out what I need to study. Sometimes, we spend too much time discussing the readings. I would rather just focus on what I need to know for the tests."

Instructor B:

Schuzan: "I really didn't think I was going to like this course. I heard a lot about this instructor, how hard he is. But his lectures are really good. I can tell how much work he puts into them. I do not see how anyone can do poorly in this class. The instructor writes practically everything on the board. Also, the handouts make it easy to take notes and study for the test."

Alice: "If anything, he needs to move a little faster. He is always stopping and writing everything on the board. Also, we never get to talk about the subject. We are always listening. I have the feeling he is more interested in the subject than in his students. That makes it hard for me to pay attention."

Esther: "I can tell this instructor really, really cares about his field. It shows in his lectures and it really helps me learn. I just wish we had more opportunities to work in small groups and talk about what we are studying."

Answer the following questions.

1. Do you identify with any of the students or with any of their comments? If so, which one(s)? What do you think this says about your learning style?
2. Which instructor would you prefer? Why? How well does his or her teaching style fit your learning style? Explain and be specific.
3. Which instructor's style do you not prefer? Why? If you found yourself in this instructor's class, what could you do to increase your chances for success?

Exercise 3: Interview and Analysis

Interview.   Schedule an appointment with one of your instructors. Explain that you would like to conduct an interview with this person for a class assignment. Prior to the interview, make a list of possible questions. Include questions that cover the following points, but do not hesitate to explore other topics as well.

- What is the instructor's name and position?
- What is the instructor's professional and educational background?
- What does he or she share in common with other instructors?
- In what ways does this instructor feel different?
- How has the instructor's cultural background influenced his or her teaching?
- How does this instructor define success?
- How has the instructor's cultural background influenced his or her definition of success?

Follow-up questions are a good way to get more information or to clarify certain points brought up during the course of the interview.

Summary and Analysis.   List each question you asked. After each question, summarize the interviewee's response. Briefly analyze the interview. How do you think it went? What did you learn?

Exercise 4: Eco-Map

1. Create an "eco-map" for yourself.
2. For each relationship you have shown, explain (1) its importance in terms of your success and (2) the strengths and strains it represents.

INTERNET ASSIGNMENT

Search the World Wide Web for a site that is about some dimension of your diversity. It could refer to your cultural heritage, race, religion, learning style, sexual orientation, position at work, age, or some other dimension. This Web site should be of a positive nature, promoting the value of what you have chosen without demeaning others. After reading the Web site and going to any appropriate links, do the following.

1. Print the information you found to be particularly inspiring or insightful. Include the URL address.

2. Write a paragraph on each of the following questions: What audience does this Web site appear to target? What did you learn about your diversity? Why did you find this information inspiring or insightful?

ANSWER to Diversity Box: "Thinking Outside the Box" (see page 49)

Directions: Draw four straight lines, without lifting your pencil, that touch all the dots.

This problem illustrates the idea that sometimes the only way you can solve a problem is to go beyond your usual way of thinking. Most people when trying to solve this problem will not extend their lines past the dots—staying "in the box." The only way to solve the problem is to "think outside the box."

 NOTES

[1] C. B. Olson, "The Influence of Context on Gender Differences in Performance Attributions: Further Evidence of a 'Feminine Modesty' Effect," paper presented at the annual meeting of the Western Psychological Association, San Francisco, CA, 1988.

[2] Samuel D. Proctor and William D. Watley, *Sermons from the Black Pulpit* (Valley Forge, PA: Judson Press, 1984), 38.

[3] National Institute of Education, "Involvement in Learning: Realizing the Potential of American Higher Education," *Report of the Study Group on the Conditions of Excellence in American Higher Education* (Washington, DC: U.S. Department of Education, 1984), 17.

[4] Al Heredia, "Cultural Learning Styles," *Eric Clearinghouse on Teaching and Teacher Education,* Dec. 1999.

[5] Jacqueline Irvine and Darlene York, "Learning Styles and Culturally Diverse Students: A Literature Review," in James Banks (ed.), *Handbook of Research on Multicultural Education* (New York: Simon & Schuster, 1995), 484–497.

[6] Howard Gardner, *Frames of Mind: The Theory of Multiple Intelligences* (New York: Basic Books, 1983).

[7] Sonia Nieto, *Affirming Diversity: The Sociopolitical Context of Multicultural Education* (White Plains, NY: Longman, 1996), 283.

[8] Alexander Astin, "Diversity and Multiculturalism on the Campus: How Are Students Affected?" *Change,* Mar./Apr. 1993, 44–49.

[9] M. A. Gibson, "Parental Support for Schooling," paper presented at the annual meeting of the American Anthropological Association, Dec. 1986.

[10] Terry Huffman, "The Transculturation of Native American College Students," in *American Mosaic: Selected Readings on America's Multicultural Heritage,* Young I. Song and Eugene C. Kim (eds.) (Englewood Cliffs, NJ: Prentice Hall, 1993), 211–219; Sonia Nieto, *Affirming Diversity: The Sociopolitical Context of Multicultural Education* (White Plains, NY: Longman, 1996).

[11] Terry Huffman, "The Transculturation of Native American College Students," in *American Mosaic: Selected Readings on America's Multicultural Heritage,* Young I. Song and Eugene C. Kim (eds.) (Englewood Cliffs, NJ: Prentice Hall, 1993), 211–219.

[12] American Management Association, "What Do Organizations Really Want?" *AMA Catalog of Seminars,* Oct. 1997.

[13] Karen Dowd and Jeanne Liedtka, "What Corporations Seek in MBA Hires: A Survey," *The Magazine of the Graduate Management Admission Council* (Winter, 1994), 38.

[14] Anne-Lee Verville, "What Business Needs from Higher Education," *Educational Record,* 76(4), Fall 1995, 46–50.

[15] Daniel Goleman, *Working with Emotional Intelligence* (New York: Bantam Books, 1998).

[16] Wendy Levinson, Debra Roter, John Mullooly, Valerie Dull, and Richard Frankel, "Physician–Patient Communication: The Relationship with Malpractice Claims Among Primary Care Physicians and Surgeons," *Journal of the American Medical Association* (February 19, 1997), 553.

[17] Christina LeBeau, "Attitude Adjustment," *Rochester Democrat and Chronicle,* Oct. 19, 1997, 1e+.

[18] Roger von Oech, *A Kick in the Seat of the Pants* (New York: Harper & Row, 1986), 5–21.

[19] Lynda P. Clemens and Andrea T. Dolph, *How to Hit the Ground Running in Your New Job* (Lincolnwood, IL: VGM Career Horizons, 1995).

[20] Sheryl Silver, "New Grads: Make the Most of Your First Job," *The Washington Post High Tech Horizons,* Aug. 3, 1997, M19.

[21] Stephen Covey, "How to Succeed in Today's Workplace," *USA Weekend,* Aug. 29–31, 1997, 4–5.

[22] Daniel Goleman, *Working with Emotional Intelligence* (New York: Bantam Books, 1998), 64.

[23] Irving L. Janis, *Victims of Groupthink* (Boston: Houghton Mifflin, 1972).

[24] Scripps Howard News Service, "White Men Still at Top of the Business Heap, Study Finds," *Carroll County Times,* Mar. 16, 1995, A7.

[25] IBM, "Directory of Diversity Programs." Online, Aug. 28, 2002. Available: http://www3.ibm.com/employment/us/diverse/programs_ibm.shtml.

[26] Kara Swisher, "Diversity's Learning Curve," *The Washington Post,* Feb. 5, 1995, H1+.

[27] Dana Cannedy, "Back at the Office . . . ," *Essence,* 23 (11), March 1998, 80, 140.

[28] Brian Smedley, Adrienne Stith, and Alan Nelson (eds.), *Unequal Treatment: Confronting Racial and Ethnic Disparities in Health Care* (Washington, DC: National Academies Press, 2002).

[29] Lynne Robins, Joseph Fantone, Julica Hermann, Gwen Alexander, and Andrew Zweifler, "Improving Cultural Awareness and Sensitivity Training in Medical School," *Academic Medicine,* 73 (10), October Supplement, 1998.

[30] George Strait, "Health Care's Racial Divide." Online, March 7, 1999. Available: http://more.abcnews.go.com/sections/living/DailyNews/racial_healthcare990224.html.

[31] Ceci Connolly, "Report Says Minorities Get Lower-Quality Health Care," *The Washington Post,* March 21, 2002, A2.

[32] Ian Simpson, "U.S. Race Bias Suits on the Rise, Putting Companies on the Defensive." Online, July 14, 2000. Available: http://news.excite.com/news/r/000714/13/economy-race-suits2.

[33] Robert Smith and Richard Seltzer, *Contemporary Controversies and the American Racial Divide* (Lanham, MD: Rowman and Littlefield, 2000), 5.

Personal and Social Barriers to Success

3

Chapter Objectives

Upon completion of this chapter, you will be able to:

- Differentiate between personal and social barriers.
- List, explain, and give examples of the six barriers to success.
- Explain and give examples of each of the four combinations of prejudice and discrimination.
- Discuss the strategies for overcoming diversity barriers.

I believe that in the United States there are barriers. People get tired of bumping their heads against those invisible walls. And I speak from experience. Years ago, I went to a predominantly white college. I got in trouble for things that were overlooked for Anglo students. But that didn't stop me from trying to get an education.

I became a supervisor at a predominantly white hospital. I was told, "Don't hire too many Mexicans because we don't want this place to become a barrio." And I didn't let that stop me from being fair in my hiring. When I worked at another hospital, there was discrimination but it was swept under the carpet. They would say, "We didn't do that," or "We didn't say it that way." Or they would go back and rewrite their policies when someone would file a grievance.

I feel that for those of us who pretend this kind of thing does not happen, it's like sticking your head in a hole. But I don't feel like any of us should allow the barriers to stop us from moving ahead. Nobody can hold you back. It's your own thinking that holds you back. I don't feel like I'm looking for discrimination all the time. I just feel like I am a realist.

—Another perspective

How do we explain why some people are more successful than others? Is it simply a matter of individual talent and motivation? Cornel West, a prolific writer and widely cited scholar, is highly critical of conventional explanations of success. In his writings, West zeros in on the issue of race and its implications for climbing up the social ladder. However, his analysis could apply to gender, class, and any number of other dimensions of diversity.

At first, West takes issue with the idea that people can solve problems such as poverty and inequality simply by changing individual values and behaviors. He rightly points out that many poor African-Americans remain poor despite their strong work ethic. Second, he criticizes the notion that more government and economic programs can eliminate racial inequality. West argues that the problem is not strictly a matter of economics. In short, he views approaches to racial inequality that focus entirely on the individual *or* the larger society as simplistic and incomplete. West argues that we will be successful only if we stop pointing our fingers at a single source of the problem.[1]

We can take West's analysis and apply it to our discussion of diversity, success, and the barriers to success. Barriers to success may stem from the individual or may be found in the larger society. **Personal barriers** refer to those individual factors that get in the way of our success. Our focus is on factors that relate to diversity. These barriers include one's lack of self-awareness, cultural ignorance, and underdeveloped diversity consciousness. Personal barriers would also include a person's biases and discriminatory behaviors. **Social barriers** focus more on society. They refer to those factors that are external to the person and impede her or his success. Among these barriers are the perceptions, thoughts, and actions of others. Ethnocentrism, stereotypes, prejudice, and discrimination are barriers that can be personal and/or social, depending on the situation. Also, it is important to remember, as West mentions earlier, that interrelationships exist between personal and social barriers. For example, encountering prejudice and discrimination in the larger society may reinforce our personal biases. Similarly, our biases can adversely affect our friends, classmates, and coworkers.

> *I am from a small island in the West Indies. I have an accent where I do not speak clearly. People do not understand me, or laugh. As for my instructors, they look at me as spaced out. They think I do not know what is going on because I do not talk a lot in class. Sometimes if I think I have a good answer, I will second-guess myself. When the instructor asks me something, the first thing I'll do is get hot and sweaty and scared. I'll feel like my answers are not as good as anybody else's.*
>
> —Another perspective

THINKING THROUGH DIVERSITY

If someone were to write your life history, what would we learn about personal and social barriers?

In this chapter we examine personal and social barriers that impede our success: perceptions, ethnocentrism, stereotypes, prejudice, prejudice plus power, and discrimination. We focus on those barriers that are obvious as well as those that are not easily recognizable. Additionally, we examine a number of strategies for overcoming such barriers.

▣ SIX BARRIERS TO SUCCESS

Barrier 1: Limited Perceptions

The scene: You just return to campus after the spring break. As you approach the library, you see a number of statues. Upon closer examination, you notice that each of these statues represents a student. Two appear to be African-American students. One of the African-American students is twirling a basketball and the other is balancing a book on her head. The single Asian-American student is carrying a violin. Each of the white students is shown holding a number of books. What are you feeling as you study each of the statues? Individually and collectively, what do these statues say to you? Are you offended? Do you plan on sharing your thoughts and feelings with anyone else? Why? Will you be able to put your feelings aside and concentrate on your studies for the rest of the day?

This scene took place at the University of North Carolina (UNC). Each year the graduating class gives the university a gift. Not long ago, one class hired a well-known sculptor to create a number of statues depicting the diversity of UNC's student population. The artist sculpted the figures described earlier. Once they were placed in a prominent place on campus, they immediately caused an uproar among students. Many complained that the statues reinforced stereotypical images. The African-Americans, they argued, were portrayed as being less studious and less intelligent than the Whites and Asian-American. In their eyes, it reinforced the stereotype that African-Americans are athletes first and students second. Other students felt that people were making a big fuss over nothing. In response to the growing tension among students, the statues were relocated to another spot on campus that was much less visible.

The scenario just described provides insight into the potential barriers that limited perceptions of diversity can create. Did the sculptor consider the different messages these statues might convey? Did the sculptor have any understanding of the backgrounds and perspectives of the students, faculty, and staff at UNC? What about the people who hired this sculptor and oversaw the project? Most important, what did the students learn from this?

For a moment, put yourself in the place of certain students who might walk past these statues. What if you were a student who was constantly asked "Do you play sports?" because of your height or skin color? Suppose that you often encounter instructors and other students who make a habit of assuming that you got into college because of your athletic talent rather than your intelligence. Or imagine that people assume you are gifted and extremely intelligent simply because of your cultural background or your looks. Taking on the role of each of these students, or at least trying to, can help us understand the multiple worlds in which we live. It can also make us more aware of the barriers we create by our perceptions, thoughts, and actions.

Perceptions refer to the way in which we receive and interpret information from any of our senses. Thus perceptions can be understood as a link between a person and his or her surroundings. However, what we perceive does not necessarily reflect reality. Furthermore, two people can look at the same image or witness

FIGURE 3.1   What do you see? Two faces looking at each other? A vase? Because of the shapes and coloring in the picture, you might see either. This image, which appears in the book *Can You Believe Your Eyes?* by J. Richard Block and Harold Yuker (New York: Brunner/Mazel, 1992), was first published around 1915. *(By permission from Archives of the History of American Psychology-The University of Akron.)*

the same event and see something completely different (see Fig. 3.1). When we interact with others or even take a look at ourselves, our perceptions come into play. They can affect the way we feel, think, and act. Hence, it is important to understand those factors that can influence our perceptions.

Common sense tells us that "seeing is believing." What we see with our own eyes or what we absorb through our other senses must be true. Yet social scientists have discovered that the reverse is also true. What we *believe* may very well determine what we *see*. In other words, we do not interact with others with an entirely blank mind. Rather, our perceptions are rooted in past experiences. Throughout our lives, we are exposed to a variety of human images via our interaction with the media, school, peers, friends, family, community members, and others. The images we experience and how we interpret these images color our perceptions.

A well-known psychological experiment illustrates how our beliefs may distort our perceptions. In this experiment, a person is shown a picture of a white man standing next to a black man. The white man is holding a knife. The person is asked to describe the picture to another person, who then relays what he or she was told to the next person. This process continues until everybody in the group has a turn. When asked to describe what the first person saw, the last person explains that there are two men standing next to each other, one Black and one White, and the black man is holding a knife. The experiment shows how our racial biases can radically alter what we perceive.

Psychologists conduct extensive research on perceptions. Research indicates that we can only experience and digest a certain portion of our vast social world. Because of this, we have a tendency to take shortcuts to understanding others. We often perceive what we want to perceive. This is called **selective perception.** In other words, we focus on those things that support our thinking and ignore information that refutes it. In this way we can store and process information in neat, simple categories.

Research by Galen V. Bodenhausen illustrates the potential dangers of selective perception. Bodenhausen asked students to take on the role of jurors in a fictitious

Perceptions of People with Disabilities

The relationship between perceptions and environment is illustrated dramatically in a study of high school seniors in Berkeley, California. The study compares students' attitudes toward people with and without disabilities. Students were shown videotapes of a man who was variously identified as disabled or able-bodied. Each student then rated the man on intelligence, work, competence, morality, and sociability. In comparison to the negative ratings found in similar studies conducted elsewhere, the overall rating of the person with a disability was much more positive.

In explaining their results, the researchers point to the uniqueness of Berkeley. As the home of one branch of the University of California, Berkeley has many students with disabilities. Mainstreaming and other educational innovations are opening up opportunities for persons with disabilities and increasing their visibility. As a result, "the nondisabled population is exposed to persons with disabilities who cope and live within the community" and "get to know them and their abilities beyond the disability."[2]

court case. Some students were told that the defendant's name was Carlos Ramirez and his home was Albuquerque, New Mexico. Others were informed that the defendant's name was Robert Johnson and he was from Dayton, Ohio. Moreover, students learned of these names either before or after the evidence was presented. The study's findings revealed that students who were told that the defendant was Carlos Ramirez *before* the evidence was presented were the most likely to find him guilty. Initially, these students formed an image of the defendant based on his name. This image had a direct bearing on their perception and interpretation of the evidence.[3]

Limited perceptions work against us for a number of reasons:

- We tend to be unaware of the blinders or obstructions that distort our perceptions in some way. This makes it difficult to acknowledge, much less remove, these obstructions. The end result is that our senses do not operate at peak efficiency.
- We absorb only a small fraction of the world around us. In other words, we experience only a slice or, in some cases, a sliver of life. More often than not, we experience things from one perspective rather than from a variety of perspectives.
- We tend to tune into those things with which we agree. Although this might make it easier to make sense of the world around us, the end result is that we miss out on a lot. In an increasingly diverse world, we fail to experience and appreciate much that the world has to offer. Moreover, there is a tendency to view more and more people as homogeneous masses with whom we have little in common.
- Our perception of others reflects on ourselves. According to an African proverb, "when you judge others, you do not define them. . . you define yourself."

> *If I am to have a successful medical career, I can't afford to walk around with blinders on or refuse to treat someone because that person is "different" from me.*
>
> —Another perspective

Barrier 2: Ethnocentrism

Culture envelopes us so completely that sometimes it is difficult to realize that our perspective is one of many. **Ethnocentrism** refers to the assumption that our way of thinking and acting is naturally superior to any other. As a result, we use ourselves or our culture as the yardstick by which we measure what is right or desirable or normal. It follows that if we display ethnocentrism, we naturally assume that behaviors and customs that appear different to us are necessarily abnormal and inferior. This kind of thinking produces "tunnel vision." Rudyard Kipling, in his poem "We and They," describes how ethnocentrism locks us into an "us" and "them" mindset. "Father, Mother and Me, Sister and Auntie say All the people like Us are We, And everyone else is They."[4]

Taking a Critical Look at Maps

Consider the way we look at maps. We are taught to read maps, not question them. After all, the world can only be drawn one correct way, right? Imagine a sphere like a hollowed-out pumpkin or an orange peel. What happens if we try to make it flat? It would not be possible without damaging or wrinkling it in some way. Now think of what happens when we take the earth's curved surface and try to make it lie down on a map. There has to be some distortion. This is why mapmakers utilize projection. Over 200 techniques have been used to project the earth onto a flat map. All are distorted to some degree.

Many schools in the United States still use the Mercator Projection Map. This map was created by Gerardus Mercator in 1569 in Germany. At this time, European colonial powers dominated much of the world.

Although the Mercator Projection has navigational benefits, it also reflects the Europeans' sense of importance and power at that time. It makes European countries look bigger than the rest of the world. Other areas, such as China, Mexico, and Africa, appear much smaller than they really are.

Arthur Robinson is one of a number of cartographers who has created a projection that corrects this bias during the past few decades. Cartographers consider his map, the Robinson Projection Map, to be a major improvement. It displays the relative sizes of continents and countries much more accurately. For example, the true relative size of Africa is shown on the Robinson Projection Map; unlike the traditional Mercator Projection, the Robinson Projection shows that Africa is actually much larger than Greenland (see Fig. 3.2 on next page).

It is important to realize that no one person, group, or society has a monopoly on ethnocentrism. We are all ethnocentric to some degree. To illustrate, we might view our customs as the right way and, in some instances, the only way. When we encounter someone from another culture, we might think to ourselves: Why can't she think the way I think? Talk the way I talk? Act the way I act? That kind of thinking can build group solidarity and pride. It becomes a liability when we get so caught up in our own thinking that we cannot see the value of other ways of life. As an example, the ethnocentrism shown by some corporations has been very costly (see Diversity Box: The Human and Financial Costs of Corporate Ethnocentrism on page 76).

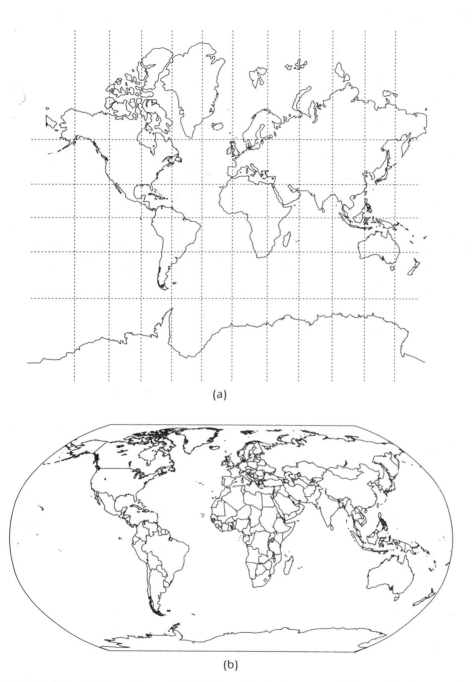

(a)

(b)

FIGURE 3.2 (a) Mercator and (b) Robinson Projection maps of the world. Compare the size of the continents on the traditional Mercator Projection and the Robinson Projection.

The Human and Financial Costs of Corporate Ethnocentrism

In the 1960s and 1970s, the worldwide infant formula industry was dominated by Nestlé of Switzerland and several U.S. companies. These firms saw the large populations in less-developed nations as a growing untapped market for their product. Nestlé planned its marketing strategy and targeted new mothers and professionals in these countries. Mass media and billboard ads showed happy mothers with their beautiful, bottle-fed babies. Free samples were given to health personnel and new mothers in hospitals. Face-to-face sales efforts pushed the nutritional value of formula.

The reaction from abroad was not what Nestlé or any of the other firms expected. Critics charged that selling formula put babies at risk. When substituted for breast-feeding, babies were denied the nourishment of their mother's milk. Many of these women were illiterate and therefore could not read the directions. In many areas, there was no refrigeration to keep the formula from spoiling.

The controversy culminated in a worldwide boycott of Nestlé from 1977 to 1984. The boycott was called off when Nestlé agreed to alter its marketing practices and comply with the marketing code established by the World Health Organization (WHO). When activists discovered that Nestlé was continuing to supply free or low-cost formula to hospitals, the boycott was reinstated. In 1991, Nestlé agreed to discontinue this practice. The company lost between $3 and $5 million as a result of the boycott.

Ethnocentrism can be very subtle and difficult to recognize. In the examples that follow, ask yourself what assumptions are being made? What are the implications for success?

1. Gloria is a manager of a large department store. She feels very proud of her success on the job and takes pride in being the only employee with a college degree. Gloria attaches considerable importance to academic degrees and credentials. When she meets with store employees, she tends to be close-minded even though she pretends to listen. She finds it particularly difficult to give much credence to the views of lower-salaried employees who only possess a high school diploma. Many of these employees sense this and keep their ideas to themselves.

2. Karlton is completing a lengthy research study in which he examines the short- and long-term effects of daily doses of aspirin. In compiling his data, he relies exclusively on research that studies only men. He operates under the assumption that what he finds true of men also applies to women. Now, a prominent fellow researcher is criticizing this assumption and questioning the validity of his research.

3. Bob is a 54-year-old, single, white male. As a veteran lawyer, he is proud of his accomplishments working for a large law firm in Chicago. He attributes his success to the tremendous amount of time and energy he invests in his job. Recently, he attended a diversity training workshop. Along with other participants, he was asked to make a list of the firm's unwritten rules. The lists were then shared. One rule mentioned by a number of minority lawyers was "If you're not a white male, you won't succeed." Although Bob did not say anything at the time, he thinks any mention of race or gender is a "cop-out." According to Bob, "These people have to be willing to sacrifice like I did."

4. Freida, a human relations manager at a large firm that manufactures disk drives for personal computers, is planning a diversity workshop. She hears of a "diversity trainer," someone who is described as an outstanding presenter with impeccable credentials. He comes highly recommended for his strong academic background and his exceptional ability to relate to diverse audiences. She is ready to ask him to facilitate the workshop until she discovers that he is White. Freida questions whether he can really understand some of the diversity issues that may be addressed in the workshop. Being relatively new on the job, she feels that choosing a person of color is a "safer" choice.

Ethnocentrism is universal. It affects us all. The challenge of ethnocentrism is realizing not *if* but *when* it influences our thinking and judgment. Similarly, it is necessary to recognize the *costs* of putting ourselves and our culture at the center of everything. We become narrow-minded and lose sight of opportunities in realms outside our own. We impair our ability to relate to others. Most important, we fail to learn and benefit from the collective wisdom and experiences of all people.

Barrier 3: Stereotypes

As you were growing up, what stories or comments did you hear about people who were viewed as different for one reason or another? They might have been members of another race, social class, or religion. From whom did you hear these things? Did you believe them at the time? What about now? Often, what we hear and accept as true takes the form of a **stereotype,** an unverified and oversimplified generalization about an entire group of people. Our social environment provides us with a set of images. Many of these images reflect stereotypes. When we stereotype, we lump people in a category and assume they are all alike.

Each of us is exposed to stereotypes starting at an early age. Wilma Mankiller, former chief of the Cherokee Nation, recalls her first encounter with stereotypes. Her schoolmates would sing a song, "Mankiller, Mankiller, how many men did you kill today?" or they would make war-whoop noises. We learn stereotypical images of Native Americans or any other group through our interaction with family, peers, school, religion, the media, and other social influences. Over the course of many years, these stereotypes are reinforced and internalized. As a result, stereotypical thinking tends to be very rigid and difficult to change.

> *I was raised in a single-parent household headed up by my mother, as were most of my friends. As a result, I grew up believing that African-American men were irresponsible, selfish, and afraid of commitment. They cared nothing about their children or the women who bore these children. As I've grown older and explored other communities and cultures, I've learned to question what I see around me. I've learned that the absentee African-American father is not the norm.*
>
> —Another perspective

Gary Foster, a sociologist, has studied the persistence of "hillbilly" stereotypes in the media and in popular culture. What is interesting, he says, is that images of hillbilly men and women endure despite the trend toward repudiation of racial and ethnic stereotyping. Foster supports his argument by pointing to television caricatures found in *The Simpsons* and reruns of *The Beverly Hillbillies* or *Green Acres*. Hillbilly men tend to be lazy and unkempt, and have a taste for moonshine. Hillbilly women come in two types: They are either oversexed and underdressed, or gaunt with unkempt hair, tattered clothes, and high-topped workboots or no shoes at all. Foster suspects that we tolerate these stereotypes, sometimes accompanied by labels such as "rednecks" or "white trash," for two reasons. First, those most offended by the stereotype, such as poor, rural whites, lack the political or economic power to effectively protest. Second, because hillbilly stereotypes are associated with Whites, we may not give these characterizations the same degree of attention and scrutiny.[5]

There is no shortage of stereotypes in today's world. Stereotypes revolve around every dimension of diversity, such as job position and function, race, ethnicity, religion, social class, language, learning style, and sexual orientation. In many instances, stereotypes relate to physical appearance, such as skin color, age, or gender. Another dimension, one that is more subtle and rarely mentioned, is physical attractiveness. Psychological research shows that many people in our society equate character with looks. According to the *attractiveness stereotype,* we view people who are attractive as "more sensitive, kind, interesting, strong, poised, modest, sociable, outgoing, and exciting, sexually warm, and responsive." Furthermore, we tend to assume that they will "hold better jobs, have more successful marriages, and happier and more fulfilling lives."[6]

Like other stereotypes, the attractiveness stereotype can affect the way we think and act. This was borne out in recent research by Wesley Kayson and Andrea DeSantis of Iona College. These researchers recruited 160 college students, faculty, and office workers. Each participant was asked to serve as a juror in an imaginary burglary case. After reviewing a fact sheet describing the crime, the participants studied the photographs of men and women described as defendants. The attractiveness of each defendant had already been rated by 10 psychology students on a scale of 1 to 7. The participants were then asked to recommend a jail sentence. On average, good-looking defendants received much shorter sentences than those rated as less attractive.[7]

Beautiful and Disabled

People with disabilities in our society constantly encounter stereotypical images of beauty that do not look like them. Some accept society's norms of attractiveness and enjoy trying to live up to them. Others, such as Ellen Stohl and James Box, do not. Stohl, who has a spinal cord injury, posed for *Playboy* in 1987. This was her way of saying that a woman with a disability can be beautiful and sexy. Box, a paraplegic and founder of a high-tech wheelchair company, uses advertising to challenge the public's perceptions of people who use wheelchairs. One ad shows a sexy blond woman lying on her back tipped over in her wheelchair. According to Box, ads such as these show that people in wheelchairs do have sexual lives. Even though some people are uncomfortable with his ads, he says that is fine. His point is to show real people in real situations.

Before we can change our thinking, we need to acknowledge our stereotypical assumptions. However, this is not easy. Coming to grips with a stereotype we have held for a long time can make us feel uncomfortable and vulnerable. Additionally, we tend to be more aware of other people's stereotypes than our own. As one of my students said, some stereotypes are "difficult to see because they are buried deep within our souls."

If students feel a certain level of trust and comfort, the classroom can be a place where students take a more critical and rational look at their thinking about diversity. In my classroom, I use an activity that brings certain stereotypes to the surface. Students and I sit in a tight circle. I ask them to recount a story or comment they have heard about members of another racial or ethnic group. One by one, each student gets a chance to share his or her story. What they share is typically negative and stereotypical.

In elementary school, I was taught that Africans lived in huts, in villages. They were starving and poor. Even though my mother is from Zambia, I still had trouble picturing Africans having the same things Americans have, such as homes, communities, and streets.

⌘

I used to believe that all white people were rich and their problems could be solved within 30 minutes.

⌘

I grew up thinking that Asians, Vietnamese, Chinese, and Japanese were all the same. For a long time, I believed that all Asians were smart.

⌘

People would say that all Jews were penny pinchers. I grew up believing that all Jews were cheap and very cautious with money.

⌘

Growing up, I viewed the English as very uptight, unathletic human beings. I pictured them as always wearing suits and trench coats. I pictured the women always dressed as if they were going to a ball and most wearing fine jewelry all the time. I figured all of the English always drank tea and ate only freshly cooked, expensive dinners.

⌘

When I was growing up, I heard that you can't trust white people. They'll act like they're your friends and they'll laugh and joke with you. But when it comes down to a confrontation, they'll turn on you.

⌘

As a child, I heard that people from Haiti and the Islands in general always lived with like 30 people to a bedroom. So many lived in an apartment they had to sleep in shifts.

—Other perspectives

Once every student has had a chance to participate, I ask each to examine critically what was shared. Do they think that any of these stories are based on fact? Why? How do we share and perpetuate these stories? What assumptions are found in each story? Can we make this assumption about all members of a racial or ethnic group? Inevitably, the students teach each other. For example, the comment, "All Whites can't be trusted" is picked apart. What does this mean? How do we know for sure? Does this apply to all Whites or just some? Can people of the *same* race necessarily trust each other? For some students, it is the first time they openly discuss issues such as this in a racially and ethnically diverse group. The value of critical thinking becomes more apparent as students weigh whether the evidence supports certain assumptions. They also begin to share how their thinking is changing as a result of personal experiences.

Interestingly, many of the stereotypes students mention revolve around two sensitive subjects we rarely discuss in public: sex and hygiene. For example, many students have been "taught" that other races are unclean and sexually deviant. Cornel West, in his best-selling book *Race Matters,* addresses the interrelationship of race and sexuality. He argues that a candid dialogue about both is virtually impossible because it is a taboo subject. When we cannot bring ourselves to address a subject openly and honestly, we rely on second-hand information that is full of inaccuracies, ignores diversity within diversity, and becomes highly impervious to change over time.

It is not enough to recognize and critically evaluate stereotypical thinking. We also need to understand that this kind of thinking can limit our opportunities. When we stereotype, we see people as labels rather than individuals. We base our actions on images that are distorted, incomplete, and usually negative. Even so-called positive stereotypes, such as all women are nurturing or all Asians excel in math and science, are damaging because they imply that everyone within a group manifests that trait, and furthermore, the group's potential is limited to that trait.

When others stereotype us, we may feel vulnerable and our self-esteem may suffer. Claude Steele refers to this as **stereotype vulnerability,** the danger of not performing up to our ability because of our anxieties and fears about perpetuating a stereotype.[8] For instance, Paul is an older employee who hesitates to ask for help when he has computer questions at work. He has to deal with a supervisor and others who assume that he cannot keep up with younger coworkers when it comes to computer know-how. Because of this stereotypical assumption, he keeps to himself and does not ask questions because he does not want to appear computer illiterate. Consequently, his skills never improve.

Steele, a social psychologist at Stanford University, has conducted experimental studies revealing that vulnerability to stereotypes is a significant factor in academic achievement. According to Steele, certain groups of students find themselves constantly wrestling with stereotypes. As an example, women deal with the image of being mathematical klutzes and African-Americans contend with assumptions about their lack of academic ability. Steele maintains that fear of conforming to stereotypical expectations creates a pressure-packed situation for these students. As a result, students who are otherwise competent often do not perform up to their ability.

"They Think I'm Dumb"

Carol, a visually impaired African-American student, is a friend of mine. Recently she confided in me that she was having problems in school. When I asked her if she had met with her teachers to discuss her poor grades and some of the difficulties she is having, she said no. Surprised by her response, I asked why. After a moment of hesitation, Carol said, I didn't want them to think I was dumb. Still I did not understand. Carol is intelligent, outgoing, and a hard worker. She then elaborated. "My teachers think I'm dumb because I'm blind. They think I'm dumb because I'm black. And they think I'm dumb because I'm a female. I just don't want to give them another reason to think I can't do the work."

Steele's research focuses attention on cultural expectations that undermine achievement, but it is equally important to examine the reactions of many different students. For some, stereotypes can motivate them to work that much harder. Some students manage to turn the negatives they encounter at school into a positive.

I believe my cultural background has definitely affected my success in school. My parents, who are not very familiar with this country and did not feel very safe, push me in the only way they know to secure a decent future for me, and that is through studying and working hard. My gender and skin color also make a difference. In some instances, I feel that being a female makes it more of a challenge for me, and that I have to prove myself. In other instances, the color of my skin makes me instantly stupid. In still other instances, I am expected to be a genius. These dramatically contrasting experiences teach me more than anything to do the best I can. In instances when less is expected of me, I actually work harder to prove the teacher wrong. It is almost a personal challenge that I am determined to win.

⌘

I sat down in my statistics class, looked around, and saw that the students appeared to be about 10 percent African-American, and 90 percent Asian and European mixed. As the African-American students entered the class, they would look around to see who was in the class. This did not appear to be unusual to me. Once the instructor entered the class, the majority of African-American students grabbed their book bags and exited the room. I found it hard to believe that they were all in the wrong class. Later on that day, I ran into one of the African-American students and asked him why he left. He informed me that he noticed that the majority of the class was Asian and the probability of him getting a good grade was slim because Asians "mess up a curve." As one of the few remaining African-American students, this made me even more determined to stay in the class and be successful.

—Other perspectives

Stereotyping is a way of putting people in our own mental boxes. The problem with these boxes is we do not individualize them; rather, we use a "one size fits all" mentality. Therefore, something important gets left out. Imagine trying to solve a mathematical problem without being given all the necessary information. Maybe your information is inaccurate as well as incomplete. Stereotyping is no different. When we put others into a "box," we lose or distort potentially valuable information and diminish our ability to relate effectively to others. Plus, in those cases in which we are targets of stereotyping, we may feel vulnerable and less confident in our abilities.

Barrier 4: Prejudice

I think my instructors feel that because I am older, I should perform at a higher level. Some don't seem to understand that some of the material is just as new to me as to my younger classmates. I notice some irritation and disappointment from some of my instructors when I do not perform up to their expectations.

⌘

There are people who assume certain things about me because I am white. Even though they don't know me, they act like they're angry at me. They assume that I think I'm superior. They assume my parents did not have to struggle to make ends meet. They assume that being white is a ticket to success.

—Multiple perspectives

Prejudice is an irrational and inflexible opinion, formed on the basis of limited and insufficient knowledge. The derivation of the term *prejudice* can be traced to two Latin words, *prae* "before" and *judicum* "a judgment." Hence, prejudice represents a judgment before all the facts are known. In *The Nature of Prejudice,* Gordon Allport points out that prejudice is based on inaccurate information and/or illogical arguments. Therefore, it is not only a *pre*judgment; it is also a *mis*judgment.[9]

Stereotypes, discussed earlier, often give rise to prejudice. Exposure to exaggerated and rigid images of a particular group might lead us to prejudge anyone we identify with that group. A good example is what happened immediately after the

1995 Oklahoma City bombing. Because of prior news events and media coverage that had connected Muslims to terrorist acts, many Muslims in the United States became prime suspects even though there was no evidence to support this. Several mosques were vandalized and a number of Muslims received bomb threats. Even Arabic and Islamic schoolchildren were viewed suspiciously and mocked by some.

In the flood of anger and hostility that followed the attacks on September 11, 2001, innocent Muslims or people who appeared to be Muslim were targeted again. Muslims throughout the United States were indiscriminately blamed for terrorism. Not only was their safety threatened, but also many Muslims found their patriotism questioned. It is worth remembering that people did not make similar prejudgments about all fair-skinned, Christian army veterans when it was discovered that Timothy McVeigh was responsible for the Oklahoma City bombing.

Sikhs, who practice a religion that is distinct from Islam, felt particularly threatened because their faith requires them to wear turbans and grow beards. Mistaken for followers of Osama bin Laden, Sikhs endured harassment, beatings, and vandalism, and one Sikh gas station owner was murdered in Arizona a few days following the attacks. Although some Sikhs tried to blend in and hide their identity, others sought to educate the public about Sikhism, a religion founded in India in the fifteenth century. Ravjot Singh, a 19-year-old student at George Washington University, created a Web site (http://www.doubleedge.net). A picture of a Sikh appears on the site with the words, "I am not a terrorist. I am an American. I am not a 'Towelhead.' I am a Sikh. My turban and beard symbolize my religion. Is every white man a member of the KKK? Is every man with a turban a terrorist? STOP THE HATE."[10]

THINKING THROUGH DIVERSITY

When you met the instructor in this class for the first time, had you already formed certain impressions of him or her? If so, were your opinions based on what you had already heard from other students? Did your instructor's race, gender, or age influence your first impressions?

More often than not, talk about prejudice focuses on "them" rather than "us." Many of us can readily sense prejudice in others, but seeing it in ourselves is a challenge. When someone mentions the word *prejudice,* what comes to mind? Is prejudice something ordinary or extraordinary? Do prejudiced people look and act like you?

It is important to understand that we learn prejudice just like any subject at school. The lyrics of a song from the Broadway musical *South Pacific* tell us that the learning process starts very early in life. "You've got to be taught before it's too late, before you are 6 or 7 or 8, to hate all the people your relatives hate." Research indicates that children as young as 4 or 5 years of age begin to show signs of racial prejudice. At a young age, we are more apt to simply believe what we hear. By the time we are adults, prejudging people for whatever reason can become almost an unconscious habit. Additionally, prejudice affords us a quick and easy way of categorizing all the new and

> *Common sense is the collection of prejudices acquired by age 18.*
>
> —Albert Einstein

different people we meet each day. It takes much more time and effort to withhold judgment until we really know someone.

If we view prejudice as something that each of us learns, it is easier to examine ourselves. We begin to realize that uncovering prejudice in ourselves does not make us bad people. Rather, it simply shows us that we have some work to do. Ask yourself the following questions:

■ Do you feel uncomfortable around certain people? Does your body language provide you with any cues? For example, are you comfortable talking to someone whose sexual orientation is different than yours? Are you comfortable sitting next to such a person?

> *As a gay man, I don't live my life looking for sex. My relationships are based on friendship, not sex. As a student, I remember being confronted by a student who lived in the same living unit as I did. He said "I don't care if you live here as long as you don't come on to me." His assumption was that if you were gay, you wanted to have sex with any man. Who that man was did not matter.*
>
> —Another perspective

■ Do you have a tendency to judge other people because of the way they look, dress, and speak? Even the cars we drive can give rise to certain assumptions. Lorenzo, a young male student who describes himself as White, Black, and American Indian, drives a nice car to school. He constantly runs into people who assume that he stole the car or bought it with drug money. Getting stopped by police is a daily occurrence. "It messes my whole day up," says Lorenzo. He now carries his pay stub beneath his license to prove he can afford the car.

■ Are there times when you form an opinion about a person because he or she belongs to a particular group? Rafael Olmeda, a reporter for the *New York Daily News,* resents it when people assume they know something important about him because of his name. He remembers being a senior at the Bronx High School of Science. One day, Olmeda received a packet of unsolicited Harvard admission materials. Included was a Minority Student Information Request Card and information about the experiences of Hispanic students at Harvard. Even though he is proud of his Puerto Rican heritage, he resents being categorized this way. What did the people at Harvard really know about him?[11]

THINKING THROUGH DIVERSITY

Are you aware of your own prejudices? What do you do when you recognize prejudice in yourself? Specifically, how do you respond?

If we are honest with ourselves, we can begin to be more critical of our mental pictures of others. Only then can we begin to acknowledge that prejudice does exist. If somebody does complain about prejudice, it is important not to discount it. As one of my students says, sometimes the greatest gift you can give to other people is just to listen to them.

A while ago, I had developed a strong hatred for all white people. This hatred was caused by the deaths of some young black boys while under the custody of the police. The situation became so bad that my grades started slipping in school. I thought about just forgetting about school and I even thought about converting to the Nation of Islam. I was hearing all kinds of things about what happened and the police investigation. The story was in the news almost every night. Then, at school one day, I got a chance to express my feelings about the incident in one of my classes, as did every other student. Getting a chance to express what I was feeling really released some of the pressure that had been building up inside me. I realized that what I had been doing by assuming that all white people are bad was wrong, and I could not judge a whole nation of white people based on what a few dirty cops had done.

—Another perspective

Some people minimize the importance of prejudice in the workplace. Since an employer cannot know what you are thinking, they argue, prejudice becomes an issue only when we act on it. Consequently, you can be held accountable only for your actions, not for your thoughts. The problem with this argument is that we cannot analyze behavior and perceptions as distinct entities.

Picture yourself driving to work. Your commute takes you by two men who appear to be Latino standing on a street corner. You pull up next to them as you stop at a red light. You wonder why they are not working. Trying to be as inconspicuous as possible, you check to make sure that your door is locked and continue on to work. At the office, you ready yourself for a series of job interviews you will be conducting throughout the day. When the last interviewee walks into your office, you notice that he is one of the two men you passed on the way to work. What are the chances that you will be able to judge this person fairly?

We cannot neatly compartmentalize prejudicial thinking. It is messy and can influence our behavior at the most inopportune times. Just ask people who are fired from their jobs because a racial slur they use at home finds its way into their conversation at work. We cannot turn prejudice on and off like light from a lamp. Whether or not we are conscious of it, our thinking can and does affect how we behave.

Prejudices, no matter how much we think we can cover them up, work against us. This is true of prejudices that we hold or those we encounter. Consider the implications when prejudice:

THINKING THROUGH DIVERSITY

Why is it that we can see prejudices all around us but not in us?

■ *Prevents us from making accurate judgments about people.* According to various studies and court rulings, sometimes police stop a disproportionate share of minority drivers simply because of their racial or ethnic background. Many are searched as well. This practice is called *racial profiling.* According to a recent national survey, more than half of all African-American men report they have been the victims of racial profiling by police some time in their lives. One in five Latino and Asian men report they have been victims of racially motivated police stops.[12] Police, as well as the public, have recently focused more attention on the role of racial bias in police–citizen interaction and possible safeguards to ensure the equal treatment of all motorists.

■ *Becomes a source of distraction.*   *Race,* a book by Studs Terkel, captures the feelings of ordinary Americans about the sensitive subject of race. One person interviewed by Terkel shares what it is like to deal with racial prejudice in the United States. He compares it to wearing a shoe that does not quite fit. "It squeezes, it pinches, it cuts off circulation and sometimes it drives people to varying forms of distraction."[13] He goes on to say that it is not your race that has this effect. Rather, it is the assumptions that people make about you because of your race.

Religious Profiling

Recently, concerns about terrorism and security have made religious profiling more common and visible. Passengers who appear Muslim have complained that airport security authorities single them out for scrutiny and possible abuse. An American-Islamic civil rights organization has received complaints from a number of Muslim women who have been forced to remove their head scarves, or hijab, in front of others at airports. Since removing head scarves in public violates Muslim teachings about modesty, the organization says it should be done in a private area and in front of a female security screener.

■ *Results in resentment and fear.*   Consider **xenophobia,** people's unreasonable fear of foreigners. People who are xenophobic often resent the academic and economic success of certain groups of immigrants. Furthermore, they devalue cultural differences, and no one benefits. A series of *Doonesbury* cartoons makes this same point. In the cartoon, neighbors complain to the parents of an Asian-American student. The parents are told that teaching their daughter to value discipline and hard work gives her an unfair advantage.

■ *Damages a person's ability to function.*   A recent study from Yale University suggests that prejudices can impair a person's mental and physical health. Ninety men and women between the ages of 60 and 90 were divided into two groups. Using a technique known as subliminal priming, researchers flashed words on a computer screen. One group saw entirely negative messages, including words such as *decrepit, senile, decline,* and *confused.* With the other group, all the messages were positive, including *alert, astute, enlightened,* and *creative.* Participants who got negative messages were more likely to show a greater response to stress and a significant increase in blood pressure. Conversely, those exposed to positive messages tended to improve memory performance and views of aging. Becca Levy, an assistant professor of epidemiology and public health at Yale University, suggests that these results show the potential consequences when older people in our society internalize chronic negative messages.[14] An earlier study conducted by Levy and her colleagues raises the possibility that prejudices might also contribute to memory decline associated with age in the absence of disease.[15]

■ *Results in "coping fatigue."*   Through interviews with successful black professionals, Ellis Cose discovered that many of them suffered from psychological wear and tear that he terms "coping fatigue."[16] Howard Ehrlich, research director at the Prejudice Institute, reviewed research on the effects of prejudice on students at a number of college campuses. Based on his research, Ehrlich estimates that one in four minority students is "victimized for reasons of prejudice."[17] Many of these students report that prejudice interferes with their ability to study. For them, stress and discomfort may be an everyday occurrence.

THINKING THROUGH DIVERSITY

Some government officials have argued that profiling is needed to track potential terrorists. They argue that it is negligent not to look at everything, including racial and religious factors. Others say that the United States should not use any kind of profiling in the war on terror. They argue that it is reckless and there is no proof that it works. What is your opinion? Is profiling justified in order to combat terror, and if so, under what circumstances?

Blue Eyes and Brown Eyes

In 1968 Jane Elliott was a third-grade teacher in a small, rural town in Iowa. She conducted an experiment in her classroom so that her students could learn a valuable lesson about the workings and effects of prejudice. She divided them into two groups based on the color of their eyes. For Elliott, it was essential that her students experience just how easy it is to prejudge people, explain behavior in terms of that prejudgment, and build a reward system around virtually any characteristic that distinguishes one person or group from another. Even though everyone does not neatly fit into distinct categories of eye color, the same is true for other socially constructed categories upon which prejudice is based, such as race and social class.

Over the period of a week, Elliott treated the children differently based on the color of their eyes. Elliott and the blue-eyed students initially treated the brown-eyed students as if they were inferior. The "brown eyes" were told to wear collars around their necks so they could be identified easily. It was not long before their schoolwork suffered and they felt angry and frustrated. Furthermore, blue-eyed students who had always been their friends turned on them.

Midway through the experiment, Elliott convinced her students that she had made a mistake—in fact, the brown eyes were superior. Each brown-eyed student was instructed to take off his or her collar and put it on a classmate with blue eyes. Almost immediately the brown-eyed children started feeling better about themselves and the quality of their schoolwork improved dramatically. A group lesson that had given them trouble when they were assumed to be inferior was now completed with ease. Now that they were viewed as superior, they refused to associate with the inferior "blue eyes". At the end of the experiment, even Elliott was amazed by the students' transformation. When asked what they learned from the experiment, one student mentioned how the collar made it difficult for her to think and pay attention. Another student said the collar made him feel like "a dog on a leash".[18]

Your prejudices, or the prejudices you encounter, can make it that much more difficult for you to achieve your goals. Prejudice can be a source of distraction and stress. It can produce resentment and fear. When people are prejudged, misunderstandings and ill feelings get in the way. For example, your work in school may suffer when prejudice comes between you and a teacher or another student. Ultimately, no one wins in a situation such as this.

Barrier 5: Prejudice Plus Power

When people in power show prejudice, the consequences can be that much more severe. **Power** refers to the ability to influence and control others. Therefore, people with power are in a position to affect many more people by virtue of their prejudices. Imagine that you are looking for a highly competitive job and no one in upper-level management considers you a serious candidate because of your gender or class or ethnic background. Prejudice of this nature is more potent because it is backed up by economic power. This is particularly true if you encounter this kind of thinking everywhere you go.

THINKING THROUGH DIVERSITY

What is the first image that comes to mind when you hear the word *racism*?

The various "isms" are at work when we talk about prejudice plus power. **Isms** refer to the thinking by those in power that certain types of people are inherently inferior; therefore, unequal treatment is justifiable. A variety of isms exist, each focusing on a different dimension of diversity (ageism, sexism, classism . . .). Of all the isms, probably none is more volatile or difficult to understand than racism.

Definitions of **racism** vary. In some instances, it refers to discrimination based on the belief that one race is superior to another. According to this definition, anyone can be a racist. From another point of view, racism requires more than just acting out racial prejudice. It requires power. This means that those in power are the only ones who can be racist. The question then becomes who has the power. For some, only Whites can be racist because they have the economic, political, and social power in the wider society. Still there are those who maintain that power shifts from place to place. For instance, in a specific locale, Latinos or African-Americans may be in a dominant position in terms of their economic or political status.

No matter how we define racism, we need to understand the importance of power and its implications. David Shipler examines the effects of racism in his book *A Country of Strangers*.[19] A former reporter for *The New York Times*, Shipler describes a workshop in which white participants are paired up with minorities. The facilitator asks participants to stand if they have to leave their culture at the door when they go to work. He then asks participants if they believe they have been stopped by police because of their color. Finally, did any of the participants consider not having children because of racism? After each of these questions, a number of minority participants stand up—but none of the Whites.

When I ask these same questions in a number of my racially mixed college classes, the pattern of responses is the same. It is important to note that *acknowledging* racism is not the same as *using* racism as an excuse for not getting ahead. When we discuss social inequality, minority students in my classes are generally highly critical of those who blame their lack of success on white racism or "the system." The views of some of my white students, especially those who are poor, are noteworthy as well. They repeatedly cite instances where being White and poor works against them or someone they know, in part because people assume they do not need help because they are White. They feel denied rather than privileged. Clearly, it is difficult to talk about racism without addressing isms that connect with class and other dimensions of diversity.

In the larger society, we rarely talk about the issue of racism in public or in racially mixed company because it can be such an inflammatory and divisive issue. However, there have been times when discussions of racism have become more open and inclusive. One example in recent history is the trial of O.J. Simpson and the dialogue it triggered on college campuses.

Viewing Racism Differently

In the mid-1990s, an African-American man, O.J. Simpson, was charged with killing his ex-wife and someone thought to be her lover. Both of the murder victims were White. Simpson was a well-known actor and sports commentator who had gained fame as a star football player in college and the pros. For many, the trial and society's reaction to the trial provided a window into race relations in the United States.

The lengthy and widely publicized trial elicited a wide range of reactions from students on college campuses throughout the country. Some Latino and Asian-American students complained about the media's portrayal of race-related issues in strictly white and black terms. When the jury found O.J. Simpson innocent, the response from many students was decisive and immediate. Media pictures of students showed African-Americans and Whites reacting quite differently. The image of African-Americans shouting and smiling was in striking contrast to the absolute silence and disbelief of Whites. The following comments provide a glimpse into students' feelings regarding the trial and the verdict:

- In my opinion, O.J. is guilty. I know my English is not good enough and maybe I did not understand something in his trial. But in fact two people died. He was beating and kicking his ex-wife. And what is the solution of jury? O.J.—absolutely free man, he is not guilty. My heart was broken. . . . I thought there was no justice only in my former country now I think—no justice here.

- O.J. was able to beat the system. He was able to do something that most African-Americans don't get to do—that is, prove himself innocent beyond a reasonable doubt.

- You call that justice?

- O.J. came across as articulate and calm. He was handsome and well dressed. This is so different than most of the black male images we see on TV.

- I don't like how the media talked about "playing the race card." Putting it this way trivializes race as an issue.

The different reactions to the verdict prompted some to exclaim that Whites and Blacks must be "living on different planets." Polls indicated that roughly two-thirds of the Whites in the United States thought O.J. was guilty. About the same proportion of African-Americans contended he was innocent. Keeping in mind that one-third of African-Americans and Whites surveyed did not follow this pattern, how can we explain this difference?

continued

Viewing Racism Differently (continued)

Research by sociologist Robert Blauner shows that Blacks and Whites see racism differently. Blauner's research, described in his book *Black Lives, White Lives,* surveyed the opinions of a group of black and white people over a 20-year period. His findings reveal that Whites tend to accept older definitions of racism, equating it with feelings of superiority on the part of an individual. Consequently, Whites are more apt to view racism as a peripheral, sporadic concern that may be triggered by an event that comes to their attention through the media or a personal experience. Black respondents, however, are more apt to see racism as central to society, as ever-present. They embrace newer definitions of **institutional racism,** racism that is built into the systems of power and social institutions.[20] Among these institutions are religion, education, government, and the economy. For example, it is one thing to talk about an individual's belief in racial superiority. It is quite another when that belief or doctrine becomes embedded in the way a company does business, a school system distributes resources, or a police department targets criminals and enforces the law. Individual racism cannot be examined apart from institutional racism. They are interconnected and reinforce each other.

One recent example provides insight into the difference between individual and institutional racism. In 1999, James Byrd, Jr., a 49-year-old black man, was beaten, bound with a logging chain, and then dragged to his death for three miles behind a pickup truck in Jasper, Texas. It was one of the worst racially motivated killings since the murder of Emmett Till in 1955. Three young, white supremacists were convicted of his murder. In her book, *A Death in Texas,* author Dina Temple-Raston shares her extensive interviews with the residents of Jasper regarding the killing. A number of them, particularly white residents, claimed that

the problem of race relations in Jasper "was mostly in the minds of the black community."[21] They saw the crime as the work of three drunken, racist troublemakers. The sheriff is quoted as saying, "those boys didn't learn to hate here."[22] Pettigrew and Martin refer to this kind of racism as "raw, overt bigotry."[23] Because it stems from an individual's belief system, dealing with racism becomes a strictly personal matter. Individual racism, including hate crimes and intolerance by individuals with ties to hate groups, typically receives extensive coverage in the media.

Dina Temple-Raston's interviews with Blacks living in Jasper reveal explanations that point to *institutional* racism. They were more inclined to see this terrifying hate crime as a reflection of historical, habitual racial tensions in Jasper and in the larger society. Blacks talked of an unwritten social code that dictated subservience. Deviating from that code, or forgetting your "place," could very well result in retaliation. Black Jasperites described the racial hierarchy that permeated the city's businesses. Whites managed most of the restaurants, motels, gas stations, and grocery stores even though the black and white populations were roughly equal in size. The history of Jasper brought back memories of lynchings and other violent expressions of racism. To black residents, James Byrd's murder was further evidence that little had changed.

Our views of racism illustrate that even though we inhabit the same society, we see the world in distinctively different ways. In her book *Why Are All the Black Kids Sitting Together in the Cafeteria?,* Beverly Tatum compares the images and messages that convey racial superiority to the smog that each of us breathes in each day because it surrounds us. In other words, sometimes racism is thick and visible and sometimes it is less apparent and harder to see, but it is still there.[24]

Viewing Racism Differently (concluded)

No one is immune from the effects of racism. In his book *No Future Without Forgiveness,* 1984 Nobel Peace Prize recipient Desmond Tutu examines the long history of racism in South Africa and its insidious impact. On his first visit to Nigeria, he recounts traveling in a plane piloted by Nigerians. After taking off smoothly, the plane hit turbulence, shuddered, and dropped suddenly. He remembers with shock his immediate reaction. "I found I was saying to myself, 'I really am bothered that there's no white man in the cockpit. Can these blacks manage to navigate us out of this horrible experience?'" He continues, "It was all involuntary and spontaneous. I would never have believed that I had in fact been so radically brainwashed. I would have denied it vigorously because I prided myself on being an exponent of black consciousness, but in a crisis something deeper had emerged. I had accepted a white definition of existence, that whites were somehow superior to and more competent than blacks. Of course those black pilots were able to land the plane quite competently."[25] From this experience, Tutu learned to be a little more forgiving of others when they succumb to racism.

When prejudice is coupled with power, diversity becomes a negative rather than a positive for everyone. Mistrust and divisiveness interfere with communication. Teamwork suffers. It becomes a matter of my group versus your group. People may start doubting themselves and assuming the worst about others. What is certain is that human potential will be wasted.

Barrier 6: Discrimination

Unlike prejudice, *discrimination* refers to behavior. More specifically, **discrimination** is defined as the unequal treatment of people on the basis of their group membership. Treatment varies because of race, age, gender, social class, or any number of other dimensions of diversity. As an example, a study by the Massachusetts Commission Against Discrimination reveals the pervasiveness of age discrimination.[26] The commission sent teams of "testers" to look for employment. With each pair, the older and younger tester were matched in terms of personality and qualifications. They were taught to interview in a similar fashion. After a series of 24 job interviews in Atlanta, certain patterns emerged. The younger testers were generally complimented, encouraged, and accommodated. In contrast, the older testers were patronized and subtly discouraged. The response, "I'm sorry, but you're overqualified" was a common mask for age discrimination.

Results from this study are consistent with other research findings. Age stereotypes can and do influence who employers hire, promote, train, and evaluate positively. Too many managers mistakenly believe that older workers get sick more often, are less productive, have more accidents, and are more difficult to manage. Consequently, they deny many talented people the chance to compete on an equal footing.

Combinations of Prejudice and Discrimination

While some people seem to see prejudice and discrimination everywhere, others are certain that prejudice and discrimination no longer exist. As difficult as it is, try to evaluate each situation with an open mind. Although prejudice and discrimination often go hand in hand, they do not have to. Four combinations may occur in a variety of situations (see Table 3.1).

1. *The prejudiced discriminator.* This is someone who holds personal prejudices and discriminates. Example: A manager's age-related prejudices influence her decisions in a variety of personnel actions. The manager evaluates a younger worker more favorably than she does an older person who performs just as well.
2. *The prejudiced nondiscriminator.* In this case, a person's prejudicial attitudes do not lead to discriminatory behavior. Example: A male employee feels prejudice toward his female supervisor because of her gender but does not show it for fear of the consequences.
3. *The unprejudiced discriminator.* Someone who is not prejudiced discriminates

nonetheless. There are times when a person may discriminate unknowingly by following certain commonly accepted policies or practices. In addition, someone may belong to a group and discriminate to conform to group expectations. Example: Even though a person is open-minded about the subject of homosexuality, he caves in to group pressure at school and discriminates against certain people who "act gay."

4. *The unprejudiced nondiscriminator.* This person is not prejudiced and does not discriminate. Example: An employer conducting a job interview notices that an interviewee with a noticeable accent shies away from direct eye contact. As in every other interview, the employer puts the candidate at ease and focuses solely on the person's ability to do the job.

It is important to remember that each of these combinations applies to situations, not to individuals. We may or may not show any of the foregoing combinations depending on the situation.

TABLE 3.1   Prejudice and Discrimination

Combinations of Prejudice and Discrimination	Is this Person Prejudiced? (Attitude)	Does this Person Discriminate? (Behavior)
Prejudiced discriminator	Yes	Yes
Prejudiced nondiscriminator	Yes	No
Unprejudiced discriminator	No	Yes
Unprejudiced nondiscriminator	No	No

Source: Adapted from Robert Merton, "Discrimination and the American Creed," in *Sociological Ambivalence and Other Essays,* Free Press, New York, 1976.

As long as I can remember, my grandfather was always telling jokes about Jews, though he used a more offensive term. Yet he worked in public education, was highly respected, even by many of the Jewish students that had been in his care. In fact, his boss was Jewish! He apparently worked quite well with the man, yet the continuous barrage of ethnic slights revealed the true nature of his heart.

—Another perspective

Discrimination assumes many forms. There are times when it is obvious and clear-cut. At other times, we are not so sure that behavior is in fact discriminatory. Although a person might be at fault, there are situations in which we need to look further. What follows are some major forms of discrimination:

1. *Blatant versus subtle discrimination.* Discriminatory acts, some more obvious than others, are an everyday occurrence in public places. In towns and cities throughout the Southwest, certain people are stopped on a regular basis and required to prove their citizenship for no other reason than because of their skin color, accent, or surname.

The prevalent practice of harassment or name-calling constitutes another example of blatant discrimination. Research reveals that deliberate insults and derogatory remarks toward women and minorities or anyone labeled as different are standard practice in some workplace settings. What's more, workers and supervisors often close their eyes to such mistreatment and subscribe to the attitude of "That's the way it is."[27]

Instances of more subtle discrimination are also commonplace, such as certain looks or what one Hispanic woman terms that "spoken or unspoken word." "Because I'm dark and have dark eyes and hair. . . . If I entered a department store, one of two things was likely to happen. Either I was ignored, or I was followed closely by the salesperson. The garments I took into the changing room were carefully counted. My check at the grocery store took more scrutiny than an Anglo's. My children were complimented on how 'clean' they were instead of how cute."[28]

Joe Feagin, of the University of Florida, recently interviewed 210 upper-middle-class African-American professionals living in 16 cities. Those interviewed reported less "door-slamming exclusion" but more subtle discrimination, such as exclusion from informal networks that increase chances for promotion.[29] Because such discrimination is so indirect and inconspicuous, it is unlikely to lead to a formal grievance or lawsuit. Knowing how to respond to subtle discrimination can be a challenge.

THINKING THROUGH DIVERSITY

What subtle forms of discrimination have you encountered? How have you dealt with them?

2. *Individual versus institutional discrimination.* Individuals are not the only ones who discriminate. Sometimes, institutional policies and procedures put certain people at a disadvantage. For example, a waiter at a restaurant may consciously

How Much Discrimination Exists?

People often disagree about the extent of discrimination at the present. For instance, is it common or rare? How we answer this question has a lot to do with our race according to recent public opinion polls. Results from a Gallup Poll show that Blacks and Whites tend to see things differently when asked "Are Blacks treated less fairly than Whites?"[30]

Are Blacks Treated Less Fairly than Whites . . .	Whites Saying "yes"	Blacks Saying "yes"
In the workplace?	14%	45%
In stores/malls?	19%	46%
In restaurants?	16%	42%
In interactions with police?	30%	60%

or unconsciously give better service to some customers because of their looks, race, or gender. This is individual discrimination. When unequal treatment becomes a company policy, it is institutional.

Discrimination of this nature allegedly existed at Denny's not too long ago. In a class-action suit against the international restaurant chain, a former Denny's manager described how he was instructed by his district manager "to implement policies designed to limit or discourage black patronage." According to the manager, a term used at district meetings was *blackout,* meaning that there were too many black customers in a restaurant at one time. He recalled: "We were taught to avoid blackouts by requiring black customers to pay for their meals in advance or simply to close the restaurant for a few hours when we started getting too many black customers."[31]

3. *Intragroup versus intergroup discrimination. Intragroup discrimination* occurs *within* groups, whereas *intergroup discrimination* takes place *between* groups. We often assume that discrimination occurs only *between* groups such as Latinos and Whites. However, intragroup discrimination is common and may be just as painful. One African-American student recounts how she got teased because of her skin complexion. In her case, most of the people who treated her differently were not Whites; they were people of her own race and even members of her family. "I was seen as a white girl and an albino. People gave me names like 'goldie locks' and 'light bright.' They called me 'light bright' because they said I was 'light, bright, and damned near White.' It was very humiliating as a kid because I got teased constantly about my complexion. My sister was the worst of them all because when she got mad with me she would tell me that I was the mailman's baby."

Putting a Price Tag on Discrimination

Andrew Hacker's widely acclaimed book *Two Nations* analyzes inequality between black and white Americans.[32] Hacker, a college professor, discusses an experiment he conducted with his white students to illustrate the costs of being treated unequally. He creates a scenario in which an official visits students to tell them a mistake has been made. Newfound evidence shows that the race of these students was identified incorrectly. They should have been identified as Black at birth. The official emphasizes that the mistake must be corrected immediately. From now on, the students will live their lives as Blacks. The official's organization is willing to pay them for the inconvenience of changing their race. When Hacker asked his white students how much money they would request, most of them asked for approximately $1 million a year for the rest of their lives. Hacker analyzed this amount as the price these students attach to prejudice and discrimination.

For a moment, consider what Hacker might discover if he varied this experiment. In my classes, I modify Hacker's experiment to take into account that race, however important, is only one dimension of diversity and one possible reason for inequality. Moreover, I give students a choice. I simply ask students how much money they would want to change any of the following: race, sex, sexual orientation, or age (add 10 years to your age). Interestingly, the vast majority of them would not change any of their statuses for any amount of money. They express satisfaction with their current status, even if it makes them the object of discrimination. Of those who do elect to change their status, most choose to add 10 years to their age. The price tag for doing this is typically in the millions. Interestingly, one category that is rarely changed is sexual orientation. When I ask students why, many respond by talking about the constant ridicule they feel they would have to endure if they became gay or lesbian.

Discrimination is a losing proposition for everyone. When discrimination occurs, factors other than merit become important. The financial and human costs are undeniable. Beside costly lawsuits, valuable human resources are lost. Discrimination feeds anger, tension, and fear. As one of my students says, it can "eventually get to you." When this happens, we sabotage teamwork and close lines of communication. Consider the amount of time and energy that is spent discriminating or coping with discrimination and its aftereffects. What would happen if we could somehow refocus this time and energy in a more positive direction?

 ## OVERCOMING DIVERSITY BARRIERS

Take a Mexican-American man in his early 20s and put him in a situation where he forces himself to go out into an all-white or predominantly white community. He's going to get some negative feedback, whether it's just looks or whispering. It can be

anything. . . there's all types of negative feedback. It doesn't have to be verbal or physical. When things like that happen, that in turn makes that person not even want to try to interact or push himself into that kind of situation. It's like a foreseeable risk.

⌘

A person's race should not make a difference. I am a white male and I have lost out on scholarships and other opportunities because I was the wrong race.

—Other perspectives

Effectively dealing with barriers is a challenge. Although particular barriers by themselves may seem insignificant, the cumulative effect of all types of barriers can be overwhelming. Joe Feagin calls this a **pyramiding effect,** meaning the cumulative impact of encounters with barriers is much more than the sum of individual instances. In his research, Feagin discusses how one respondent compares the pyramiding effect to ergs of energy. To paraphrase, the mind only has so many ergs of energy. If we use up 50 percent of those ergs doing the creative things that we want to do each day, 50 percent remains. But if we need to use a good portion of those precious, remaining ergs to deal with innumerable, everyday barriers, we don't have as much energy left. Because our mind is not free, we cannot do what we are capable of doing.[33]

THINKING THROUGH DIVERSITY

Given the magnitude of this challenge, how do you summon the energy that is necessary to deal effectively with prejudicial beliefs, discriminatory behaviors, and other social barriers that you may encounter? To flourish in the face of adversity, what might you do differently?

How do you deal with prejudicial beliefs, discriminatory behaviors, and other social barriers that you encounter in your environment? It is important to realize there is no single strategy that is right for everyone or appropriate for all situations. What may work for you may be ineffectual for someone else. One CEO says that he counters prejudice by doing his job beyond expectations. His habit of doing more than he is asked to do wins people over. A student of mine resorts to writing whenever she feels the sting of prejudice. For her, writing provides an emotional release. "Writing down what happens and how it feels puts some distance between me and the incident. I can look at it later with less emotion." Still another effective strategy was employed by author Zora Neale Hurston. When people discriminated against her, Hurston did not get angry. Instead, she saw discrimination as a way in which others lost out. In effect, they denied themselves the pleasure of her company.[34]

Regardless of what strategy or strategies work for you, keep mindful of the following:

1. *Recognize that barriers sometimes exist.* Before we overcome barriers, we have to acknowledge them—in ourselves, others, and in our communities. That does not mean that you have to let them get in your way. In Ellis Cose's book *The Rage of a Privileged Class,* one highly successful African-American observes that business executives' attitudes and behaviors may be judged differently because of racial prejudice. "Recognize the fact, don't necessarily accept it, deal with it as the reality."[35] He goes on to say that, like every other obstacle, it can be overcome.

> *Prejudice. . . I can get over it, around it, above it. Sometimes I'm just too busy to even deal with it.*
>
> ⌘
>
> *When you feel comfortable in your own skin, you simply find a way to get around the obstacles that roll down the road.*
>
> —Other perspectives

2. *Develop and maintain pride in yourself.* Eleanor Roosevelt once said: "No one can make you feel inferior without your consent." Stephanie, a former student of mine, has had to deal with what she describes as "life's little cruelties and discomforts" because of her obesity. She recalls standing in a college biology class for two hours at a time, week after week, because she could not find suitable seating. No one, including the instructor, seemed concerned. Additionally, she remembers the instructor maintaining almost constant eye contact with her one day as he lectured about the dangers of being overweight. As she left the college campus that day, she had no plans to return and continue her college education. But she drew strength from her obese mother, who taught her that she is unique and deserves to be heard. Stephanie gradually changed her thinking. "I learned that I have a place in this world that is beyond the shadows. I learned I don't have to accept whatever is given to me. I have a right to be out there and make a living for my children."

3. *Develop and maintain pride in your culture.* When combating intolerance, cultural pride can be a source of strength. Jorge, a student from Mexico who attends a small, rural college in Maryland, emphasizes how important it is for him to be grounded in his culture. People who lack this grounding, according to Jorge, tend to be more confused and vulnerable. In Fig. 3.3, he is shown with folk art he brought with him from Mexico.

> *I am proud to be an Orthodox Jewish woman for several reasons. My fellow Jews are always looking out for one another, forming a special bond that I'd like to call a "cultural network." I know that in any time of need, regardless of the problem or barrier, my fellow people will help me out. It is known among Jews that if you have a flat tire on the side of the road, then Jews will stop alongside of you and be of assistance. I'd like to share a story that illustrates this point. A Hispanic man, on his way to New York's Catskill Mountains, got a flat tire. The man was very upset, particularly because no one stopped to assist him. Luckily, he remembered*

FIGURE 3.3   Jorge, a student, shares his Mexican heritage with his college community by assembling an altar in memory of a Mexican hero, Emiliano Zapata.

that his grandmother once told him that whenever he needs any kind of help, he should put on a head covering that Orthodox Jewish males wear on their heads. This man always kept this head covering, called a "kippa," in his car, but never used it before. He hesitantly placed the kippa on his head and within minutes cars stopped to help him out. They were Orthodox Jews. Without the advice of his grandmother and the kindness of the Jewish people, he might have never made it to the Catskills. I am so lucky to be part of this special network of Jews.

—Another perspective

4. *If you encounter diversity barriers directed at you or others, speak out if at all possible.*   What you say does matter, according to research. In one study, individual students were interviewed after hearing people express their views about racism. Those students who heard someone else condemn racism were more likely to express anti-racist sentiments than those students who heard someone express equivocal views or condone racism.[36] Using the *I feel formula* to convey how you feel about an incident can be particularly effective. Explain to others how *you* feel and why *you* consider it inappropriate (see "Conflict and Communication," page 205). If you or others are personally offended by something that takes place in a group setting, consider the pros and cons of dealing with it immediately. If it involves only one or two members of a larger group, you might be better off waiting and talking to these people in private. However, speaking right away may result in a valuable learning experience for the entire group.

In determining how to respond to discrimination and other barriers, consider whether your safety is an issue. If it is, use your common sense and do what is in your best interest. You may elect to ignore it, at least for a period of time, or deal with it indirectly and remain anonymous. If you think that a law has been broken, report the incident to someone in authority—preferably a person or group you know and trust. Depending on the situation, this might be an instructor or manager whom you know and respect. It may be necessary to consult a lawyer or the local human rights commission. If you record what happens, this can be useful if you pursue the matter further at a later date.

5. *When people judge you immediately because of your distinctive looks or behavior, try to be as patient and understanding as possible.* In interviews with minority men and women who have thrived as community leaders and advisers, researcher John Moritsugu found that showing compassion was one of their most important coping responses. Even though the respondents were enraged by racism and other acts of intolerance, they were not angry at the perpetrators. Instead, they considered them to "be victims of miseducation or a lack of experience." Furthermore, the respondents addressed the importance of acting rationally and weighing the alternatives. Rather than acting on emotion alone, they considered what they hoped to accomplish by responding a certain way.[37] Did they want to change behavior, raise awareness, or simply "blow off steam"?

It helps to remember that the perceptions of others may have nothing to do with you as a person. More likely, they result from ignorance, mistrust, and even fear. Viewing other people's prejudices in this manner helps us deal with the walls of misunderstanding and mistrust that we encounter. Keep in mind those times when *you* jump to conclusions about others.

Because of numerous past encounters with prejudice, sometimes you may sense prejudice where none exists. To illustrate, parents of a child with severe facial anomalies were attending a high school musical. The child remained at home with a relative. Throughout the entire performance, the parents could not help but notice two young people seated in front of them who continually turned around to look at something. On the way home that night, the parents tried to make sense of the strange looks from the couple. Only then did they realize that if their son had been with them, they would have been overcome with emotion. Moreover, they would have been *positive* that the looks were directed at him.

As a graduate student, I attended a small, rural, private college. I had just moved from a large city. I was very open about being gay. I felt like "I'm gay and damn you're going to like it." One night, I remember visiting one of my friends in his dormitory. On the way up to his room, I saw the quarterback of the football team. We knew each other and had talked before. Up to that point, I had always looked at him as a "dumb jock" and he saw me as a "stupid faggot." This time it was different. We related as humans, not as categories. I came to realize that if I tried to push my "category" on someone else, we would end up relating as categories.

—Another perspective

6. *Fine tune your anger.*   Many people who constantly face petty and not so petty slights find it necessary to pick their battles. Some pick their responses: shouting, whispering, or conversing. It may depend on the situation or how one feels that day. Karen Bates and Karen Hudson recently coauthored an etiquette book for African-Americans entitled *Basic Black: Home Training for Modern Times.*[38] Part of the book offers advice to those who suspect they are being treated a certain way because of how they look. Bates and Hudson give the example of poor service at a restaurant. Perhaps the waiter is rude to you and polite to others. What if the maitre d' ignores you and your guests or your request for seating in a certain area of the restaurant? The authors suggest asking the person in charge if the waiter is having a bad day. If you suspect that your race is the reason for your treatment, ask the manager: "Can I assume that your restaurant does not want customers who look like me?" Low-key responses to subtle but hurtful slights can get results.

7. *Resist the urge to scapegoat.*   When we **scapegoat,** we unfairly blame others for our own problems. In essence, scapegoating allows us to look outward, not inward. For example, some majority group members blame affirmative action for the ills of society. They argue that affirmative action has given minorities an unfair advantage and puts Whites at a disadvantage. When a close relative or friend is not promoted or hired, an underqualified minority is assumed to be the reason. In reality, maybe this relative or friend was simply not the strongest candidate for the job. Similarly, some minority-group members see the white man as the root of all evil. One student of color comments: "A lot of the blame is toward the white man. When do we stop blaming and just accept that it happened and go on? They say the white man has oppressed us and is still oppressing us. I think in the long run we're oppressing ourselves because of our attitude. We have a lot of opportunities we are not taking advantage of."

8. *Try to keep the focus on the behavior in question rather than the person.*   This can be done by maintaining one's composure, using the "I feel" formula, or possibly turning a question around. Instead of trying to answer an insensitive question by justifying or defending your behavior, turn the question around. By doing this, you keep the focus on what is said. For instance, a student who is gay might respond to the following questions this way:

Question: When did you know you were gay?

Answer: Well, when did you know you were straight?

Question:	When did you come out of the closet?
Answer:	Good question. When did you come out of the closet?
Question:	Why do you like someone of the same sex?
Answer:	Why do you like someone of the opposite sex?

9. *Seek out others for support.* Harvard psychiatrist Alvin Poussaint emphasizes the importance of sharing one's experiences and emotions with others.[39] Mentors, or people who serve as guides, role models, and teachers, can provide much needed support, counsel, and friendship. Mentors can offer a different perspective, help you understand the issues that you and others like you may be facing, and reinforce your confidence.

Often, people assume that what they are going through is unique to them and may be their fault. By building relationships with others who have had similar experiences, you can release emotional pressure, make new friends, raise your consciousness, and work for change. Support groups take many forms. You can join or create one at school, work, or in any social setting. If your hectic schedule makes this impossible, consider using your personal computer to network online with people who experience similar problems.

10. *Work with others to find new and effective ways to combat barriers and promote the value of diversity.* Consider joining a community-, work-, or school-based organization. For example, at one college, a conflict resolution team offers assistance to students who request it. Team members include racial and ethnic minorities who speak a variety of languages, students with physical and learning disabilities, as well as students who are gay, lesbian, and bisexual. After a period of intense training, they work in small, diverse groups to help disputants settle their differences.

Combating Genetic Discrimination

Community groups, such as the Council for Responsible Genetics (CRG), play a crucial role in educating and mobilizing the public. This nonprofit, nongovernmental group of scientists, public health advocates, physicians, lawyers, and concerned citizens disseminates information and promotes dialogue regarding the social and ethical implications of biotechnology. According to CRG, there have been a number of cases of genetic discrimination across the United States. In such cases, employers have used genetic information to dismiss workers in order to minimize potential healthcare costs. The group's efforts include providing public education in areas such as cloning and genetic privacy, creating model legislation, and writing position papers.

11. *Combat the ignorance and intolerance that exist within each of us.* When we look for barriers to diversity and ultimately our success, all too often we look outward rather than inward. Irving Horowitz described our way of life as becoming a "culture of victimization," in which "everyone is a victim" and "no one accepts responsibility for anything."[40] A culture of victimization encourages us to look for simple answers to complex problems, to distrust entire categories of people who we identify as "the oppressor." One of my students describes victimization as "the barracuda syndrome," the feeling that you are constantly under attack and cannot trust anyone. When we look for barriers to diversity, we need to start with ourselves. Only then can we develop a perspective that allows us to recognize and combat both personal and social barriers.

Each of us has the power to choose our reactions and overcome barriers that get in our way. One of the things I admire most about my students is their resiliency. When we talked about this in class one day, one student recalled how she has spent most of her life crying because of something somebody said. "There comes a time," she said, "when you simply have to stop crying and move on." In the course of the discussion, someone else talked about her "survival kit." When I asked her to describe its contents, she said, "a large sketching pad, colored pencils, free year-round movie passes, a full-sized notebook to write down my thoughts each day, uplifting self-help and spiritual books, and phone numbers of supportive people I can call and chat with."

THINKING THROUGH DIVERSITY

If we open up your survival kit, what will we find?

Throughout this chapter we have examined a number of personal and social barriers that may interfere with our ability to be successful. These include limited perceptions, ethnocentrism, stereotypes, prejudice, prejudice plus power, and discrimination. Additionally, we have explored a variety of strategies that can help us acknowledge and overcome these diversity barriers.

In the next chapter, we examine the impact of our social isolation. We take an in-depth look at the process by which we develop our awareness, understanding, and skills in the area of diversity. We also explore a number of strategies that can help us open our minds and learn more about diversity.

 ## CASE STUDIES

Case Study One

Ligua's desire to continue her education makes her feel like an outsider in her community. A number of neighbors have made it clear that she should reevaluate her priorities and spend more time at home. Ligua feels as though she is a dutiful wife who puts the needs of her family ahead of her own. She works because she has to work. While her family takes priority, she knows that her husband will help too if there is a crisis at home. Nevertheless, she feels guilty because she can't "have it all," that is, be a supermom, a superworker, and a superstudent.

At school, Ligua constantly feels like she is under a spotlight, especially when people want the "minority" point of view, or expect her to be knowledgeable about certain subjects because of her looks and name. When she interacts with certain professors and staff members, she encounters subtle stereotypes. Some people expect her to be inarticulate, submissive, and unexceptional. For example, although she is an active participant in her English literature class, her professor never seems to call on her or look her way when he asks a truly challenging question. In her history class, she feels it's subtler than that. If Ligua answers a difficult question well, she is apt to detect an element of surprise in her teacher's face like wow, did that come from her?

Questions:

1. Role conflict is a constant struggle for Ligua. This conflict is exacerbated by traditional cultural expectations in her community that view motherhood as a full-time responsibility. Are Ligua's expectations unrealistic? What can she do to alleviate her sense of guilt?

2. As a student, Ligua feels like some professors do not expect her to excel. Additionally, she feels as if she is being asked to speak for all Latinos anytime one of her professors discusses topics such as affirmative action, immigration restrictions, or profiling. Even though she doesn't want to alienate these professors, she feels that she needs to say or do something. What might Ligua do and why?

3. Which of Ligua's dilemmas do you see as personal barriers? Which are social barriers? Explain your reasoning.

Case Study Two

Society can be very judgmental. For instance, Mary has noticed a lot of negative responses from all sorts of different people regarding her personal expression with body modifications (tattoos and piercing). Mary says, "What people don't realize is how much they mean to me, how much beauty I see in them. It's a chapter in my life that I have opened to the outside world. Each one represents a certain moment in my life or defines a part of who I am, little pieces of me stained on my skin in beautiful contrast." Unfortunately, Mary says she encounters people time and time again who prejudge her because they don't understand.

Suspicious looks and comments, or negative "vibes," are more common in the summertime according to Mary. "There's a seasonal discriminatory policy in effect," she says jokingly. Sometimes she gets bombarded with rude questions or smirks. Occasionally, she does get the occasional compliment since her artwork is done professionally and she puts a lot of time and money into it.

What really worries her is the impending fear that has been placed on her by her parents and some friends. They have told her that she will never find a decent job or gain recognition or respect with "all those tattoos." Her mother has even gone so far as to beg her to consider tattoo removal. Despite what they say, Mary believes there is a high-paying and respectable job opportunity in her future in the field of social work. She argues that her skills and her credentials are what matter, not how many different colors are on her skin.

Questions:

1. Do you agree with Mary's insistence that her skills, not her extensive body modification, will determine her opportunities in the field of social work? Explain why.

2. If you were one of Mary's friends, what advice would you give her?

3. Do you think Mary's problems are due more to personal or social barriers? Explain.

Case Study Three

Everyday encounters with profiling make Michael distrustful of people. When he goes out at night, he cannot walk close to a woman without thinking what she is going to think of him. Usually, he assumes they're negative thoughts.

Michael finds that if he dresses in business attire early in the morning or late in the day, he has virtually no trouble getting a cab. However, if after work he has on jeans and tennis shoes, that same cab driver who picked him up in the morning will leave him standing on the corner.

When Michael shares these stories with his white coworkers, they say he is making way too much out of it. To prove their point, they describe similar situations in which people ignore or avoid them for no apparent reason. For Michael, experiences like these make him extremely reluctant to share anything of a personal nature with his white coworkers, especially if it deals with race.

Questions:

1. What do you think is the cumulative psychological impact of Michael's daily encounters with profiling?

2. What accounts for Michael's response to his coworkers and his reluctance to discuss race-related issues at work?

3. If you were one of Michael's coworkers and he shared these stories with you, how would you react? Be specific.

 EXERCISES

In-Class

Exercise 1: Feeling Different

Directions for Instructor

1. Ask each student to think of a real-life situation in which he or she felt different: for example, being the only person in a group with a particular skill, look, or lifestyle. This should be a situation you feel comfortable sharing with another student.

2. Instruct students to answer the following questions briefly in writing.

  a. How did you feel in this situation?

  b. How did you react? How did others react?

  c. If this situation occurs again, would you try to react differently? Explain. Would you like others to react differently? Explain.

3. Divide students into small groups, preferably three students in each. Instruct them to take turns describing the situation in which they felt different and their responses to parts a, b, and c of question 2.

Exercise 2: People with Disabilities: Barriers at Your School

Directions for Instructor

1. Divide the class into groups of four. Each group should appoint a recorder, a leader, a mediator, and a reporter. Provide the recorders in each group with a flipchart and a felt-tip marker. The tasks are as follows:
   - *Recorder:* takes notes
   - *Leader:* keeps the group on task and encourages everyone to participate
   - *Reporter:* speaks for the group, uses recorder's notes
   - *Mediator:* makes sure everyone understands and listens

2. *Brainstorming Activity.* The idea behind brainstorming is to generate as many ideas as possible. There are no "right" or "wrong" ideas for this exercise. The recorder should write down *all* the group members' responses to the following questions.
   a. What barriers do people with disabilities encounter at your school? (These barriers might take many different forms. The attitudes of students, faculty, and staff are possible barriers. Services and facilities that are or are not provided for students with disabilities represent another.)
   b. Which barriers are based on the thinking and behavior of individuals?
   c. Which barriers are institutional, meaning they are more closely related to the school as a whole?
   d. Which barriers could be removed within the next year? What needs to be done to remove each barrier?

3. *Consensus Building Activity.* This activity requires that all members of each group reach a general agreement on:
   - *One* barrier that could be removed within the next year
   - What needs to be done to remove it

   Be as specific as possible. The recorder should take notes and later type this information on a single page. A copy of this goes to the instructor.

4. Instruct each group to share this information with an administrator who is in a position to consider the feasibility of your recommendations. If possible, the group should arrange a meeting to discuss their concerns.

Out-of-Class

Exercise 1: Media Images of the Elderly

Journal. Keep a journal for two weeks. During this time, collect at least 10 magazine/newspaper articles and/or advertisements that contain pictures or news about older persons. For each article or advertisement, record information on a chart with the headings shown below:

Source: Article/Ad/What Is Being Sold/Role of Elderly/Analysis. Given the entries in your journal, do you notice any patterns in the images you observed? For example, are the images of the elderly primarily positive or negative? Are there any stereotypical roles associated with old age?

Exercise 2: Reflections on Being an Insider and an Outsider

Being an insider:

1. Describe a situation in which you feel like an insider. In other words, when do you feel people accept and respect you? Why do you feel this way?
2. What privileges do you have as an insider? Did you do anything to deserve these privileges? Explain.

Being an outsider:

1. Describe another situation in which you feel like an outsider. In other words, when do you feel a lack of acceptance or respect from others? Why do you feel this way?
2. What disadvantages do you have as an outsider? Did you do anything to deserve these disadvantages?

Being an insider and an outsider in different situations teaches us something:

1. What do you learn about yourself and others by being an insider? What do you learn by being an outsider?

Exercise 3: Memory Maps

1. Draw a map of the world from memory alone.
2. Compare your map to a map of the world found in an atlas or other reputable source. What are the major differences? For instance, which hand-drawn continents are closest to their actual size and shape? Which are the least accurately drawn or missing?
3. What does your map reveal about you and the way you view the world? What biases or gaps in knowledge does it show? Which areas are the easiest and most difficult for you to visualize? Why?

Exercise 4: Hate Incidents

On college campuses, an increasing number of students are victims of hate incidents. These incidents affect students directly and indirectly. Indeed, the entire college community can feel the repercussions of a single act of intolerance. Pick *one* of the following real-life examples. Describe how you could respond effectively as a student. What would you do? Why? At whom would your response be directed? Why?

- In the entranceway to a dormitory, a student writes on the dry erase board a message that describes Blacks as welfare recipients and STD spreaders.
- A columnist for a student newspaper refers to Whites as "irredeemable racists" and calls for Blacks to "execute" Whites who pose a threat.
- A college fraternity holds a "Mexican Border Party." To gain entrance, students have to crawl under a barbed wire barrier.
- Leaflets depicting the Holocaust as a hoax are handed out in front of a building housing a Jewish student organization.

- A group of students take it upon themselves to sell T-shirts with anti-homosexual slogans. One of the T-shirts advocates violence against gays and lesbians. Another has the words "Homophobic and Proud of It" printed on the front.

 ## INTERNET ASSIGNMENT

Web sites of hate groups have proliferated in recent years. According to a recent report by the Southern Poverty Law Center, there were a total of 405 U.S.-based hate sites on the World Wide Web in the year 2001, up from 366 the year before.[41]

1. Locate a hate group on the World Wide Web. Print the home page and include the URL address.
2. Analyze the site by responding to the following questions. What appear to be the goals of this hate group? How does this group try to rationalize and "market" hate? What prejudices, stereotypes, and "isms" are revealed in this Web site? Be as specific as possible and give examples.

 ## NOTES

[1] Cornel West, *Race Matters* (New York: Random House, 1993).

[2] Howard Schwartz, "Further Thoughts on a 'Sociology of Acceptance' for Disabled People," *Social Policy,* Fall 1988, 36–39.

[3] Galen V. Bodenhausen, "Stereotypic Biases in Social Decision Making and Memory: Testing Process Models of Stereotype Use," *Journal of Personality and Social Psychology,* 55, 1988, 726–737.

[4] Angus Wilson, *The Strange Ride of Rudyard Kipling: His Life and Works* (New York: Viking Press, 1978), 290.

[5] Richard Morin, "Needed: A Hillbilly Anti-Defamation League," *The Washington Post,* May 4, 1997, C5.

[6] E. Berscheid and E. Walster, "Beauty and the Beast," *Psychology Today,* Mar. 1972, 46, 74.

[7] Andrea DeSantis and Wesley Kayson, "Defendants' Characteristics of Attractiveness, Race, and Sex and Sentencing Decisions," *Psychological Reports,* 81, 1997, 679–683.

[8] Claude Steele, "Twenty-First Century Program and Stereotype Vulnerability," unpublished study and program, Stanford University, Stanford, CA, 1995.

[9] Gordon Allport, *The Nature of Prejudice* (Reading, MA: Addison Wesley, 1954).

[10] Ravjot Singh, "Stop the Hate," Online, September 19, 2001. Available: http://www.doubleedge.net.

[11] Jim Slepper, "Liberal Racism," *The New Democrat,* July/Aug. 1997, 8.

[12] Richard Morin and Michael Cottman, "Most Black Men Profiled by Police, Poll Says," washingtonpost.com. Online, June 21, 2001. Available: http://www.washingtonpost.com/ac2/wp-dyn?pagename= article&nodc= &contentId= A30338-2001Jun21&notFound= true.

[13] Studs Terkel, *Race: How Blacks and Whites Feel about the American Obsession* (New York: New Press, 1992), 124.

[14] Becca Levy, "Improving Memory in Old Age Through Implicit Self-Stereotyping," *Journal of Personality and Social Psychology,* 71 (6), 1996, 1092–1107.

[15] Becca Levy and Ellen Langer, "Aging Free from Negative Stereotypes: Successful Memory in China and Among the American Deaf," *Journal of Personality and Social Psychology,* 66 (6), 1994, 989–997.

[16] Ellis Cose, *The Rage of a Privileged Class* (New York: Harper Collins, 1993), 63.

[17] Howard J. Ehrlich, *Campus Ethnoviolence: A Research Review,* Institute Report 5 (Baltimore: National Institute Against Prejudice and Violence, 1992), 8.

[18] ABC News, *The Eye of the Storm* (video) (Mount Kisco, NY: Guidance Associates, 1981).

[19] David Shipler, *A Country of Strangers* (New York: Alfred A. Knopf, 1997).

[20] Bob Blauner, *Black Lives, White Lives* (Berkeley, CA: University of California Press, 1989).

[21] Dina Temple-Raston, *A Death in Texas* (New York: Henry Holt, 2002), 266.

[22] Karen Olsson, "Bad Old Boys," *The Washington Post Book World,* Feb. 10, 2002, 4.

[23] T. F. Pettigrew and J. Martin, "Shaping the Organizational Context for Black American Inclusion," *Journal of Social Issues,* 43 (1), 1987, 41–78.

[24] Beverly Tatum, *Why Are All the Black Kids Sitting Together in the Cafeteria?* (New York: Harper Collins, 1997).

[25] Desmond Mpilo Tutu, *No Future Without Forgiveness* (New York: Doubleday, 1999), 252.

[26] Massachusetts Commission Against Discrimination, as reported on ABC News Primetime Live, "Age and Attitudes," June 9, 1994.

[27] Barbara Larcom and Allyson George, "First Glimpse of New Workplace Research," *National Institute Against Prejudice and Violence Forum,* March 1992, 1+.

[28] Gabriela Kuntz, "My Spanish Standoff," *Newsweek,* May 4, 1998, 22.

[29] Karen Winkler, "While Concern over Race Relations Has Lessened among Whites, Sociologists Say Racism Is Taking New Forms, Not Disappearing," *Chronicle of Higher Education,* Sept. 11, 1991, A10–A11.

[30] "Inclusion, Not Rejection, Will Spur Racial Harmony," *USA Today,* June 16, 1997, 18A.

[31] Stephen Labaton, "Denny's Gets a Bill for the Side Orders of Bigotry," *The New York Times,* May 29, 1994, E4.

[32] Andrew Hacker, *Two Nations* (New York: Ballantine Books, 1995).

[33] Joe Feagin, "The Continuing Significance of Race: Anti-Black Discrimination in Public Places," *American Sociological Review,* 56, 1991, 101–116.

[34] Zora Neale Hurston, as quoted in Dorothy W. Riley, ed., *My Soul Looks Back, 'Less I Forget: A Collection of Quotations by People of Color* (New York: Harper Collins, 1995), 318.

[35] Ellis Cose, *The Rage of a Privileged Class* (New York: Harper Collins, 1993), 168.

[36] Fletcher Blanchard et al., "Reducing the Expression of Racial Prejudice," *Psychological Science,* 2, 1991, 101–105.

[37] Bill Shapiro, "Speakers Call for Greater Effort in Combating Racism," *American Psychological Association Monitor,* 28 (10), Oct. 1997, 39.

[38] Karen G. Bates and Karen E. Hudson, *Basic Black: Home Training for Modern Times* (New York: Doubleday, 1996).

[39] Ellis Cose, *The Rage of a Privileged Class* (New York: Harper Collins, 1993), 169.

[40] Irving Louis Horowitz, *The Decomposition of Sociology* (New York: Oxford University Press, 1993).

[41] Southern Poverty Law Center, *Intelligence Report,* Spring, 2002.

Developing Diversity Consciousness

4

Chapter Objectives

Upon completion of this chapter, you will be able to:

- Explain the importance of diversity consciousness.
- Define cultural encapsulation and discuss its impact.
- List and explain the six areas of development.
- Discuss at least three strategies for developing diversity consciousness.
- Explain why the development of diversity consciousness is a continuing process.

> *Not to know is bad.*
> *Not to want to know is worse.*
> *Not to hope unthinkable.*
> *Not to care unforgivable.*
>
> *—Nigerian proverb*

THE IMPORTANCE OF DIVERSITY CONSCIOUSNESS

In this chapter we look at how each of us can develop our diversity consciousness. We examine the roots and impact of our cultural isolation, as well as how we can become more aware of ourselves and others. This ongoing process is not sequential; it does not occur in steps that follow one another neatly. Rather, many things feed into this nonlinear process as we continually open ourselves up to other perspectives.

Regardless of your educational or career goals, diversity consciousness is important for a number of reasons:

1. *It enhances your diversity skills.* These skills, discussed throughout the book, include:

- Teamwork
- Ability to balance "fitting in" and "being yourself"

- Flexible thinking and adaptability
- Ability to network and learn from everyone and anyone
- Ability to recognize and respect diverse intellectual strengths and learning styles
- Ability to appreciate and maintain pride in your background and culture
- Ability to deal effectively with barriers to success
- Interpersonal relations and communication
- Self-evaluation
- Pluralistic leadership
- Conflict management
- Critical thinking

These skills will open up your mind to opportunities in all realms of life.

2. *It expands your horizons and empowers you.* Knowledge is power. Learning about yourself and others helps you to cope with all kinds of situations. Knowledge can give you confidence and instill pride in yourself and your culture. Unlike material possessions, it cannot be taken away from you. Vu Duc Vuong, a Vietnamese immigrant, makes this point when he talks about the economic hardships endured by refugees. They "often lose everything they have; everything can be taken away from a refugee: money, house, car, gold, souvenirs, job, status, friends, relatives, spouses, and even their own lives. You have heard these stories, and some of you may have even witnessed them firsthand. But among all the losses, there is one thing that will always be yours, that is your learning. No person, no circumstance, no law, and no catastrophe can take away what is inside your head. So, you owe it to yourself to learn as much as you can the rest of your life. That is one possession that is completely within your control, that is completely yours."[1]

Knowledge is better than riches.

—Cameroonian proverb

3. *It promotes personal growth and strengthens your social network.* By making contacts and developing relationships with people from a wide variety of backgrounds, you expand your social network. Social networking is not only a matter of who or how many people you know. The nature of the relationship and your skills in nourishing and strengthening that relationship can be even more critical. Carol Gallagher, author of *Going to the Top,* conducted in-depth interviews with 200 top executive women at Fortune 1000 companies. She found that the term *networking* did not resonate with many of these women because they thought it implied developing relatively superficial relationships. Instead they talked about the importance of developing close relationships that helped them learn and grow and provided them with the connections they needed to get ahead.[2] Being able to draw on a variety of diversity skills will help you expand your circle of friends and develop substantive relationships with new and different kinds of people.

In school, diversity consciousness allows you to relate more effectively to a wide variety of instructors with diverse teaching styles. It enables you to learn more from other students. Additionally, the skills you develop as you become more conscious of diversity increase your value at work. Your assets will include your flexibility, creativity, and ability to communicate and work with all kinds of people. These are the same qualities that will make you a more effective leader or manager.

> *Opportunity isn't necessarily going to come along looking, talking, dressing, and acting like you. The more different kinds of people you can get along with, the more opportunities you will have.*
>
> —Another perspective

CULTURAL ENCAPSULATION

Recently, I heard a student describe college life as living in a bubble. She went on to say that her college experience insulates her and in some ways makes her oblivious to the outside world. When culture has that same effect on our awareness, it is called **cultural encapsulation,** meaning a lack of contact with cultures outside of our own that promotes insensitivity to cultural differences. Being encapsulated in a cultural bubble alters our view, making it difficult to transcend our cultural assumptions or even realize how culture shapes those assumptions. Therefore, we are more prone to define reality in terms of our set of experiences and assumptions, making it possible to sort and evaluate people and their cultures all too quickly and easily.

When we think of what is typical, we tend to start with ourselves and our own little worlds: our families, neighborhoods, schools, and communities. This kind of thinking often gives rise to ethnocentrism, a concept we discussed in the last chapter. Ethnocentrism leads us to judge others or the larger world by our own limited experiences.

Sometimes, our narrow perspective expands a bit through exposure to the media. Indeed, for most people in the United States, various media are their primary source of information about the larger world. This can be dangerous since many people do not critically evaluate what they see or hear on television, in the newspapers, or elsewhere. According to research, the media often provide information that is stereotypical, superficial, and incomplete.

For example, the research group Women, Men, and Media periodically reviews the gender of newsmakers found on the front page of large and small newspapers. In a survey of news coverage, this group found that women rarely make the front page of newspapers. When they do, it is often because of a tragedy such as death or due to their relationship to a male newsmaker.[3] Another survey by the National Council of La Raza found that television and film often depict Hispanics as low status and criminals.[4] Many stories on poverty that appear in the media reveal a bias as well. According to a recent Yale University study by Martin Gilens,[5] stories about the poor in national news magazines picture African-Americans 62 percent of the time. This is likely to create the impression that most poor people are African-Americans. However, U.S. Census data paint a different picture of poverty. While roughly 25 percent of Americans who fall below the poverty line are African-American, 75 percent are not.[6]

If we cannot rely on the media, what about our personal lives? Why can't we simply fall back on what we know as a result of our past and present experiences? At the beginning of the semester, we discuss this very subject in my Introduction to Sociology classes. One of the criticisms of sociology is that it is common sense. After all, why spend a semester studying human behavior when "street knowledge" or personal experiences will suffice? We analyze a number of statements that reveal the pitfalls of relying solely on experiences, such as "Most of the poor in the United States are non-white minority-group members." Many of my students agree with this statement because they have lived most, if not all, of their lives in large, impoverished urban areas with large minority populations. Others disagree, noting their exposure to white poverty, which they argue is pervasive but more hidden. Still others take issue with the ambiguity of the statement, arguing that *most, poor,* and *non-white* need to be clearly defined. For example, what does *most* mean? Does it refer to the percentage or number of poor? In the course of dissecting this statement, we begin to realize that because of our cultural encapsulation we view the world differently.

Cultural encapsulation starts at a young age. It is apparent throughout **socialization,** the lifelong process of social interaction that enables us to learn about ourselves and others. We are inclined to make friends with other people who are like us. In many cases, we attend schools and live in neighborhoods that are racially and ethnically segregated. Cultural encapsulation prior to college is one of the major reasons why college life can be such an adjustment. After living in relatively segregated communities, students tend to become much more aware of their cultural identity when they enter college. One student comments: "Like now, I feel white. I feel different. I feel really different compared to other people."[7]

Students may find it difficult to adjust to college life when the cultural backgrounds of their fellow students are unlike those of people in their home communities. Similarly, adjusting to a new cultural environment at work may pose an equally formidable challenge. Faced with this situation, people typically become more focused on their own culture or minority status. As one college student remarked, "I'm used to being the minority, but I wasn't used to living it day by day by day, morning, noon, and night."[8]

Prior to college, exposure to other groups and ways of life takes place largely through the media and popular culture. Students tend to experience exposure to some groups more than others. Larger groups, such as Latinos and African-Americans, tend to be more visible than smaller groups, such as Asian-Americans and Native Americans. Even when images in the media are accurate, they may lack balance. By way of illustration, a movie such as *The Joy Luck Club* provides us with certain negative images of Asian-American males. These images might accurately reflect *some* Asian-American men. However, these images are not adequately balanced by other, more positive portrayals.

Cultural Encapsulation at College

In a poll conducted by Zogby International in 1999, 18- to 29-year-olds felt, on average, that campus diversity was as important to the quality of a college as grades and high test scores in college admissions.[9] The value of diversity at all levels of education is increasingly being acknowledged by people of all ages. In particular, the college experience serves to broaden our cultural horizons and make us more aware of our cultural encapsulation.

Nonetheless, exposure to a diverse mixture of students does not necessarily lead to greater acceptance and interaction across group boundaries. This is due to a number of factors.

1. *Research shows that throwing diverse students together in the same setting is no guarantee that they will interact or get to know each other.* Whites, African-Americans, Latinos, and other minority students often are unlikely to develop personal relationships outside their group. Students in general may find it easier to socialize with others who they perceive as being more like them. Also, negative prior experiences or personal biases may make some students hesitant to develop any kind of meaningful relationship with someone who does not share their background or even their physical appearance.

This kind of self-segregation, in which people "keep with their own kind," is relatively common on college campuses. It occurs in residence halls, athletic teams, social clubs, and support groups. Contrary to popular belief, research findings indicate that self-segregation is more common among white students than among students of color. This is one of the major conclusions found in *The Impact of Diversity on Students,* a research report published by the Association of American Colleges and Universities.[10]

THINKING THROUGH DIVERSITY

Take a look at your close circle of friends. How diverse is this group?

2. *The campus climate is "chilly" for some students.* **Campus climate** refers to the level of comfort that students experience in the classroom and on campus. Students may feel uncomfortable for any number of reasons, including gender. In *The Classroom Climate: A Chilly One for Women?,* a female student recalls: "I was discussing my work in a public setting when a professor cut me off and asked me if I had freckles all over my body."[11] A chilly climate can make it more difficult for students to focus on their schoolwork, communicate with others, and develop relationships with faculty and students. Unfortunately, research findings show that students feel there are very few opportunities to express their concerns about campus climate.[12]

3. *Opportunities to learn about diversity, and students' inclinations to take advantage of these opportunities, vary greatly.* When it comes to providing students with opportunities to become more knowledgeable about diversity, some colleges do a lot and others do relatively little. At certain colleges, all students are required to take at least one course dealing with cultural diversity. An increasing number of college instructors are infusing diversity in their courses. Student and faculty programs, workshops, and activities dealing with diversity issues are commonplace.

Nevertheless, learning about diversity is not always a college-wide priority. Sometimes, it is only an issue if a particular student or faculty member makes it an

THINKING THROUGH DIVERSITY

Look at what is being taught in your
college classes. Do the readings,
lectures, and discussions reflect the
contributions of many cultures?

issue. At some schools, diversity is seen as relevant only for
a small group of students majoring in the social sciences or
related areas. Consequently, many students discover that during their years in college, learning about diversity is up to
them. If you take responsibility for learning more about others regardless of the college you attend, your diversity consciousness will grow. If you don't, it won't.

Cultural Immersion Program

The University of Indiana has recently begun
what it calls a *cultural immersion program* for
education majors. As part of their educational
program students are required to teach and live
in a predominantly bilingual/bicultural setting.
The program addresses the growing need for
elementary and secondary school teachers with
multicultural skills and training.

Through this experience, student teachers
learn to consider the cultural, cognitive, and
linguistic backgrounds of their students.
Further, they gain valuable insight into the
development of effective curricular and
instructional approaches for students whose
first language is not English.

SIX AREAS OF DEVELOPMENT

Diversity consciousness is not an ideal level of awareness and understanding that we
reach, after which we remain static. Rather, it is dynamic. Developing our diversity
consciousness means committing ourselves to constant learning and change. In this
sense, it is a lot like developing computer know-how. There is always something
new to learn and practice.

*Many people want to change
the world; only a few want to
change themselves.*

—Leo Tolstoy

The development of diversity consciousness can be broken down into six areas (see Fig. 4.1): (1) examining ourselves
and our worlds, (2) expanding our knowledge of others and
their worlds, (3) stepping outside of ourselves, (4) gauging the
level of the playing field, (5) checking up on ourselves, and
(6) following through. In the following sections we describe
each of these areas.

Examining Ourselves and Our Worlds

It is a huge mistake to assume that we already have full knowledge of our own history and culture. Zora Neale Hurston, a well-known writer and anthropologist, stated:
"I couldn't see it [culture] for wearing it. It was only when I was off in college, away

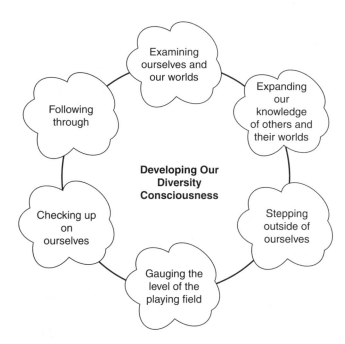

FIGURE 4.1 Diversity consciousness: Six areas of development.

from my native surroundings, that I could see myself like somebody else and stand off and look at my garment. I had to have the spyglass of Anthropology to look through at that."[13] Like many of us, Hurston was unaware of her culture because she was so immersed in it. When she went to college, she found herself in a different cultural and academic setting. By experiencing and learning about cultural diversity in this new environment, she was able to "stand back" and take a more critical look at her culture.

Before we begin to make sense of other cultures and cultural differences, we need to become aware of who we are. We do this by focusing on ourselves and the enormous diversity that exists within each of us. Each person is different and each is unique.

Our uniqueness is a reflection of both nature and nurture, which work together. **Nature** refers to our biological makeup. This includes our inborn or genetic traits. "Who we are," therefore, has something to do with nature. However, we cannot examine nature apart from nurture. **Nurture** refers to those aspects of the environment that mold and shape us, such as schools, families, and peer groups. Each of us is reared in a distinctive environment. Even children from the same family interact differently with other family members, watch different television shows, read different books, and have different friends.

You can begin to reveal your own diversity by asking a number of questions about your background. What makes you unique? Is it your work ethic, talents, personality, sense of humor, or maybe all these things? Your upbringing, schooling, family background, and cultural roots further distinguish you from other people. Your answers to the following questions will provide greater insight into your diversity.

1. What is your name? What is the meaning or significance of your name?
2. Where and when were you born?
3. What is your family background? Who raised you? As you grew up, who did you consider "family"? Where did you live? Who were your closest friends?
4. What schools did you attend? In general, did you feel like you belonged, or did you feel like an outsider at school? Were the values you learned at school similar to the ones you learned at home? Did you feel the need to "leave your culture at home" in order to be accepted at school?
5. How has your identity been influenced by your race, gender, religion, ethnic background, sexual orientation, and/or social class?
6. What about your personality makes you unique? How are you different from other members of your family?
7. What motivates you? What are your interests and hobbies? What are your goals in life? How do you want to be remembered?
8. What kinds of learning experiences are meaningful for you? What kinds are not?

Every person has a name, and also his own story about his name. My name is Yuan Cai. I don't know what you think about that, but to me it just feels upside-down because I used to be called "Cai Yuan" or "Yuan Yuan." That's why when I speak English I just tell you my name is "Yuan." "Yuan" is the end character of my name, so I feel I have told you all. You know, giving best names to children is so important in China. They look up in dictionary and search for the most beautiful sounds, perfect meanings, special and elegantly simple characters, and require the characters to have some relationships between family members. So you can imagine how hard a job it was for my parents to give me my name.

—Another perspective

Examining our own diversity entails learning about our culture. This is a bigger job for some than others. How much do you know about your ancestors? Although most of us have an immigrant past, few of us know much about it. Whereas some students are very conscious of their cultural backgrounds, others are hardly aware of it at all. Still others wrestle with the history of their culture and how it reflects on them.

Sometimes, learning about your history can be difficult. In *Tearing the Silence,* Ursula Hegi talks about "what it means to be linked to two cultures."[14] Hegi, a German-American, devotes much of her book to the personal histories of Germans who were born during or after World War II and later migrated to the United States. When they arrived, they expected to find an open and tolerant society. Instead, they encountered many who scorned and mocked them because they were assumed to be Nazis.

Many of the German-Americans interviewed by Hegi wanted to leave their past behind. As one person put it: "I have a very difficult time dealing with the Holocaust. I think there is a collective burden in our generation because it is just so tremendous, so horrible. On the other side, I must say that we have this 'Gnade der spaten

Geburt'—the grace of late birth. It's an easy way out. . . . But it came to my mind that there is a shadow of a collective guilt. At the same time, I feel it is not my personal guilt, and there's nothing I can do."[15]

Your own cultural identity may be more or less visible to you for a number of reasons. For example, some people are more apt to be reminded of their cultural background on a daily basis. Bong Hwan Kim, a Korean-American man, recalls that his first childhood memory about difference revolved around bringing lunch to school on the first day of kindergarten. His mother had made him kimpahp, rice balls rolled up in dried seaweed and wrapped in aluminum foil. All morning he remembers looking forward to having this special treat for lunch at school. As soon as the lunch bell rang, he pulled out the kimpahp from inside his desk. When he unwrapped it, his classmates "pointed and gawked, 'What is that? How could you eat that?' they shrieked." He continues, "I don't remember whether I ate my lunch or not, but I told my mother I would only bring tuna or peanut butter sand-wiches for lunch after that."[16]

Language, music, food, holidays, and customs all serve to reinforce our sense of cultural belonging. Being treated as an outsider serves as a reminder as well. Because of their background, some students continually find themselves in situa-tions in which they must decide whether to try to "fit in." Frequently, they may have to weigh the pros and cons of being "true" to their cultural roots, assimilat-ing, or some combination of the two. However, other students do not have to make these choices. Their culture is the norm at school, among friends, and at work.

There are also times when some feel their culture is slipping away. "I was so anx-ious to assimilate, to blend in, that I started to forget who I was. . . . I just felt it wasn't cool to be a poor Latina girl from Harlem. It was better to mosh than merengue and to be able to go to a country home on the weekends. I almost forgot who I was and where I came from, and it's important not to do that. Remember, you come from beautifully vibrant cultures filled with rich music and traditions. Share that. Enlighten others with your history. . . . Try new things but don't forget the old. . . . Remember who you are."[17]

In the course of becoming aware of our cultural roots, it is important to re-member that our identities are inextricably linked to the surrounding cultural land-scape. An African proverb states: "A person is a person through other people." We cannot escape the influence of culture; we are not the totally independent thinkers and learners we may think we are.

Up to this point we have focused on who we are and how we are interconnected with others. Frequently, it is difficult to make that connection for a number of rea-sons, including the following:

1. *The emphasis on individualism in U.S. society makes it difficult to see social influences.*   In most cases, people in the United States are raised to believe that they think and act on their own. Consider the sayings, "Be all that you can be," "Pull your-self up by your own boot straps," and "You are your own worst enemy." Now con-trast those with the African proverb, "It takes an entire village to raise a child." Asian cultures also tend to be more oriented toward "we" than "me." As an example,

Japanese have a saying, "the nail that stands up gets pounded down." This notion that personal goals are not as important as the goals of the group is at odds with the saying in this country that "the squeaky wheel gets the grease."

Baseball: A Cross-Cultural Perspective

Think for a moment about how we view baseball in the United States. How might people in other countries, such as Japan, view it differently? Some differences are captured in an article that appeared in *Sports Illustrated*:[18] While U.S. professional ballplayers are encouraged to do their own thing," *kojinshugi* (the Japanese term for individualism) is frowned upon in Japan. In the United States, it is commonplace for a player to hold out for more money and sell his services to the highest bidder. This is highly unacceptable in Japan because it shows that a player is more concerned about himself than about his team. In the United States, each player gets himself into shape, whereas in Japan, everyone follows the same training regimen, even the superstars.

2. *Our cultural environment is so close to us that sometimes we do not see it.* This can lead to **enculturation,** immersion in a culture to the point where that way of life appears only natural. Often, we do not even think about certain beliefs that are deeply embedded in each of us. Consequently, it is hard to step back and take a long hard look at our environment or imagine that anyone could think any other way. In *Patterns of Problem Solving,* Moshe Rubinstein provides us with insight into how people from different cultures might view the following hypothetical situation.[19] Imagine that you are in a boat on a lake, along with your mom, spouse, and child. The boat capsizes. If you could save yourself and only *one* of these three people, who would you save, and why? Most students in my classes answer child. They argue their children have their whole future ahead of them. Some students mention that their children are "part of them." Very few choose mom or spouse. Rubenstein relates how a man from an Arab culture chose "mother." Given this man's cultural background, he could not imagine choosing anyone else. His reasoning was that you can always have another child or spouse. However, you can only have one mother.

3. *Some people rarely experience* **social marginality,** *meaning exclusion that results from being seen as an "outsider."* Because of this, they have a difficult time seeing beyond their own world. However, if you are constantly being judged because of your race, class, or religion, you are apt to be more aware of its social significance. For example, consider an American history instructor who repeatedly calls on the only Mormon student in class to get "her people's" point of view. This experience may make this student feel like an outsider because she is constantly being singled out. In addition, the student may realize that other students in class are not called upon to represent their religions.

THINKING THROUGH DIVERSITY

How can learning about others help us learn more about ourselves?

Expanding Our Knowledge of Others and Their Worlds

Learning about others is instrumental in laying the foundation for diversity consciousness. Furthermore, it enables us to learn more about ourselves. Anthropologists, for example, do not just study cultures that differ from their own. They also work to understand and interpret their own culture, often using what they learn about other cultures to do so. Visiting another country, similarly, can make you more aware of your cultural biases and provide you with a basis for comparison. After your visit, you may have a whole new outlook on parts of your culture that you take for granted, such as housing, recreation, education, or friendship.

I come from Zaire and one thing that I miss here most is the friendship of my neighbors and friends. In my country, and in Africa in general, people are hospitable. Friendship is the most important thing in life. In my country, you can't perish from hunger or illness, because members of your family must assist you and help you to improve your life. It's an obligation. Even the neighbors give you their assistance. For instance, when you are sick and you can't go to a hospital because you don't have enough money or you don't have a car, the one in your neighborhood who has a car must transport you to the hospital without hesitation. He has to do it with all his heart. You can even stop a car passing your way, to get help.

In America, however, I think this is not the same. People live in mistrust of each other. You can't count on your neighbors because either they don't know you or don't want to be involved. You are condemned to live without any moral support from anyone in the neighborhood. You can be ill and can die alone in your apartment and no one is likely to notice it. Here I think friendship takes place only when there is an interest. Last week I finished my milk and went to ask a neighbor for a half cup of milk. She gave it to me, but a few days later, she asked for some sugar from me and gave it back to me in the evening. I was very surprised because this is not done among neighbors.

Maybe I am wrong in my opinion, but the facts show that friendships in America are very different from friendships in my country.

—Another perspective

Malcolm X, in his autobiography, talks about his visit to Saudi Arabia as well as a number of countries in Africa as being one of the turning points in his life.[20] His experiences in that part of the world gave him an entirely different view of race relations in the United States. Moving to another country can provide students with new insight into their ethnic background. A college student from Colombia talks about her interaction with other Latin Americans in the United States. "I have met a lot of Latin Americans. Although we have the same cultural background, we are different. We have different accents in our language and use different words to mean the same things. I have learned about exotic foods from other Latin American countries that I have never seen before. It's incredible that I have learned about Latin American culture in a non-Latin American country. When you are in a foreign country, you have the opportunity to recognize your own roots because you see things from a different point of view."

Differences

Typically, students learn about cultural differences by sampling and studying a few noteworthy events and people. A good example of this is the "group of the month" approach adopted by many schools. With this approach, students are exposed to various elements of African-American culture during Black History Month. Similarly, there are months reserved for women, Latinos, Native Americans, people with disabilities, and other groups.

This kind of approach may be attractive because it is simple and easy to implement. Unfortunately, it promotes a superficial and distorted view of differences. The historical experiences of African-Americans or women, for example, cannot be separated and studied in any kind of meaningful way in a single month. At best, this approach gives us a "taste" of a few noteworthy people or events. At worst, it excludes some students who wonder why their groups are never a "group of the month." Such an approach can also lead to even more stereotypical assumptions.

Although sampling different ways of life may have some value, it is not without dangers. After riding in a wheelchair for 15 minutes or attending a one-hour lecture on disability awareness, some people may begin to feel that they now know what it is like to have a disability. They may generalize what they learn or experience to all people with disabilities. In addition, they may forget the lesson learned shortly thereafter, unless it is reaffirmed time and again.

What then is the best way to learn about differences? A number of specific strategies will be discussed later in the chapter. It is impossible to know every aspect of every culture. However, we need to approach cultural differences with a number of things in mind:

1. *Do not simply sample differences from a distance.*   This promotes an "us" versus "them" attitude. Awareness and understanding changes as we get closer to people and engage differences. In the mid-1970s, I remember a student in one of my classes correcting me on something I had said about Black Muslims. The student, Lola X, was a Black Muslim. She then invited me and my wife to her local temple. We accepted. When we arrived, we were frisked for our own safety. At that time there were concerns about the threat of violence. We were then taken into the temple. My wife was seated with the women on one side and I took my seat with the men. We discovered that we were the only two Whites in a congregation of more than 300 people of color. The sermon was powerful and positive. Everybody, it seemed, tried to make us feel welcome. After the service, a number of people came up to us, introduced themselves, and invited us back. As I look back at that experience, I realize how being there helped me learn and appreciate Lola and her religion. Based on what I had read and heard, I fully expected to be surrounded by people who were angry and hateful toward Whites. What I saw and felt were strong, loving people who went out of their way to make my wife and me feel at home.

2. *Seek to understand how the histories, perspectives, and contributions of different cultures are interconnected.* In 1927, the American historian Carter Woodson made this point with regard to "Negro history." Woodson argued that the focus should be on the Negro *in* history rather than on Negro history.[21]

3. *Try to decrease the social distance between you and those about whom you know little if anything.* **Social distance** is a concept that was coined by a scientist named Emory Bogardus.[22] It refers to the degree to which we are willing to interact and develop relationships with certain racial and ethnic groups. Bogardus created a scale to measure whether we would accept certain people as neighbors, classmates, coworkers, or even spouses. He found that we tend to separate ourselves from others who we think are not like us. This is particularly true of our inner social circles. Take a look at your close friends. How closely do they resemble the racial, ethnic, and social class mix of the students in your school? Would you be comfortable bringing someone of a different religion or sexual orientation home for a few days to spend some time with your family? Our tendency to gravitate toward people who are like us promotes cultural encapsulation, a concept discussed earlier in this chapter.

THINKING THROUGH DIVERSITY

In your life, what groups or cultures are most socially distant?

4. *Focus on ordinary people and occurrences.* Learning about a few remarkable people and events from another culture is not sufficient. Often, stories like these tell us very little about a culture. You can learn a lot more from people who do not make the headlines or the history books, such as a friend, a fellow student, or the employee who works in the cafeteria. Think about the "perspectives" that appear throughout this book. What have you learned from them?

Similarities

Arthur Ashe, in his autobiography *Days of Grace,* writes, "I see nothing inconsistent between being proud of oneself and one's ancestors and, at the same time, seeing oneself as first and foremost a member of the commonwealth of humanity, the commonwealth of all races and creeds. My potential is more than can be expressed within the bounds of my race or ethnic identity. . . . If I had one last wish, I would ask that all Americans could see themselves that way, past the barbed-wire fence of race and color. We are the weaker for these divisions and the stronger when we can transcend them."[23]

THINKING THROUGH DIVERSITY

Describe a specific life experience that made it possible for you to see yourself as a member of the "commonwealth of humanity."

Too often, we preoccupy ourselves so much with individual and cultural differences that we ignore our similarities. Some similarities are harder to see because they lie beneath the surface. In a poem entitled "Underneath We're All the Same," a student addresses the fact that we all share certain feelings.

> *He prayed—it wasn't my religion.*
> *He ate—it wasn't what I ate.*
> *He spoke—it wasn't my language.*
> *He dressed—it wasn't what I wore.*
> *He took my hand—it wasn't the color of mine.*
> *But when he laughed—it was how I laughed,*
> *and when he cried—it was how I cried.*
>
> —Amy Maddox, as quoted in *Teaching Tolerance* Magazine[24]

Picture yourself in one of your classes. With whom do you have the most in common? Perhaps it is someone who looks like you or shares your cultural background. It might be the Hispanic student who sits next to you: Even though your race is different, you both grew up in a middle-class, urban neighborhood and are very close to your families. Then again, it might be the white woman who sits in front of you. Unlike you, she is married and has five children. Yet she is the one person in class who shares your passion for computers. Both of you hope to find jobs as computer programmers. Our differences often hide our similarities. Until we really get to know a person, we often fail to realize just how much we share in common.

As students encountering each other for the first time, we tend to notice differences. During the course of a semester, similarities among races, cultures, and other groups can become more apparent. The following comments were written by students who were part of a semester-long study group on racial and ethnic diversity.

> *I look at things differently because with me being a single parent, I do struggle and I realize that it's not just a "black thing." Everybody struggles.*
>
> ⌘
>
> *I learned that Whites hurt just like I do, they cry just like I do. I never knew that some Whites have the same fears about race that I have.*
>
> ⌘
>
> *I remember the day we listed the qualities that make us who we are. I realize most of us are alike in a lot of ways, and different in fewer ways. It was very reassuring to see other students agree with me on the same qualities.*
>
> —Other perspectives

Stepping Outside of Ourselves

We understand others or at least try to understand others by stepping outside of ourselves; that is, we try to put ourselves in their shoes, so to speak. In effect, we "simulate" how we would feel, what we would perceive, and how we would respond in a given situation. In *Surviving in Two Worlds,* Terry Tafoya describes this ability as being "able to borrow other people's eyes, to see to learn, and learn to see." For many Native-American people, Tafoya says, "there's the idea of understanding life as a crystal. A crystal of quartz has different facets. Every time you turn it you discover a new facet."[25]

The ability to "put ourselves in somebody else's moccasins" increases our awareness, understanding, and diversity skills—our diversity consciousness. By stepping outside of ourselves and our culture, we can gain a deeper appreciation of other people's experiences. As a result, our ability to think flexibly and to communicate effectively improve.

Stepping outside of ourselves is important for other reasons as well. It increases our awareness of our own frame of reference and how this shapes what we see. By adopting another perspective, we become more aware of our own. We also begin to realize that our perspective is just one of many.

THINKING THROUGH DIVERSITY

Imagine that you are being forced to change your sex (select male/female) or your race/ethnicity (select a "new" racial/ethnic group) or your sexual orientation (select homosexual/heterosexual). Which would you change, and why?

Only Skin Deep

Joshua Solomon, a white student at the University of Maryland, remembers the day he read the book *Black Like Me* by John Howard Griffin.[26] He spent the entire day reading it and thinking about little else. Back in 1959, Griffin, a journalist, took a drug to change his skin from white to brown. He then traveled throughout the South and recorded his experiences. (A white woman by the name of Grace Halsell did something similar in the 1970s. Over the course of three years, she wrote three books about life as a Hispanic, Native American, and African-American woman.)

Solomon decided that he too would change the color of his skin and venture into the South. He did some research and talked to a physician at Yale University. He found the drug that Griffin had taken. Once he started taking it daily and spending time at a tanning salon, the effects became very noticeable.

Solomon decided to visit Atlanta, Georgia first. Almost immediately, he found himself trying to be polite when people stared at him or looked away. Even though he had never had any difficulty making friends, this was no longer true. People acted differently toward him. A hostess at a half-filled restaurant made it clear to him that there would be a long wait. A police officer stopped him and gave him a warning even though he had done nothing wrong. And a lady who sat next to him while he was eating warned him not to venture into an all-white area north of Atlanta. She made it clear that "you people" ruin white neighborhoods.

Solomon cut short his experiment after a couple of days because he had grown increasingly angry and depressed. He had always thought that many black people use racism as a crutch or an excuse. Because of this experience, he developed new insight into how pervasive and debilitating racism can be.

For some, learning to step outside of your own world can be a matter of survival. W. E. B. Dubois addresses this issue in his book *The Souls of Black Folk.*[27] According to Dubois, **double consciousness** refers to a person's awareness of his or her own perspective and the perspective of others. It is like looking at the same thing in different ways. Double consciousness makes it possible to shift your perspective back and forth continuously.

Why is shifting one's perspective so important? Imagine driving through the Deep South years ago. For many, driving through Mississippi or Texas on a long trip was like driving anywhere else. They drove as far as they wanted and then stopped for gas, food, or rest. They stopped when it was convenient. Others may recall their trips through this part of the country differently. They had to be constantly aware of where they were at all times. Some remember filling their car with gas and then driving for miles without stopping for gas, food, or lodging. Given the racial climate in the area, they may have even feared for their lives. They found themselves in two worlds divided by race. As they drove, they had to understand the perspective of people who lived in the surrounding areas. If they did not, their safety might be at risk.

Perspective shifting, when done repeatedly, allows us to develop greater awareness and then retain and refine it over time. In some situations, switching positions and roles with another person may seem virtually impossible, such as when a person's behaviors or belief systems seem repulsive or incomprehensible. If this is the case, we may develop the understanding that we do not understand. In the process of trying to understand, however, we may unknowingly begin to loosen up our mindset and emotions.

Gauging the Level of the Playing Field

For some of us, college is the first time we really wrestle with inequality. This is particularly true of students who have lived around people of similar means all of their life. George Pillsbury, heir to the Pillsbury Flour Company family fortune, recalls that he never saw people living in poverty during his youth. He grew up on a private estate, attended an elite boarding school, and spent his leisure time at a country club. When he started attending classes at Yale University in New Haven, Connecticut, he was exposed to a radically different social world. "It was the first time I'd ever lived in the city—a real city with housing projects with poor people. I began to see poverty where I never had before. . . . I saw the inequities and felt them personally for the first time. I felt a lot of guilt at first, but then it became an emotional and intellectual process toward dedicating myself to positive social change."[28] As Pillsbury discovered, learning about diversity means coming to grips with social inequality.

THINKING THROUGH DIVERSITY

Are you *solely* responsible for opening and closing the doors of opportunity in your life?

Social inequality refers to the unequal distribution of resources, such as wealth, power, and prestige. In *Where Do We Go From Here,* Martin Luther King addresses the fact that people have different amounts of power.[29] He says, "There is nothing essentially wrong with power. The problem is America's power is unequally distributed."

As a result of social inequality, we belong to different social classes. A **social class** is a category of people who share similar amounts of wealth, power, and prestige. As mentioned earlier, social class is one dimension of diversity. Social class in the United States is not simply a matter of economics. Education, lifestyle, interests, and values relate to one's class position as well.

Diversity and social inequality are closely related. A sense of worth is often attached to differences. For example, in the United States we attach a lot of significance to age. We distinguish between old and young people, and unlike many other countries, we value youth. Billions of dollars are spent each year by people trying to avoid being perceived as old. A relationship exists between social inequality and people's perceptions and behaviors. One example of social inequality is **ageism**, an ideology that asserts superiority on the basis of age. In the United States, ageism may be used to rationalize economic, political, and social discrimination against older people. Other examples of social inequality revolve around other dimensions of diversity, including gender, race, ethnicity, class, religion, and sexual orientation. In each case of social inequality, we categorize certain people as different and treat them unequally.

Gauging the level of the playing field is difficult. Living in this society constantly exposes us to advantages and disadvantages tied to social inequality. However, in our own lives, we somehow fail to see many of our *advantages*. Think back to the example of George Pillsbury. He was surrounded by economic advantages throughout his childhood, yet he was not really aware of them because of his social isolation.

Why do we remain oblivious to many of our advantages or privileges? Why are we more aware of our disadvantages than our privileges? Why do we assume that we deserve these privileges and that others do not? **Unearned privileges** are those benefits in life that we have through no effort of our own. Perhaps we were born into a wealthy family or maybe we have certain benefits in school because of our religious background, gender, or race.

Unlike my wife, I was challenged by my teachers to pursue science or math as a possible career. I did not think twice about this unearned advantage until my wife shared with me that she was always led to believe that math was for males: As a result, she opted not to pursue her interest in math even though she exhibited a tremendous amount of potential in this field. After graduating from college and teaching music for a number of years, she went back to school to pursue her lifelong dream of being a mathematician. She is now teaching this subject to high school students.

Privileges are invisible for a number of reasons. When we have something, we tend to take it for granted. For example, we might not truly appreciate freedom until we lose it. Those with privileges naturally want to hold on to them as long as possible. One way of preserving privileges is to discount or ignore them. The education we receive in schools typically focuses on how certain groups are disadvantaged, not advantaged. Discussing individual privileges is seen as too personal and threatening. We also live in a society that values individual achievement, competition, and equality. Because of this, we do not like to acknowledge our privileges, especially those that we do not earn. If we are privileged in some way, we assume that we deserve it. If others are not, we assume that they are not as good or worthy or qualified.

Thinking through privileges and disadvantages requires more than just learning about these things in an abstract way. Rather, we need to recognize them in our own life and in the lives of others. In each of our lives, we have an assortment of privileges as well as disadvantages. The power, number, and consequences of these privileges or disadvantages vary from person to person. Ask yourself: How are you privileged? What privileges do you enjoy? Did you earn them? Writing them down might help you bring them into sharper focus. One of the exercises at the end of this chapter will ask you to do this.

In *White Privilege and Male Privilege,* Peggy McIntosh talks about some of the privileges of being White. She examines an "invisible, weightless knapsack of special provisions, assurances, tools, maps, guides. . . ." McIntosh cites some of the privileges operating in her own life, such as "I am never asked to speak for all the people of my racial group." Another one of the 47 unearned privileges mentioned by McIntosh is: "I can be pretty sure that if I ask to talk to 'the person in charge,' I will be facing a person of my race." In addition, she states, "I can easily buy posters, post-cards, picture books, greeting cards, dolls, toys, and children's magazines featuring people of my race."[30]

Perhaps another privilege of being White is thinking of oneself as an individual devoid of race. Ruth Frankenberg, in her book *White Women, Race Matters: The Social Construction of Whiteness,* writes about one of the white women she interviewed. "Beth was much more sharply aware of racial *oppression* shaping Black experience than of race *privilege* shaping her own life. Thus, Beth could be alert to the realities of economic discrimination against Black communities while still conceptualizing her own life as racially neutral. . . ."[31]

In interviews with white subjects, Joe Feagin and Hernan Vera asked, "What does it mean to be White?" They found that the most common answer was, "I never thought of it."[32] When a white person in our society does something, such as commit a crime or star in a movie, it is individualized and his or her own race is not likely to be seen as relevant. But when a person of color does the same thing, it is more likely to be racialized, meaning that race is seen as relevant.

There is considerable disagreement when we attempt to explain why everybody in the United States does not have an equal "piece of the pie." Recent polls show that the vast majority of white Americans believe racial and ethnic inequality is a thing of the past. When inequality is acknowledged, Whites tend to view it as a personal problem. People of color are more apt to see inequality as a problem that is rooted in society and is still very much with us.

Evidence of the perceptual gap between races is found in data from the most widely used academic survey of public opinion—the University of Chicago's National Opinion Research Center's General Social Survey (NORC-GSS). NORC-GSS data (see Table 4.1) reveals that a majority of Whites (52 percent) see lack of individual motivation rather than past discrimination as the "main" cause of the lower status of Blacks, whereas 64 percent of Blacks see past discrimination as the main cause. Another significant gap is found in the responses of Blacks and Whites to the statement, "If the Irish, Jews, and other groups overcame prejudice and worked their way up, so should Blacks." Seventy-seven percent of Whites agreed with this statement compared to 54 percent of Blacks.[33] In spite of the interracial differences, it is important to note significant disagreement *amongst* Whites and *amongst* Blacks regarding what they see as the main causes of black inequality.

TABLE 4.1   Racial Differences on "Main" Causes of Black Inequality

	Blacks	Whites	Gap	Gulf
Past discrimination	64%	35%		29%
Lack of individual motivation	41	52	11	
Lack of chance for education	54	45	9	
Blacks should overcome prejudice; work their way up like Irish, Jews, etc.	54	77		23
Conditions of Blacks improved in recent years	36	65		29

Source: General Social Survey, 1996.

People who do not encounter discrimination on a daily basis are more apt to see it as an aberration; it happens but it is rare and relatively inconsequential. In an ABC news segment entitled "True Colors," the everyday activities of a white and a black male were videotaped for two and one-half weeks in a large metropolitan area in the Midwest. Both of these men were "testers," meaning that they were trained in presenting themselves in exactly the same way. One white student's reaction to the video is found in the following perspective:

When it comes to discrimination, I don't think I am as naive as some of my friends. I realize that it still exists in America. Before seeing this video, I assumed that maybe the cameras would catch a few things, like a salesman tailing the black man in a store, or perhaps a few not giving the black man the same friendly service. I was amazed when I saw not one but two car salesmen charging the black man a higher price than the white man for the exact same car. I saw a landlord giving the white man the keys and a welcomed tour of an apartment. The same landlord, however, told the black man this apartment was not available: a blatant lie. When the reporters entered the landlord's office with both the black and white man, they showed the landlord footage of the tape and asked him for an explanation. Although he had obviously just discriminated against the black man, he got upset and replied, "I am not a racist, I got Mexicans, and 'Jewies,' I got 'em all here." Not only was this man extremely racist when telling the black man that there was no apartment available, but he didn't even realize it. It seems to me that some people think that as long as you are not calling Blacks by derogatory names or telling them to their face they cannot do something because they are Black, that they are not discriminating.

—Another perspective

The use of testers as shown in "True Colors" has yielded similar results in many other cities and suburbs throughout the United States. If you were constantly subjected to the kind of treatment that was documented in this video, what would be its cumulative effect on you? What would be the psychological *and* economic implications?

In gauging the level of the playing field, it is important to ask yourself the following questions:

1. *Are you blaming the individual or society?*   When we blame individuals, we find fault with their characters, work ethics, attitudes, or some other individual difference. We assume that individuals are holding themselves back. Blaming society changes the focus from problem people to people with problems. These problems or barriers, which are found in the larger society, act as obstacles or detours. Social barriers might take the form of racism (a concept discussed earlier), sexism, and classism. **Sexism** refers to the thinking that one sex is superior to another and that unequal treatment is therefore justifiable. **Classism** can be defined in the same way, with the focus on social class. Both the individual and societal points of view are shortsighted and incomplete. One assumes total control over one's fate, the other assumes almost a total lack of control. The individual and society are both important and interconnected. Individuals do have the freedom to choose. People are not at the mercy of their environment. However, inequality does exist. We do not live in a **meritocracy,** a system in which people get ahead *solely* on the basis of merit. Factors that have nothing to do with ability can affect your move up the economic ladder, regardless of your motivation. These factors include who you know, your looks, and other people's preconceived notions about you.

2. *Are you assuming that if one person can succeed, anybody can?*   How do you feel when people in the public eye are held up as evidence that anyone can make it to the top? What about when someone compares your school grades with someone else in your family or with a close friend? We are all different and unique, with our own strengths and limitations. A goal that is realistic or obtainable for one person may be out of someone else's reach or vision. Holding up one person as an example that anything is possible is an example of tunnel vision. People, for example, may point to a female CEO or Supreme Court Justice and cite her success as proof of equal opportunity for men and women. We cannot assume that what happens to one person necessarily applies to the entire group. If we focus exclusively on the one or two who "make it big," we may ignore the vast majority who do not. Circumstances vary from person to person and from one field of employment to another. To draw meaningful conclusions, we need considerably more data about the experiences of men and women in general. Moreover, we cannot gather and analyze evidence haphazardly.

3. *Do you see power and privilege as an all-or-nothing proposition?*   Part of the problem with the terms *minority* and *majority* is that they create the impression that we are one or the other. When discussing social inequality, majority and minority refer to power, not numbers. **Majority** refers to the group with power and privilege. **Minority** is the group at a disadvantage in terms of power and privilege. In reality, the division between the more and less powerful is not that easy to see. As an example, a student's majority statuses might include being White, male, and upper class. This same student's minority statuses might be that he is gay and has a disability. Depending on the situation, people may consider him a majority- or a minority-group member. It is a mistake to ignore our multiple statuses and their impact on us.

4. *Do you immerse yourself in your own victimization to the point that you cannot see or comprehend the victimization of others?* Perceiving ourselves as victims may not only distort our sense of personal responsibility for our actions, but it may also restrict our vision of the role inequality plays in the lives of others. By way of illustration, we may overstate the presence of social barriers for ourselves and underestimate or completely deny their existence for others. We may feel like victims because of our minority and/or majority statuses.

Well-known columnist Leonard Pitts discusses the dangers of blaming one's victimization on the white man. He writes, "Everybody should have a white man. Because when you have a white man, nothing is ever your fault. You're never required to account for your own failings or take the reins of your own destiny. The boss says, 'Why haven't you finished those reports, Bob?' and you say, 'Because of the white man, sir.'" Pitts adds that while it is naïve to think that racism no longer exists, we are obligated to "live without excuses" in the face of that reality.[34]

We *can* empower ourselves. Learning from our own experiences and observing how others have resisted victimization can help us think through social inequality. Experiencing what it is like to be a victim may sensitize us to the subtle and not so subtle ways in which our actions victimize others.

Checking Up on Ourselves

Many of us shy away from self-examination. We would rather focus on other people and their shortcomings. In a way, it is much more difficult to confront our own prejudices, stereotypes, and ethnocentrism because it requires us to closely examine our assumptions. These assumptions can be difficult for us to see. They are often so embedded in us that we take them for granted.

A good example is the belief that "women, by nature, make better nurses than men." For some of us, this is an absolute truth. The media, school, and family cultivate and reinforce this assumption. It is difficult to step-back and look at this commonplace assumption in an uncommon way. What are the sources of this assumption? Are these sources reliable? Historically, why did the nursing profession become predominantly female? How does this assumption affect our thinking and behavior toward male and female nurses? Wrestling with questions such as these is difficult. It also requires **critical thinking,** the ability to freely question and evaluate ideas and information.

Critical thinking is a diversity skill that enables us to recognize our biases and those of others. It can help us understand that our point of view is one of many. Critical thinking can also reveal gaps or inconsistencies in our assumptions. Research has shown that one key factor in reducing bias is the ability to think critically. In general, students who question what they hear from others and think things through show less prejudice than those who simply accept things at face value.

Checking up on ourselves requires constant questioning, reevaluation, and self-reflection. Questions, such as those that follow, provide us with valuable insight into our thinking and behavior throughout the day.

1. *Are you more comfortable around certain types of people?* Why? For example, are you uncomfortable doing business with men who come across as aggressive? If so, are you equally uncomfortable around white and black men who act this way? What does this teach you about with whom you are comfortable and with whom you are not? James Box, a paraplegic and founder of a high-tech wheelchair company, suggests that we need to confront our discomfort and wrestle with it. If something "turns us off" or repulses us, we need to examine it for a while and ask questions of others and ourselves until we can figure out why we are uncomfortable.

2. *Do you make snap judgments about people?* When you are walking through a shopping mall, for example, what assumptions do you make based on clothing, hairstyle, and physical features?

3. *Who do you tend to include in your social circle?* Who do you tend to leave out? How might you expand and diversify your social circle?

4. *When you communicate, what messages are you sending?* What about your body language? Do you simply assume that people interpret your communication as you intend? If not, how do you check for possible misunderstandings?

5. *Is your behavior consistent with your thinking?* In *To Be Equal,* Whitney Young addresses the need to do more than use language that is inoffensive. A change of vocabulary, according to Young, is something quite different from changes in behaviors and attitudes.[35]

Self-examination is ongoing. Since our environment is constantly changing, our awareness and understanding needs constantly to keep pace. We need to grow and adapt as our world and life experiences expand. Checking up on ourselves gives us direction. Companies, for example, regularly conduct assessments before they draw up a plan of action. Since individual workers need to do the same thing, Northwestern University asks its first-year MBA students to keep a Feeling Journal. The aim of the journal is to help students become more aware of their feelings and the role they play in their work. Before we are able to improve and develop skills such as teamwork, leadership, and communication, it is necessary to think through where we are and in what direction we are going. This takes time, commitment, patience, and awareness of self.

Following Through

Diversity consciousness does not refer simply to our awareness of ourselves and others. It extends to how we behave and interact with others. In order to apply our knowledge and awareness to real-life situations, we need to practice, practice, and practice. We learn by doing. For example, hearing lectures about computers or reading textbooks is not sufficient to develop your computer skills. Think how much more you learn by sitting down at a computer and actually using it time and time again.

We can only develop and refine diversity skills through constant use and self-evaluation. For instance, many of us regard listening as passive. However, we can improve our listening skills through **active listening,** taking a more active role in hearing and digesting what is being said as well as encouraging the speaker. Specific techniques for developing this skill are found in Chapter 5.

A Personal Pledge to Listen

Brett Banfe, a student at William Patterson University in Wayne, New Jersey, learned to develop his listening skills by making a personal pledge to keep silent for an entire year. During his freshman year, he carried a text pager to class to type notes and used e-mail to keep in touch with family and friends. Banfe says this year-long experience taught him more about communication and interaction than the first 18 years of his life.

Mainly, he grew acutely aware of how little time and effort we invest in listening. "Listening is the most important social interaction we as humans can make to improve human relations, yet we spend the least amount of time on it because it is outward, not inward. We spend our time on appearance, on hairstyle. . . when in my opinion, listening is far more important than all of these, yet it hardly even seems like an interaction."[36]

It is very important for me to maintain control of my wandering mind. I try to avoid all of the listening traps, such as dwelling on one thought while the person continues speaking or thinking about tomorrow's list of errands. I focus on the one thing the speaker says that enlightens me for the moment. Also, I always carry a note pad and pen so that I will not cause my own frustration by forgetting my own opinion about whatever is being shared. Often, everyone is so intent on being able to speak that no one actually listens for content, but for cues that the end of the last sentence is about to arrive. A lot is missed in that kind of environment.

—Another perspective

Practicing a diversity skill is not a feel good activity. There is an element of risk taking. Try not to get too down on yourself or allow others to frustrate you. As time goes by, you will realize that it is worth the struggle.

STRATEGIES FOR DEVELOPING DIVERSITY CONSCIOUSNESS

Developing diversity consciousness is an uneven process, meaning that it is very unpredictable and sporadic. There is no magical moment when you develop diversity consciousness and say to yourself; "Ah ha, I got it." You may find the more you learn about diversity, the less knowledgeable you feel. As you grow, you may go from feeling, "I'm not prejudiced" to "maybe I am" to "I am prejudiced."

In the process of developing our diversity consciousness, we change the way we feel, think, and act. Sometimes, changing the way we feel is the most difficult because it is so deep-rooted and holistic. Moving from fixed to flexible thinking requires us to suspend judgment and question received knowledge. Finally, the process is incomplete unless we show the openness, humility, and willingness that is necessary to modify our behavior.

Ultimately, each of us must take responsibility for our development in this area. The following eight strategies, which revolve around education, self-examination, and networking, can help you move toward that goal.

1. *Take an active role in educating yourself.* Developing diverse relationships results in incidental learning, meaning that we often unknowingly learn much more about others and ourselves by widening our circle of friends, coworkers, and acquaintances. Reading helps us expand our knowledge too.

Articles, novels, and personal narratives can provide us with realistic and dramatic portrayals of diversity. This is especially true of first-person accounts. These accounts or stories tend to be much more real, intimate, and varied. They remind us that Americans represent many cultures and come from many countries. When we read about history, different accounts emerge. To illustrate, the westward expansion by early European settlers is a different story when told by Native Americans. For them, the expansion meant encroachment, death, and disease. A number of first-person accounts are included in the Bibliography and Suggested Readings at the end of the book.

2. *Put yourself in a learning mode in any multicultural setting.* Try to suspend judgment and adopt a childlike kind of inquisitiveness when trying to make sense out of a situation. One of my students compared this to starting over or "wiping the slate clean." She went on to say that her English instructor told her on the first day of class to forget everything that she had learned about English. The instructor was pushing her to relearn the subject matter and undo her bad habits. In a similar vein, each of us has to shed what we know in certain situations. Only then can we look at people and lifestyles as if we were encountering them for the first time.

3. *Remember that your own life experiences are one of many important sources of knowledge.* This applies to everyone. In the book *Women's Ways of Knowing,* women who live ordinary lives are interviewed about how they perceive themselves and the world around them.[37] Many of these women had little respect for their own minds, ideas, and experiences. At work, school, and home, they relied on others to feed them information and felt voiceless much of the time. Despite their own feelings of inadequacy, the interviews revealed that these women were extremely knowledgeable as well as talented.

4. *Move beyond your personal comfort zone.* Sometimes, learning can be difficult and uncomfortable. However, this is a necessary part of opening up intellectually and emotionally. The company, Hoechst Celanese, requires its top executives to join two organizations in which they are an "outsider," so to speak. The rationale for this policy was summarized by the CEO: "The only way to break out of comfort zones is to be exposed to other people. When we are, it becomes clear that all people are similar."[38]

5. *Be modest.* A few years ago, Bill Cosby told a graduating class at George Washington University: "Don't ever think you know more than the person mopping a floor." Everybody has something of value to share. Be aware that no matter how much you know or have seen, you can still learn from anyone. This perspective will make you more open to differences and more willing to learn from those around you.

6. *Don't be too hard on yourself if misunderstandings arise.* No matter how hard we try, there will be situations in which we show our lack of knowledge of other cultures. We may do this without even knowing it. The important thing is to acknowledge our mistakes and learn from them.

7. *Realize that you are not alone.* There are other people out there who care about you and will support you as you grow, learn, and wrestle with diversity issues. Surround yourself with these kinds of people.

THINKING THROUGH DIVERSITY

Do you think you can honor and respect diversity without working on understanding it?

8. *Never stop learning.* Opportunities to learn and grow can arise at any moment. Learning can be triggered by any number of experiences, such as overhearing an insensitive comment, attending a workshop on diversity, or doing something that might seem totally unrelated to diversity. People learn, unlearn, and relearn in a myriad of ways. In the next section we describe a wide range of learning opportunities.

Diversity Education—A Range of Opportunities

Diversity education is one of the primary ways of increasing diversity consciousness (see Fig. 4.2). We are surrounded by opportunities to learn more about diversity. Whether we avail ourselves of these opportunities to develop our diversity consciousness, and whether we allow ourselves to be transformed, is up to us. For example, a wide range of diversity education programs and courses are available on most college campuses. If these opportunities are not available, you might suggest them to your instructor or someone in charge of student programming.

Vacationers, Prisoners, and Explorers

Lin Dawson, a former professional football player for the New England Patriots, is part of a three-member diversity awareness team that works on behalf of Northeastern University's Center for the Study of Sport. In his work with professional and college sports teams, Dawson knows that members of his audience fall into three categories: *vacationers*—those who are apathetic and attend because they have to, *prisoners*—those who are forced to attend and want nothing to do with training, and *explorers*—those who are open-minded and feel there is something to be gained.[39]

Individuals, groups, and entire communities can initiate and participate in diversity education. Seven possible activities follow:

1. *Computer technology.* New uses of technology, such as the Internet/World Wide Web (WWW), distance learning, and teleconferences, make it possible to cross cultural boundaries very easily and quickly. The WWW provides a window to the

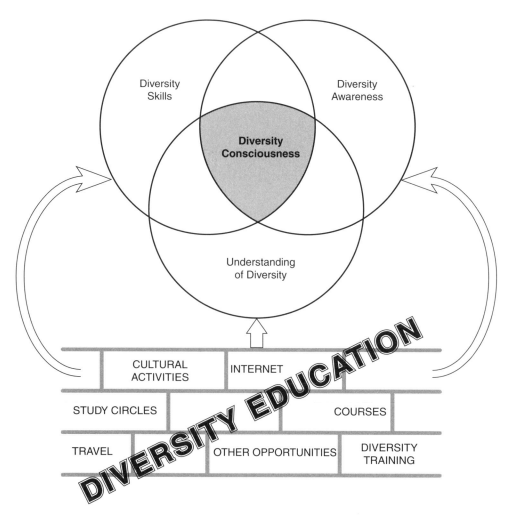

FIGURE 4.2 Diversity education, in its many forms, is the foundation upon which we develop our diversity consciousness.

world. Using listservs, newsgroups, chatrooms, e-mail, and links to a variety of resources and information, we are able to dramatically increase the cultural, geographical, religious, and political diversity we encounter daily. Still, a lack of computer access in many parts of the world—especially low-income countries in much of Africa and Asia—continues to limit the inclusiveness of this global network. Diversity Links, a section found toward the end of this book, provides a list of some excellent Web sites on diversity.

2. *Courses.* More and more teachers at all levels of education are integrating diversity into the curriculum. This is true of a wide range of disciplines including lit-

FIGURE 4.3 Students visit a museum in Cairo, Egypt. The students, who are spending a semester on board a cruise ship, are enrolled in the University of Pittsburgh's "Semester at Sea" course. Each semester, more than 600 students take classes on board a cruise ship and then experience what they study by visiting countries throughout the world. *(Courtesy of the Institute for Shipboard Education, University of Pittsburgh, Pittsburgh, PA.)*

erature, art, business, math, allied health, student success, and social sciences. If diversity is not the focus of the entire course, it is likely to be discussed in one or more units of a course. Even though the content of the curriculum is important, research suggests that the nature of intergroup interaction is also critical.[40] To maximize learning, we need to feel comfortable interacting with others from diverse racial, cultural, and language backgrounds. This includes discussing controversial issues, working on group projects, or learning about differences in other ways.

3. *Travel and opportunities for study abroad.*   Students who study abroad learn the importance of a world view. This is particularly true of extensive trips abroad which provide opportunities for studying, working, and socializing (see Fig. 4.3).

4. *Racial/cultural awareness training and workshops.*   Schools, workplaces, and community groups frequently offer this type of learning opportunity. Although one two-hour workshop is not going to change your thinking and behavior dramatically, it can deepen your understanding of diversity issues and put you in touch with people who may have similar interests and concerns. In his comprehensive study of undergraduates throughout the country, Astin found that participation in workshops increases students' awareness that (1) discrimination is still a problem and (2) individuals can bring about change in society.[41]

5. *Diversity programs.*   Many programs seek to promote the respect and celebration of cultural differences. Many organizations offer these programs in connection with Black History Month, International Women's Day, AIDS Awareness Day, and other events. Lectures, dramatic presentations, art exhibits, and field trips tap a wide range of learning modalities and interests.

6. *Cultural activities in the community.*   Plays, movies, ethnic festivals, and museums are just a few of the community resources and events that provide numerous opportunities to learn about diversity. Sometimes it makes sense to do this with others so that you can share your thoughts and feelings afterward. With a minimal amount of expense or planning, a group can rent and watch videos such as *Philadelphia, Beloved, Schindler's List, The Joy Luck Club, Rain Man, Smoke Signals, Hoop Dreams,* and *A Walk in the Clouds.* This type of experience can "break the ice" and provide insight into history, culture, and different life experiences. It can also make it easier to talk about a variety of issues dealing with diversity.

> *Music and art have shown me the common ground between people and what we can do for each other.*
>
> —Another perspective

7. *Study circles/groups.*   As discussed earlier, study circles are small group discussions that focus on any number of issues, including diversity. The basic idea is that a group of perhaps 8 to 12 people commit to meeting regularly over a period of time. This type of discussion allows people to get to know each other, discover common ground, and take action. Schools, businesses, and communities throughout the country have adopted the study circle concept.

▣ A LIFELONG, CONTINUING PROCESS

> *The greater our knowledge increases, the greater our ignorance unfolds.*
>
> —John Fitzgerald Kennedy

A study by Pascarella and associates examined what factors had the greatest influence on college students' openness to diversity. What they found should not surprise us. Even though students' academic and social experiences in college made a difference, "precollege variables" had the largest effect. This points to the need to foster openness in early childhood and in the elementary and secondary grades. Children are susceptible to what Carlos Cortés calls the "societal curriculum" very early in life.[42] This curriculum, which includes all those lessons that we learn in school, the family, our places of worship, and throughout society, has a profound and lingering effect on our openness to intolerance and diversity consciousness in later years.

Imagine observing 3- and 4-year-old children at a preschool. At nap time, you notice a 3-year-old white girl resting on a cot. She says, "I can't sleep next to a nigger. Niggers are stinky." Later on, during play time, a 4-year-old tells a 3-year-old, "Get off, white girl! Only black folks on the swing, you see?" These comments, recorded by sociology professors Debra Van Ausdale and Joe R. Feagin, appear in their study entitled *The First R: How Children Learn Race and Racism.*[43] Their examination of the racial attitudes of 58 children at a racially diverse urban school is cause for concern. Notwithstanding the childrens' progressive teachers who taught from an anti-bias curriculum, many lessons about race and intolerance were learned outside of the classroom. As an example, Whites and Blacks do not occupy the same social space, nor do they share the same social status. What's more, according to the authors, this "lesson" does not go unnoticed by children. Who mops the floors at school, who bags the groceries, and who mows the lawns are important components of a societal curriculum that teaches children what the authors term the "first R"—race.

By doing nothing or very little, we leave our own and our children's diversity consciousness in someone else's hands. By constantly educating and transforming ourselves, we help to restructure the societal curriculum in a way that sheds a more positive light on diversity. To accomplish this, we need to bear in mind that diversity consciousness is not something we can develop, store, and then consult periodically. It is not something that "kicks in" at school or work. Rather, the term *consciousness* implies that these thoughts and feelings become a way of life, second nature, a permanent part of who we are. Developing this is an unending process. We need to reevaluate our knowledge of ourselves and others continuously as we gain new knowledge. As our thinking changes, so does our behavior. This kind of change requires both time and effort.

As we develop diversity consciousness, a number of positive changes will gradually occur:

- Our thinking will become less rigid and more flexible.
- Our awareness and appreciation of human differences will heighten our ability to see and value similarities.
- We will move from a perspective that centers on ourselves and our immediate environment to one that is more inclusive and global.

It should be clear from this chapter that it is extremely difficult to develop a high level of diversity consciousness. For many of us, just tolerating certain differences requires radical change. In many cases it means unlearning much that we have been taught. Diversity consciousness moves us well beyond tolerance. Rather than putting up with differences, it makes it possible for us to understand, respect, and value differences. This kind of personal transformation requires not only time but also commitment.

> *Education is all a matter of building bridges.*
>
> —Ralph Ellison

In the next two chapters we examine two diversity skills: communication (Chapter 5) and teamwork (Chapter 6). As our society becomes more diverse and the larger world becomes more interconnected, it is increasingly important for us to understand the significance of these skills and their relationship to diversity consciousness.

 ## CASE STUDIES

Case Study One

Ligua is taking a class entitled, "Cultural Diversity." It is required of all students majoring in education. The class examines issues and concepts related to diversity and education, such as cross-cultural communication, teaching tolerance, barriers to understanding, and managing diversity in the classroom. Given her life experiences as a minority, Ligua feels as if *she* could teach this course. Ligua understands its value, particularly for those students who have led very sheltered lives. For these students, according to Ligua, a semester-long course on diversity is not nearly sufficient.

Questions:

1. Do you think a course dealing with cultural diversity should be a requirement for all education majors? Why?
2. What do you think Ligua might learn from a course such as this?

Case Study Two

Mary is fascinated by different cultures. However, because of her cultural encapsulation as well as her fear of being put in an awkward situation, she has chosen to interact with people from cultural backgrounds that are similar to hers. As a social worker, she realizes that this will no longer be an option.

Questions:

1. What are three things Mary can do to develop her diversity consciousness?
2. If she chooses to remain culturally encapsulated *outside of work,* do you think this will affect her job performance? Explain.

Case Study Three

Michael, who lives in a well-to-do suburban area, sends his son Aaron to a private school. The students at Aaron's school are predominantly white. Most of them come from wealthy families. Michael struggles with this. On one hand, he wants to prepare Aaron to live in the real world, full of prejudice and poverty, a world in which race is an issue. On the other hand, he wants to protect his son from the racial intolerance that Michael feels is still rampant in our society today.

Ideally, Michael would like his son to attend a quality school in a diverse setting. However, he knows of no such school in his area. Michael worries about the consequences of Aaron's isolated existence. He wonders whether Aaron will develop stereotypical notions of inner-city Blacks. He is wary of Aaron becoming what he calls an "oreo cookie," black on the outside and white on the inside. Because of concerns such as these, Michael does what he can to expand Aaron's world. For example, a segment on the news might turn into a mini-lesson on race relations or black history. In the aftermath of the terrorist attacks on September 11, 2001, the issue of profiling became a lesson on diversity.

Michael is already starting to weigh the advantages and disadvantages of sending Aaron to a historically black college. He thinks that this kind of experience might be good for Aaron, although he is not sure.

Questions:

1. Michael expresses the concern that his son's life is culturally isolated or encapsulated. Do you agree? Why?

2. How might Aaron's education influence his diversity consciousness? Outside of school, what might Michael do to help Aaron develop diversity consciousness?

 EXERCISES

In-Class

Exercise 1: The Name Game

Directions for Instructor

Ask each student to respond to the following questions in writing:

1. Throughout our lives, each of us learns about many famous people who have shaped history. Draw on this knowledge and name three well-known people (living or dead) who are:
   a. Upper class
   b. Lower class
   c. Gay/lesbian
   d. Asian-American
   e. Native American
   f. Female
   g. Male
   h. Disabled

2. Have students pair up. Ask each pair of students to review the names each of them listed for the eight categories. Which categories of people were the easiest to name? Why? Which categories of people were the most difficult to name? Why?

3. As a class, discuss what this exercise reveals about you and your upbringing. Discuss what it reveals about your education.

Exercise 2: Family Stories

The African proverb "a person is a person through other persons" applies to each of us. In particular, it describes our relationship with family members. As we get older, we become more aware of these relationships.

Directions for Instructor

1. Ask each student to think of stories that have been passed down from generation to generation in her or his family. Students should select one story that has influenced their lives in some way, such as making them more resilient or altering how they view what is really important in life. They should try to remember as much of the story as possible.

2. Have students pair up. Each student shares his or her story. Also, the student should explain how the story affects her or him.

3. As a class, discuss the following questions: Is there anything that your stories have in common? In what ways are they different? Why do you think some family stories are forgotten and others remain with us? What have you learned from these stories?

Exercise 3: Unearned Privileges

Each of us has privileges as well as disadvantages. Many of these relate to different dimensions of diversity, such as race, ethnicity, class, gender, sexual orientation, and religion. In the case of privileges, some are earned whereas others are unearned.

Directions for Instructor

1. Ask each student to list in writing three privileges he or she has that are *earned*. Then list three that are *unearned*. Be as specific as possible. Share these with the class.
2. As a class, discuss which of our privileges—earned or unearned—are easier for us to identify. Why?

Out-of-Class

Exercise 1: Shifting Perspectives in the Classroom

You are sitting in a college classroom. It is the first day of class. Your instructor, whom you have never met, walks in, introduces himself, and hands each student a course syllabus. Prior to going over the syllabus, the instructor reviews his expectations for classroom interaction.

- Students should act as if they understand everything and never ask any questions.
- Students should never raise questions about tests or grades at any time.
- Students should not look directly at the instructor when he speaks.

Answer the following questions.

1. In general, how do you feel about these expectations? Why do you feel this way? How does your cultural background relate to your feelings?
2. Talk to other students who have attended schools outside the United States. How do they feel about the expectations outlined above? How have their educational experiences differed from yours?

Exercise 2: Cross-Cultural Interview and Analysis

Interview. Interview someone who was born and grew up in a country other than your own. This person should be a fellow student or a member of the faculty or staff. When interviewing someone, find a comfortable place to talk. Begin by getting acquainted with each other. Then focus your questions on the following topics related to the interviewee:

- Family background
- Cultural background

- Educational background
- Community in which (s)he was raised
- Leisure activities as a child
- Religious background
- Development of his/her diversity consciousness
- Other areas of interest

Analysis. Once the interview is completed, think through how you might respond to these questions. Compare your responses with those of the interviewee.

1. List some of the major differences in your backgrounds. What are some of the major similarities?
2. Create a poster that represents these differences and/or similarities. Do not use any words; rather, express yourself through images. The images may be drawn by hand or created on the computer. You may include clippings from newspapers and magazines as well as photographs.

Exercise 3: The Challenge of Diversity Consciousness

What do you think will be your most difficult challenge as you work on increasing your own diversity consciousness?

INTERNET ASSIGNMENT

1. Go to the Web site for your organization/school. Search it thoroughly for activities (courses, workshops, programs) relative to diversity. Make a list of all you are able to find.
2. Go to a Web site for another organization/school. Find one that has significantly more or fewer diversity activities. List these as well.
3. Contrast and compare the activities offered at the two organizations/schools. What possible explanations might account for the differences?

NOTES

[1] Juan L. Gonzales, Jr., *The Lives of Ethnic Americans,* 2nd ed. (Dubuque, IA: Kendall/Hunt, 1994), 98.

[2] Carol Gallagher, *Going to the Top* (New York: Viking Press, 2000).

[3] "Women, Men, and Media," in M. Junior Bridge, *Marginalizing Women* (Alexandria, VA: Unabridged Communications, 1996).

[4] National Council of La Raza, *Don't Blink: Hispanics in Television Entertainment* (Washington, DC: Center for Media and Public Affairs, 1996).

[5] Martin Gilens, "Race and Poverty in America: Public Misperceptions and the American News Media," *Public Opinion Quarterly,* 60, 1996, 515–541.

[6] Associated Press, "Number Living in Poverty Drops for 3rd Year in a Row, U.S. Says," *The Sun,* Sept. 25, 1998, 3A.

[7] Charles Gallagher, "White Reconstruction in the University," *Socialist Review,* 24, 1994, 165.

[8] Cheryl Tan, "For College Students, Degrees of Ethnicity," *The Washington Post,* Sept. 3, 1996, B1.

[9] Erin Texeira, "Young See Race Divide, But Give Reason to Hope," *The Sun,* Aug. 17, 1999, 3A.

[10] Morgan Appel, David Cartwright, Daryl Smith, and Lisa Wolf, *The Impact of Diversity on Students* (Washington, DC: Association of American Colleges and Universities, 1996), x.

[11] Roberta Hall and Bernice Sandler, *The Classroom Climate: A Chilly One for Women* (Washington, DC: Association of American Colleges, 1982), 3.

[12] Ansley A. Abraham, *Racial Issues on Campus: How Students View Them* (Atlanta, GA: Southern Regional Education Board, 1990), 2.

[13] Zora Neale Hurston, as found in Dorothy W. Riley (ed.), *My Soul Looks Back, 'Less I Forget* (New York: Harper Collins, 1993), 81.

[14] Ursula Heigi, *Tearing the Silence* (New York: Simon & Schuster, 1997).

[15] Jonathan Yardley, "Coping with History," *The Washington Post: Book World,* July 6, 1997, 3.

[16] Karen Aguilar-San Juan (ed.), *The State of Asian America* (Cambridge, MA: South End Press, 1994), 74.

[17] John Lahr, "Speaking across the Divide," *The New Yorker,* Jan. 27, 1997, 41–42.

[18] Robert Whiting, "You've Gotta Have 'Wa'," *Sports Illustrated,* September 24, 1979, 60+.

[19] Moshe Rubinstein, *Patterns of Problem Solving* (Englewood Cliffs, NJ: Prentice Hall, 1975).

[20] Malcolm X, *The Autobiography of Malcolm X* (New York: Ballantine Books, 1965).

[21] Carter Woodson, as quoted in Dorothy W. Riley, ed., *My Soul Looks Back, 'Less I Forget: A Collection of Quotations by People of Color* (New York: Harper Collins, 1995), 189.

[22] Emory Bogardus, "Measuring Social Distance," *Journal of Applied Sociology,* 9, Mar./Apr. 1925, 299–308.

[23] Arthur Ashe, *Days of Grace* (New York: Ballantine Books, 1993), 186.

[24] Amy Maddox, "Underneath We're All the Same," *Teaching Tolerance,* Spring 1995, 65.

[25] Louis Crozier-Hogle and Darryl Babe Wilson, *Surviving in Two Worlds: Contemporary Native American Voices* (Austin, TX: University of Texas Press, 1997), 139.

[26] John H. Griffin, *Black Like Me* (New York: NAL/Dutton, 1999).

[27] W. E. B. Dubois, *The Souls of Black Folk* (New York: Fawcett, 1961).

[28] George Pillsbury, as quoted in John Sedgwick, *Rich Kids* (New York: William Morrow, 1985), 120.

[29] Martin Luther King, Jr., *Where Do We Go from Here: Chaos or Community?* (Boston: Beacon Press, 1968).

[30] Peggy McIntosh, *White Privilege and Male Privilege* (Wellesley, MA: Wellesley College Center for Research on Women, 1988), 7.

[31] Ruth Frankenberg, *White Women, Race Matters: The Social Construction of Whiteness* (Minneapolis, MN: University of Minnesota Press, 1993).

[32] Joe Feagin and Hernan Vera, *White Racism* (New York: Routledge, 1995), 139.

[33] Robert Smith and Richard Seltzer, *Contemporary Controversies and the American Racial Divide* (Lanham, MD: Rowman and Littlefield, 2000), 34.

[34] Leonard Pitts, "It's Time for Men to Act Like Men," *The Sun,* July 16, 2001, 7A.

[35] Whitney Young, *To Be Equal* (New York: McGraw-Hill, 1966).

[36] Samantha Critchell, "Silent Since September and Learning a Lot," *The Washington Post,* May 15, 2001, C4.

[37] Mary Belenky, Blythe Clinchy, Nancy Goldberger, and Jill Tarule, *Women's Ways of Knowing* (New York: Basic Books, 1986).

[38] Fay Rice, "How to Make Diversity Pay," *Fortune,* Aug. 8, 1994, 82.

[39] Mark Murphy, "Rocker a 'Prisoner,' At Least When It Comes to Treatment." Online, Jan. 11, 2000. Available: http://cbs.sportsline.com/u/ce/multi/0,1329,1878900_52,00.html.

[40] Association of American Colleges and Universities, "The Educational Value of Diversity: Research from Louisville High Schools," *Diversity Digest,* Winter 2001, 10, 11.

[41] Alexander Astin, "Diversity and Multiculturalism on the Campus: How Are Students Affected?" *Change,* Mar./Apr. 1993, 47.

[42] C. E. Cortés, "The Societal Curriculum: Implications for Multiethnic Education." In J. A. Banks (ed.), *Education in the 80's: Multiethnic Education* (Washington, DC: National Education Association), 1981.

[43] Debra Van Ausdale and Joe R. Feagin, *The First R: How Children Learn Race and Racism* (Lanham MD: Rowman and Littlefield, 2001), 1.

5

Communicating in a Diverse World

Chapter Objectives

Upon completion of this chapter, you will be able to:

- Explain how communication and culture interrelate.
- Discuss the effects of electronic communication.
- Explain the relationship between diversity consciousness and communication.
- List and give examples of barriers to effective communication.
- Define and give examples of "hot buttons."
- List the ground rules for difficult dialogues.
- Describe strategies for communicating inclusively.

I think that people within my culture and from other cultures may mistake my lack of eye contact for dishonesty. I feel that staring into someone's eyes lets them see into my soul so instead I focus on something else when speaking. This way is more comfortable for me. I find that when I try to give eye contact, I often end up focusing on some other feature of the individual's face. I think that I offend many people when I don't look them eye to eye.

I usually fold my arms and I don't walk around smiling. People always comment to me "Is it that bad?" or "Smile; there is nothing to be sad about." I have been told that I look unapproachable because of my stance and facial expressions, but I think I am one of the most approachable people on the streets.

One day, a man called my house taking a survey and he started asking me questions. Before I got a chance to tell him my race, he was already writing down that I was White. I interrupted and told him that I was Black and he apologized and told me that I sound White. I was wondering what Whites sound like.

A communication style I have that other cultures may find offensive is my openness about personal feelings or experiences. I have to be careful not to overwhelm people with "too much information" about a certain subject. This tends to make many people feel uncomfortable. I have learned to think before I speak; however, it is sometimes difficult.

⌘

When I smile, there are men who think I'm "coming on to them." All I'm trying to do is be friendly.

⌘

I have felt like I have represented all Kenyans in all my classes since I'm the only one from that part of the world; standing out sometimes when I dress in African dress or when I speak. There is pin drop silence every time I begin to speak. All eyes are on me when a dub of British is detected in my accent. I wonder what goes through their minds, from my pronunciation to the spelling of certain words. After the first day of class when I introduce myself I face questions about Africa on a daily basis—questions often of places and things I don't even know.

—Other perspectives

Communication takes place whenever meaning is attached to a message. The meaning may be intended or unintended. By developing our diversity consciousness and, in particular, our communication skills, we become more aware of the messages we are sending and receiving. This empowers us and enriches our lives. However, poor communication skills can make it difficult for us to achieve our goals and can alienate, confuse, and hurt others. Communication skills are one specific form of diversity skills.

COMMUNICATION AND CULTURE

Communication and culture interrelate. Culture is reflected in the way we communicate, and the way we communicate shapes our culture. Because of our upbringing, we attach specific meanings to what people say and do. These meanings may vary within and between cultures. As our work, school, and community environments become more multicultural, it is increasingly important to become more conscious of our cultural differences as well as our similarities. This, in turn, will enable us to become more sensitive to the cultural context of one's words and more proficient in using language precisely and sensitively.

  Communication is the process by which people transfer information, ideas, attitudes, and feelings to each other. The word *communicate* comes from the Latin verb *communicare,* which means to share. When people use and share symbols with others who can understand their meanings, they are communicating. A **symbol** is any thing that represents something else. Symbols take many forms. Spoken and written words probably come to mind, but we also communicate with nonverbal symbols. Examples of nonverbal communication, or what we refer to as body language, include gestures, facial expressions, body positioning, touching, and eye movements.

People throughout the world send messages by a vast array of body language. In *Gestures: The Do's and Taboos of Body Language Around the World,* author Roger Axtell discusses **kinesics,** the study of body movements as a means of communication. He cites studies by a number of researchers, including Mario Pei and Ray Birdwhistell. Pei estimates that humans can produce approximately 700,000 physical signs. According to Birdwhistell, the face alone is capable of 250,000 expressions.[1] By studying the kinesics of different cultures, anthropologists have determined that people from different cultures may signal each other in very different ways.

Body language throughout the world is culturally specific. If a gesture is **culturally specific,** it may mean one thing to one culture but something quite different to another. When he was vice president of the United States, Richard Nixon learned this lesson the hard way. On a goodwill tour of Latin America in the 1950s, he stepped off his airplane and was met by a cheering crowd. He responded by flashing the "A-OK" sign, his thumb and forefinger forming a circle. The crowd immediately began to boo and show their disapproval. The next day, large pictures of Nixon making the gesture made the news from Mexico City to Buenos Aires. The gesture generated so much attention because in this part of the world, it means "screw you."

Communication allows us to dialogue and feel a sense of togetherness. Also, it can illustrate our differences and drive a wedge between us. This is especially true of intercultural communication. **Intercultural communication** refers to a process in which messages created in one culture must be processed and interpreted in another culture. Misunderstandings can also occur between people who may be different in other ways. Maybe they have different styles of communication. Perhaps differences in gender, age, marital status, or social class make it difficult to connect with someone.

Miscommunication often results because we attach different meanings to the same symbol. As an example, Nike marketed some of its products a few years ago by displaying their logo, the word *Air,* in stylized letters. They soon discovered that the logo resembles the Arabic word for Allah. Under threat of a worldwide boycott of its product by Muslims, Nike agreed to recall and stop selling any shoes with this logo. Muslims did not object to this logo on caps and tee shirts. However, they felt that its appearance on shoes was a sign of disrespect. By communicating a totally different message than they intended, Nike learned a costly and important lesson. According to one spokesperson for Nike: "Our company has to be more vigilant and work more with communities on issues of sensitivity."[2]

Most of us think of ourselves as literate. Because of our educational background, we can read and write. But we are literate only in a particular cultural environment. In another setting within our society or abroad, we may have no idea how to communicate ideas and feelings.

Men and Women, Divided by Language

Deborah Tannen is a professor of *linguistics,* the science of language. In her research, Tannen focuses on the different communication styles of men and women. She has written extensively on this subject. Her books, entitled *You Just Don't Understand, That's Not What I Meant,* and *Talking from 9 to 5,*[3] offer some examples of gender differences.

- Men engage in report talk, women in rapport talk. *Report talk* is a way of showing one's knowledge and skill. *Rapport talk* allows one to share with others and develop relationships.
- When making requests, women tend to be indirect. A female supervisor might ask, "Could you do this by 5 P.M.?" Something more direct and to the point is more typical of a male supervisor: "This needs to be done by 5 P.M."
- Women have a greater *information focus.* They do not hesitate to ask questions in order to understand something. Men have more of an *image focus.* Even though men may be unclear about an issue, they may forego asking questions to preserve their image or reputation.
- Women often say "I'm sorry" to express concern about something. Men, however, may interpret this to mean that women are accepting blame or responsibility. This is not at all what women have in mind.
- People tend to judge men for what they say and do, and women by how they look and dress.

Tannen makes the point that these differences do not apply to all men or women in all situations. Furthermore, she states that no one's communication style is absolute. Each person's style may change in response to social context and others' styles. By realizing that differences such as these may exist, we lessen the chances of miscommunication and conflict.

There are a lot of beautiful, favorite places in any language in which you feel yourself at home. In English, I don't have such a place yet. All phrases come out from my mouth, rough and heavy. . . the words fall with plops on the floor, like ugly frogs. And I am so waiting for the butterfly.

—Another perspective

Imagine sitting in a classroom at Gallaudet University in Washington, DC, the world's only accredited four-year liberal arts university for deaf and hard of hearing people. In *Seeing Voices: A Journey Into the World of the Deaf,* Oliver Sacks describes his first visit to Gallaudet. "I had never before seen an entire community of the deaf, nor had I quite realized (even though I knew this theoretically) that Sign might indeed be a complete language—a language equally suitable for making love or speeches, for flirtations or mathematics. I had to see philosophy and chemistry classes in Sign. . . I had to see the wonderful social scene in the student bar, with hands flying in all directions as a hundred separate conversations proceeded."[4] (See Fig. 5.1.)

FIGURE 5.1 Students at Gallaudet University communicate with each other about their weekend plans. *(Courtesy of the Office of Public Relations, Gallaudet University, Washington, DC.)*

Sign language, a visual form of communication using hand shapes and movements to talk or to express an idea, is not uniform or universal. Contrary to popular thought, deaf people all over the world cannot communicate with each other. Sign languages, which have been around since the beginning of recorded history, are as distinct and differentiated as spoken languages. Hundreds of different sign languages exist, including American, British, Mayan, French, and Chinese.

Linguistic diversity refers to the many languages spoken in the United States and throughout the world. Some people speak only one language, while others speak more than one. We refer to people who are able to speak two languages fluently as **bilingual,** and those capable of speaking more than two as **multilingual.** Language differences and the way we view these differences affect our achievement. Although proficiency in English is critically important, more and more research shows that fluency in more than one language can increase one's chances for success. Many colleges offer programs for English as a Second Language (ESL) students. These programs serve immigrants, refugees, foreign students, and other people who need to improve their English skills.

Individuals who speak a language other than English may encounter **linguicism,** a relatively new term that refers to discrimination based on language.

How do you feel when you enter a particular class for the first time and you are met by an instructor or teaching assistant who is bilingual and speaks English with an unfamiliar accent? When you are in a group with a number of ESL students, do you take the time to listen carefully and encourage full participation from everyone? Do you accept responsibility for making sure that you understand what is being communicated? When you don't understand, are you comfortable asking people to repeat themselves until you do?

Some of us are apt to view situations such as these as problems rather than challenges. Although communication with the aforementioned teacher or students might be difficult for a period of time, persistence as well as good listening skills can help a great deal. Also, consider what they have to offer. Studies show that people who speak more than one language have higher levels of *cognitive flexibility,* meaning they can adjust more easily to different situations. Someone who is bilingual or multilingual may be better able to share a variety of world perspectives.

> *Students tell me I have an accent. I usually tell them they have an accent too.*
>
> —Another perspective

ELECTRONIC COMMUNICATION

Electronic communication is the imparting or interchange of information through technology, such as phones, satellites, or the Internet. The capabilities of electronic communication are expanding rapidly. Computer technology is transforming electronic communication. College professors use the Internet and Web pages to post syllabi, class notes, related links, and other necessary information. Along with their instructors, students engage in online discussion groups. Papers are submitted and critiqued, and grades are returned online as well. In the workplace, individuals can work at home or any other location. Unlike the office setting of the past, they communicate by fax, e-mail, cell phones, PDAs, and pagers.

As more and more people throughout the world learn to use new technologies, new communication problems arise. Since Internet communication relies primarily on text, such as e-mail, chat rooms, and news groups, people cannot rely on other cues, such as tone of voice or gestures. We do not necessarily know anything about who is sending the message and his or her position, cultural background, or even the person's mood. In fact, an individual is free to create a new identity or a number of different identities. A person can negotiate a new virtual self by becoming another race, age, or profession, assuming a whole new personality, and keeping his or her personal data hidden from others. In his book, *Interaction Ritual: Essays on Face to Face Interaction,* Erving Goffman calls this **impression management**, the ways in which people attempt to control the impressions they make on others and how others see them.[5] Electronic messages may result in misunderstandings, name calling, and hard feelings if people are unfamiliar with certain rules of etiquette. For example, Internet etiquette defines communicating in all capital letters as YELLING. Some people, who like using "all caps" because they find it easier, do not realize that they may be offending others.

Uncertainties also arise because rules governing electronic communication differ depending on the organization or group. As an example, some workplaces permit personal messages while others do not. Many organizations review every message for inappropriate material.

What are the possible effects of Internet communication? The Internet offers a diversity and wealth of information as well as misinformation. Distinguishing between accurate information and hoaxes, scams, lies, and other inaccurate information is difficult. On the Internet, information travels so quickly and so much information gets produced. Anyone and any group, for example, can write a Web page and consciously or unconsciously inject their biases or points of view. In spite of the Web's capacity for spreading misinformation, it also can be used to verify information. When confronted with a "fact" that seems "too good to be true," we can use the Web to authenticate what we find, by checking sources and gathering additional sources from around the world.

Some see this form of communication as a vehicle for breaking down barriers and promoting the diffusion of language and culture in general. **Cultural diffusion** refers to the spread of objects and ideas from one culture to another. Each year, the Internet is becoming more multicultural. New software allows for instant translation of Web pages written in any foreign language. As mentioned earlier, Web developers have discovered a tremendous market for multilingual Web sites. Users click a button and see the Web site in the language of their choice.

Others view the impact differently. According to former Brown University president Vartan Gregorian, "What is being created is. . . the ability to retreat to small communities of the like-minded, where we are safe not only from unnecessary interactions with those whose ideas and attitudes are not like our own, but also from having to relate our interests and results to other communities."[6] News groups and chat rooms allow people with similar interests or agendas to gravitate to each other. This can have positive or negative consequences. As an example, the Net can bring together people who are looking for support and current information about a particular disease or disability. It can also serve as a safe haven for hate groups. Therefore, electronic communication is a tool we can use to access other perspectives and worlds or isolate ourselves even further.

E-Mail Privacy?

Many employees converse casually by e-mail each day. In many instances, they mistakenly assume that their messages are private. Consequently they often say things they would not communicate in writing or discuss in public. This includes racist, sexist, and other derogatory messages. Many companies routinely save all e-mail messages. These saved messages are now being used to provide evidence in lawsuits.

Experts say that e-mail is a matter of official record. It is no different than a memo written on company letterhead. Consequently, jokes or other offensive messages circulated through a company's e-mail system may constitute evidence of discrimination.

Energy giant Chevron paid a $2.2 million settlement to employees who sued, claiming that sexually harassing e-mails created a hostile work environment. A Washington, DC, police investigation turned up hundreds of vulgar, racist, and homophobic e-mail messages written by officers. Officers' remarks were cross-referenced with civilian complaints to determine whether any of the messages indicated illegal actions. Increasingly, organizations are responding to inappropriate e-mail by creating policies regarding e-mail usage and monitoring messages with a variety of software capable of scanning offensive words and phrases.

Business and educational publications describe the effects of communicating via computers using terms such as *empowerment* and *inclusiveness*. There are a number of reasons for this. When conferencing through the Internet, for instance, a person with relatively little status can be empowered. This same person's status may be much more of a consideration in a face-to-face meeting. In face-to-face groups, higher-status people tend to talk more, and what they say is assumed to be more important. However, numerous research studies show that the flow of communication online is more evenly distributed and respected, regardless of who occupies what status.

In their book, *Connections: New Ways of Working in the Networked Organization,* Sproull and Kiesler describe a study of decision making by college students: "When pairs of graduate students and undergraduates met face-to-face to decide their joint project, the pairs were likely to choose the topic preferred by the graduate student." When the decision was made via computers, each person's choice was equally likely to be chosen.[7]

Taking a course online offers a number of advantages. Students who are for any reason unable to attend school physically can still take courses. Online courses facilitate lifelong learning regardless of age (see Fig. 5.2). In general, students taking these courses have more time to ask and respond to questions. Moreover, they can communicate through writing, graphics, images, and sounds. Learning is *asynchronous,* meaning students can interact in the "classroom" at any time. Consequently, they never have to miss a class. The identity of the communicators remains hidden or anonymous. As a result, people may ask questions online that they would not ask face to face. People may project themselves in any way they want. In this kind of communication, race, gender, and other dimensions of diversity become less relevant. The message is more important than the messenger.

DIVERSITY CONSCIOUSNESS AND COMMUNICATION

As discussed in Chapter 4, the development of diversity consciousness occurs in six areas. These areas help us understand the communication process. For example, if we are to communicate effectively, we need to have a sense of who we

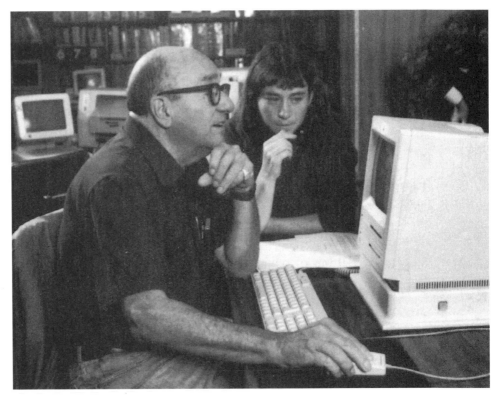

FIGURE 5.2 Computer technology provides opportunities for students of all ages to continue their education. *(Courtesy of Senior Net.)*

are individually and culturally. Additionally, we need to broaden our perspectives and develop an understanding of people from a variety of backgrounds. Finally, we need to apply and improve those skills that allow us to connect with others.

Areas of Development: Diversity Consciousness and Communication

Your communication skills will improve as you become more conscious of diversity. As discussed earlier, there are six areas of development: (a) examining ourselves and our world, (b) expanding our knowledge of others and their worlds, (c) stepping outside of ourselves, (d) gauging the level of the playing field, (e) checking up on ourselves, and (f) following through. Each of the areas, and its implications for effective communication, are discussed on the next page.

Examining Ourselves and Our World

Before we begin to make sense of communication outside our culture, we need to develop awareness of our own communication style and why we communicate the way we do. Our individual and cultural backgrounds profoundly influence the way we communicate. The most obvious example is the language we learn and use. It is easy to take our own language for granted and assume that everybody interprets words and gestures in the same way. What about the words *you* use? If you are majoring in computers, your vocabulary consists of terms such as *gigs* and *megs, operating systems, Web browsers,* and *java.* When you use these terms with people who are not familiar with computers, how do they react? In general, is communication between people who are and are not computer literate problematic?

Even material culture can be interpreted in many ways. **Material culture** is that which we create and can see, touch, or feel. Consider the clothes you wear. What do they communicate to different people in different settings? How do they connect to your culture? For example, what does a pair of $80 jeans symbolize? Does it symbolize the same thing to people of varying ages?

Social events can alter the meaning of material culture. The hajib or head scarf, worn by some Muslim women as an expression of female modesty, has taken on added significance in the aftermath of the terrorist attacks on the World Trade Center and the Pentagon. As evidenced by the following comments made by middle school students who attend a Muslim school in the United States, the hajib took on new meaning after September 11, 2001.

> "Before September 11, when we wore scarves, they made us feel special. Now we're just paranoid."
> "People, because of our scarves, they think we're something we're not."
> "Under our scarves, we're just like other girls. We like to do our hair, and we like to go shopping."[8]

Since September 11, a number of Muslim women's Web sites have held chat room discussions for those who are considering wearing the hajib. Some Muslim women have found themselves researching their own religion and reexamining their spiritual development. For those who feel misunderstood or under attack because of their faith, putting on the hajib may be a way of standing up for their religion and showing pride in being Muslim. Madeline Zilfi, a professor of Middle Eastern history, says, "It's like when you go to a foreign country as an American and you don't feel patriotic until someone starts attacking your country. Then you find yourself standing up for the good things about it. . . the interesting thing is that the American forum is very open to this kind of expression."[9]

Sometimes, we are ineffective communicators because we fail to realize that everyone does not share our interpretation(s). Furthermore, we may find it difficult to examine our own ways of communicating. In her book *Ways with Words,* Shirley Brice Heath describes a technique that students can use to stand back and look at themselves. She suggests that students put themselves "under a microscope" and take the role of an **ethnographer,**[10] a person who spends time living with people in order to research their customs. Using this method, students assume the role of a neutral observer and observe their own communication systematically. They record even the smallest details and try to discover patterns. As an ethnographer, you might focus on how you communicate with others in the classroom. What about the tone and volume of your voice? How might your body gestures influence how your message comes across to others? How do you react to lectures, discussions, and group work in class?

Expanding Our Knowledge of Others and Their Worlds

Do we even recognize the presence of others and their capacity or right to communicate? Sometimes, we view women, men, children, lower-class persons, and people with disabilities as unable to speak for themselves in certain situations. Raymond Bingham, a white male nurse, recounts the assumptions he made one morning while working in a newborn intensive care unit. A child with a heart defect needed emergency surgery. The nurse vividly recalls meeting the child's father for the first time. He was "a large black man, with unkempt clothes, somewhat slurred speech, and at 8 o'clock in the morning a hint of beer on his breath."

The nurse's first impression was not to expect too much from this man. He was soon proven wrong. The father showed a lot of caring and compassion for his son. When he needed to explain the procedure to the child's mother on the phone, he gave a complete and thorough description of the surgery and why it was necessary. Finally, the nurse remembers the father sitting at the child's bedside and crying. Toward the end of his shift, the nurse reflected back on this experience. "This man, of whom I had thought so little at first glance, who had been so strong, so calm, so resolved throughout a tumultuous day, who had so many things to worry about and take care of. . . had handled them all."[11]

THINKING THROUGH DIVERSITY

If you and other students sit in the same classroom, read the same assignments, and hear the same lectures, are all of you receiving the same education? Might each of you interpret the same lesson differently because of the social worlds in which you live?

Frequently, we are unaware of different patterns of cultural differences and the pivotal role they play in communication. Depending on the cultural setting, it may or may not be appropriate to be frank about emotions, to delegate decision making, or to deal directly with conflict in face-to-face meetings. Lack of awareness regarding these differences can result in all kinds of misunderstandings.

When you encounter cross-cultural communication difficulties, are you mindful of how your cultural background may be influencing your own reactions? Do you listen intently and try extra hard to understand? Are there times when you refuse to accommodate or even acknowledge differences? When you go to school or work, are you likely to encounter different communication styles? What do you assume when:

- *People converse with their faces only a few inches apart?*   Among some cultures, this is the norm. In others, people like to keep their distance and are uncomfortable if someone stands closer than a couple of feet.
- *A student or a coworker takes a long time to answer a question?*   According to researchers who study language, short wait times put some people at a disadvantage. For example, the cultures of many Native Americans emphasize deliberate thought. Before making a decision, they learn to consider all possible implications.
- *People do not look at you when you talk to them?*   Among many African, Asian, and Latin American cultures, it is rude to establish direct eye contact with elders or people in authority.
- *People talk informally for a period of time before "getting down to business"?*   In many cultures, this is considered good manners. Many Middle Easterners, for example, see this type of "small talk" as a necessary part of business. It is not at all unusual for Asians or Latinos to view the process of getting to know each other as important as the message itself. To many U.S. businessmen and women, it is simply a waste of time.
- *People answer a question with "yes"?*   In many East Asian cultures, it is rude to answer a question in the negative. In such situations, people may say "yes" even though they mean "no." It is a way of showing respect or "saving face," saving someone from embarrassment.
- *You see two people verbally challenging each other?*   If your cultural background is Greek, Italian, or Israeli, you might view it positively, as a sign of intimacy. If you are from certain Hispanic or Asian cultures, you would probably view this kind of verbal sparring differently. Since expressing anger in this way is frowned upon, you might consider it more appropriate to repress feelings and simply smile or change the subject.

> When you meet people on the way to class, on the street, in a store, or wherever, they say "Hi" plus they ask "How are you doing?" or "How are you?" even if you are a complete stranger to them. I like when they say "Hi" to me, but what really doesn't make sense is that they add "how are you feeling?" even though they don't care whether I am well or not. I feel like Americans ask this just because they are obliged to do it. In fact, if I answered "I am not OK," nobody would care. In a certain way, this is like a movie where the actors have to say what is written in the script. To the question, you feel obliged to answer you are well no matter whether it is the truth or not. Considering this point, I prefer Italians who just say "Hi" or nothing to the people they have never met before. They don't even think to ask about their health. It could appear colder, but it is certainly less hypocritical.
>
> —Another perspective

Intimate Talk Among College Students: Some Gender Differences

Recent research has taken a look at the degree to which male and female college students "open up" in intimate relationships. In one study, 360 college students attending universities in the South and Midwest were surveyed. The study suggests that female students:

1. Tend to disclose much more than men.
2. Are more apt to open up and discuss previous love and sexual relationships.

3. Are more likely to communicate to their partner how they really feel about them.
4. Are more apt to express what they want for the future of a relationship.

These findings are consistent with other research which shows that women tend to be more relationship-oriented than men.[12]

We cannot be familiar with all variations in communication. Furthermore, we cannot assume that all people from a given culture will communicate in the same way. However, it is important to be open to the possibility that communication differences exist. Keep in mind that despite our differences, we all want people to listen to, acknowledge, and respect us.

Stepping Outside of Ourselves

It would help if everyone could experience what it is like to be a minority for a while, to learn what it is like.

—Another perspective

One of the most important skills needed for effective communication is the ability to process and understand another person's point of view. This skill allows us to step outside of ourselves and become more open and sensitive to others, although it does not necessarily mean that we will fully comprehend or agree with their thoughts and feelings. Certain experiences may teach students the importance of putting themselves in the shoes of friends, family, and others.

Ashley is a high-school senior whose best friend is dealing with an unwanted pregnancy. Even though Ashley has never been in this situation, she can "feel her friend's pain" and this helps her know what to say. Judah, a community college student, writes about how he works with a number of people with severe cerebral palsy. Since some cannot communicate verbally, he finds it helps to "put his mind into theirs" and rely on other physical cues. Ernestine, an older female student who has a household of daughters, explains how she struggles with their thinking about life. They have watched many of their friends die violently. As a result, her daughters prefer to focus on the present and not think about the future. Says Ernestine, "I try to imagine going to countless funerals of classmates and soulmates and babies, all because somebody dissed them or stepped on their shoes or looked at them the wrong way." These three students—Ashley, Judah, and Ernestine—are more effective communicators because they have the ability to step outside of themselves. They are not locked into their own way of thinking.

When people try to understand a variety of perspectives, it opens up lines of communication. People are more willing to share when they sense that others are really listening and not judging or comparing. Also, stepping outside of yourself can make you more aware of your own thoughts and feelings. In *I Know Why the Caged*

Bird Sings, Maya Angelou talks about the development of this kind of self-awareness. "I had gone from being ignorant of being ignorant to being aware of being aware."[13] This revealing, empowering process is not easy. Yari, a college student, describes what it is like to really let herself go into the "inner world of another person." "It is one of the most active, difficult, and demanding things I do. And yet it is worth it because it is one of the most releasing, healing things that I have any occasion to do."

Gauging the Level of the Playing Field

On the surface, this area of development does not appear to relate to communication. What do concepts such as status and inequality have to do with language? Ask yourself whether you address your teacher differently than you do a fellow student. What if you are angry? Would you show that anger differently? As an employee, do you communicate any differently with your coworkers than with your supervisor? The relationship between the speaker and the receiver influences communication. One aspect of this relationship is status and power. **Status** refers to one's position. **Power** is the ability to influence people. Our interaction with others takes the form of an equal or unequal status relationship. In the classroom, an unequal status relationship exists between teachers and their students. Simply put, teachers have more authority because of their position. In another setting, this relationship might change and so might the communication between teacher and student (see Diversity Box: Communication on the Court and in the Classroom).

Communication on the Court and in the Classroom

As a new young instructor teaching sociology at a predominantly black college, I remember numerous times when I was the only white person. This often occurred when I walked into a classroom, ate in the cafeteria, or worked out at the gym. One day, I remember going over to the gym to play some basketball. There were pickup games at each of the six baskets. I was the only white person in the gym. No one knew me since I had only been teaching a few weeks and none of my students were present. When there was a break in the action, I started to take some shots at one of the baskets. Someone suggested that we pick sides. I got picked last. After a few minutes, I heard someone yell, "Hey, white boy!" Obviously, it was not difficult to figure who was being singled out by that comment. I tried to ignore it but he kept repeating. "Hey, white boy!" "Hey, white boy!"

I still remember that day as if it was yesterday. Even though I was 24 years old, it was the first time in my life I can remember my race being held against me. This experience also helped me understand the different dynamics on the basketball court and in the classroom. On the court, we were pretty much equals, especially since the other players assumed that I was just another student. Our age, class, and lifestyle did not matter. The student who called me "white boy" was treating me like he would any other young adult white male. Once in the classroom, however, the relationship as well as the communication changed. It was considerably more difficult to be open and honest because I was the teacher and they were the students. This was particularly evident when we talked about controversial and emotional issues such

continued

Communication on the Court and in the Classroom (continued)

as race and social inequality. There was an unwritten script that each of us followed.

Consequently, it was difficult for us to be spontaneous and communicate our true feelings.

THINKING THROUGH DIVERSITY

One of the challenges confronting doctors is to open up lines of communication with their patients. One doctor laments, "People put us on a pedestal. They see us as angels, and this makes communication difficult. They don't ask questions or express their concerns. But we make mistakes like anyone else." In communicating with their patients, what is one specific thing doctors might do to level the playing field and promote more open, honest communication?

Every opinion, every voice deserves to be heard. And it is a rare gift indeed to hear voices that are so very different from my own.

—Another perspective

Differences in power and status can be an obstacle to effective communication. With effective communication, the receiver interprets the message just as the sender intends. Those with less power are often ignored during the communication process. For example, we tend to listen and assign more importance to what an adult says than to what a child says. In the classroom, we want to know what the teacher thinks is important. What students say typically carries less weight. Students who sense they lack power may feel that their input is not as important. However, everybody has something important to offer. Take advantage of opportunities to hear and learn from others, regardless of their credentials or titles.

One technique used in diversity training is to instruct people in a group to completely ignore each other's titles and degrees. The idea is to focus on the message rather than the messenger. Although this technique sounds promising, it is extremely difficult to put into practice in everyday life. Actually, children are more effective communicators in this sense. Unlike adults, they do not get so caught up with the trappings of power.

Checking Up on Ourselves

The problem with communication is the illusion that it has been accomplished.

—George Bernard Shaw

Effective communication requires constant practice and self-examination. To improve our communication skills, we need to be open to *feedback*—people's responses to us. Otherwise, we do not know when we are relating well to others.

Despite our knowledge and sensitivity, misunderstandings will occur. Often, we are not even aware of a problem. Therefore, it is important to ask constantly for feedback from others. To illustrate, Michelle, a study group leader, uses several techniques to ensure that she is not simply "talking at" students in her group. As much as possible, she engages each student in a dialogue. She focuses on the students' body language as well as what they say. Furthermore, she is learning to provide more and more wait time. This encourages more thorough and thoughtful questions and answers from a larger number of people.

In any given situation, ask probing questions of yourself. This enables us to go deeper and examine what messages we send and receive. However, try not to get so caught up with analyzing yourself that it interferes with your ability to listen. Think through the following questions:

1. *Am I considering my entire audience?* This includes people who will hear the message either directly or indirectly. At work, for example, your supervisor may eventually receive your message through someone else. Consider the personal and cultural characteristics of your entire audience, and how much they know and how they may feel about the subject matter.

2. *What is the situation?* What influences outside and within this particular setting might have an impact on communication? What cultural differences may exist? Is the setting formal or informal? Elijah Cummings, a U.S. congressman, describes how he communicates differently depending on the situation. When he is in the halls of Congress, he uses what some might refer to as "paycheck" or "edited" English. But when he is back home, he communicates more informally.

3. *What options are available to me?* In other words, what form or forms of communication might I use? Your message might be written, oral, visual, or a combination of these. A case in point is police work. In response to complaints from the deaf and hard of hearing, police have increasingly reexamined the way they train officers. Some departments have started teaching sign language to selected officers, while others have sensitized officers to the importance of using pen and paper to communicate with a deaf person when requested. To better deal with emergencies, departments have begun to recognize the need for having interpreters on call and TTY telephones for the deaf.

4. *What is the specific purpose of the communication?* Perhaps the purpose you have in mind is not shared by others. As an example, Westerners tend to emphasize the end product of communication, the message. In contrast, many Asians place more importance on being together and getting to know each other.

5. *What feedback am I receiving regarding the messages being sent (content) and how they are sent (style)?* Tone of voice, volume, pauses, facial expressions, and gestures can be just as meaningful as words themselves.

6. *What might I do differently to communicate more effectively?* For example, what can I do to listen more actively? How can I make my verbal and nonverbal communication congruent? How can I communicate more inclusively? Toward the end of this chapter, some specific suggestions are offered.

7. *Am I using language that might be viewed as offensive?* Sometimes offensive terms or phrases, known as *hot buttons,* impair communication. Hot buttons are discussed in more detail later in this chapter.

A friend of mine at work told me a story about how she was home alone and two black guys came to the door selling something. Later I started wondering why she felt she had to describe them as black.

卍

In my work environment, I work with people of many cultures. When I don't understand what is being said or what is meant, I ask questions to make sure that I understand instead of assuming.

—Other perspectives

Following Through

How did you do that? How did you make it look so easy? People may ask these questions of someone who has refined a skill by practicing it a countless number of times—perhaps a great athlete, a computer whiz, or an accomplished musician. What we tend to forget is the same thing applies to communication skills. Constant practice enables us to become excellent listeners as well as competent speakers in a wide variety of settings and circumstances. This is true for all of us.

Developing, expanding, and refining our communication styles and skills is a daily challenge.

A teacher who is very task-oriented finds that her relationship with students improves if she makes a habit of engaging in a little chitchat before the start of class. An employee experiments with different ways of listening. He finds that nodding his head, using facial expressions, and making "listening noises" such as "hmmm" and "oh" allow him to show others that he does care. A father discovers that spending more time with his teenage daughter and approaching conversations with her a little differently opens up lines of communication on a variety of topics, including dating and other personal issues. Instead of trying to solve all of her problems and telling her what to do, he tries to simply listen much of the time and be more empathetic.

COMMUNICATION MATTERS

In job interviews, employers weed out prospective employees by evaluating their verbal and written communication skills. As the interview unfolds, the employer is getting a live demonstration of how well individuals get their points across to others. In *The Interview Kit,* author Richard Beatty provides numerous examples of questions employers often ask. One series of questions he cites is, "Give me an example of something complex that you needed to effectively communicate to others. What made it complex? Why was it difficult to communicate? What did you do to communicate effectively? What were the results? How might these results have been improved?"[14]

Regardless of the social arena, we can readily observe the value of good communication skills. In school, for instance, why do students like some teachers more than others? Most teachers are well liked because they "know their stuff" and they relate well to students. Relating well has to do with communication skills.

When people talk about the power of communication, what does that mean? Think of the last time you:

- *Heard a dynamic and charismatic speaker address a large audience.* The message conveyed by that person will probably remain with you for the rest of your life.
- *Had an extremely difficult time communicating with someone who is very close and important to you.* How did that make you feel? How did that affect your relationship?
- *Were part of a team whose members could not communicate very well.* How did this affect your ability to function as a team?
- *Felt hurt by what a teacher, student, or administrator said.* This kind of remark can poison your relationship with someone. At the very least, it can be difficult to forget. It can also make you view that person or even yourself in a different light.

> *Words are powerful and have physical impact on the receiver. They assault and abuse if used offensively.*
>
> —Another perspective

The Power of Language

Even one word can stick with us for a long time. Indeed, it can be the only thing that we remember about an event that took place a long time ago. In the following poem entitled "Incident," the lingering impact of a single word is described by Countee Cullen.

> Once riding in old Baltimore,
> heart-filled, head-filled with glee,
> I saw a Baltimorean keep
> looking straight at me.

> Now, I was eight and very small,
> and he was no whit bigger,
> and so I smiled, but he poked
> out his tongue, and called
> me "nigger."
> I saw the whole of Baltimore,
> from May until December,
> of all the things that happened
> there that's all that I
> remember.[15]

To a large degree, your success in all realms of life is dependent on your ability to communicate effectively. Whenever you encounter someone at school or work, you communicate something even if you say nothing. Each encounter poses a challenge. When communication is ineffective, mutual understanding and joint action are highly unlikely. However, when communication is effective, your chances for relating well are that much greater. Teaming, networking, and learning are easier and more rewarding if you can communicate effectively with different people in all kinds of situations. Consequently, many businesses report a great need for employees with cross-cultural communication skills (see Fig. 5.3, next page).

> *Once a human being has arrived on this earth, communication is the largest single factor determining what kinds of relationships she or he makes with others and what happens to each in the world.*
>
> —Virginia Satir

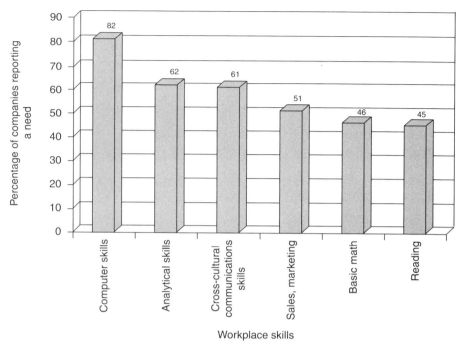

FIGURE 5.3   Workplace training skills. This information comes from a survey by the American Society for Training and Development. Companies were asked what kind of training their employees need. Although computer training is what companies cite as most needed, training that targets communication skills ranks high as well.[16]

BARRIERS TO EFFECTIVE COMMUNICATION

There can be any number of barriers to effective communication, particularly when we communicate across cultures. These barriers include cultural biases, lack of awareness of cultural differences, language differences, ethnocentrism, and inactive listening.

   1. *Cultural biases.*   In certain situations, we may make unwarranted assumptions about the person or persons with whom we are communicating. A person's dialect, for example, may trigger negative assumptions about a person's education, intelligence, or character. The term **dialect** refers to patterns in the way people use language. These patterns, which reflect people's cultural and regional backgrounds, include pronunciation or "accent" as well as vocabulary and grammar. Children learn dialect prejudice at an early age, as evidenced by comments like "You talk funny" or "Did you hear how she said that?" In the media and in the classroom, accents are described with adjectives such as foreign, hick, and weird. People who are very cautious about saying anything that might have racist or sexist overtones are much more open when it comes to belittling language differences.

In a film on cross-cultural communication, two people are shown interviewing for a job. Both answer the questions in exactly the same way. However, one of the interviewees talks with a noticeable accent. After hearing both interviews, the narrator of the film poses the question, "Who would you hire?" Too often, a person with an accent is assumed to be less intelligent or less qualified. One study by researchers at the University of North Texas lends credence to the possibility that this kind of discrimination is commonplace. Fifty-six executives listened to a CD-ROM program of ten men from different regions of the country recite the same 45-second passage. The jobs, and particularly high-prestige jobs, went to speakers with less identifiable regional accents. One of the researchers, Dianne Markley, says her research shows that companies need to monitor their job hirers more closely, perhaps by using tools like the CD-ROM program.[17]

Personally, when I have had the occasion of speaking with students from other cultures I have found myself focusing on how they differed from what I felt normal for me. While focusing on differences, I was really missing the point of what was being said. I found myself making a judgment on the person speaking based solely on his culture.

⌘

Having another language is treated like it's a disease. If you're in America, it is assumed that you ought to automatically speak THE language—that is, English.

—Other perspectives

2. *Lack of awareness of cultural differences.* If you are communicating with someone from a different culture, the two of you may interpret the same symbol differently. Several examples follow.

- What does holding your thumb up mean to you? If you are in the United States, most people would probably interpret this gesture to mean "okay." However, in another country, you might interpret this differently. In his book *Cultural Diversity in the Workplace,* George Henderson examines various meanings that people attach to this gesture in different parts of the world.[18] In Japan, it means money. In Ghana and Iran, it is a vulgar gesture, similar to raising the middle finger in the United States.

- When a teacher asks a question of the entire class and there is a long period of silence, what does this mean to you? Does it make you feel uncomfortable? In most classrooms in the United States, silence is viewed as something to fill up. This is a reflection of our cultural upbringing. According to George Henderson, many Native American cultures admire a person who has the ability to remain silent. Many Asian students learn to listen to what is not said as well as to what is said. Zen Buddhism, which is influential in many parts of Asia, reinforces this lesson.

According to a Zen proverb, "He who knows does not speak and he who speaks does not know."

- During an argument, how do you feel when other students all try to talk at once? In *Aspects of Ethnicity: Understanding Differences in Pluralistic Classrooms,* Wilma Longstreet describes how different students react during a heated debate in a seminar.[19] When a number of black students start talking at the same time, the rest of the class remains quiet. After a few minutes, the black students appear angry. They want to know why the rest of the class is no longer talking. The white students explain that they are waiting for their turn in the discussion. Meanwhile, the Asian students express a need to think and reflect for a moment before talking.

3. *Language differences.*   Communicating in an unfamiliar language can be challenging. For example, some businesses cater to customers who speak a variety of languages. When people try to communicate in a language other than their own, the results can be amusing. The following attempts to communicate in English did not come across as intended:

- "Our wines leave you nothing to hope for." (from a restaurant menu in Switzerland)
- "Ladies are requested not to have children at the bar." (from a bar in Norway)
- "Fur coats made for ladies from their own skins." (from a Swedish furrier)[20]

Even when people speak the same language, such as English speakers in the United States and other parts of the world, they may find it difficult to communicate. To lessen the confusion, the *Encarta World English Dictionary* was recently published. Linked by e-mail, more than 320 lexicographers (dictionary editors), linguists, and other specialists in 20 nations worked for more than two years to define words that can mean different things in different English-speaking countries. In South Africa, for instance, people refer to a stoplight as a "robot." The word *hotel,* in Australia, is an establishment that sells alcoholic beverages. And job seekers in Southeast Asia provide prospective employers with a "biodata" rather than a resume.[21]

4. *Ethnocentrism.*   Ethnocentrism shows itself in the language we use. When we talk about the *cultural deprivation* of a group of people, what does this mean? This once commonly used term implies more than just difference. According to this label, anyone who does not share a certain way of life is assumed to be at a disadvantage. Another example of ethnocentric language is the way we fail to differentiate between *arrival* and *discovery*. A number of years ago, many people celebrated the 500th anniversary of Columbus's *discovery* of the "New World." This touched off a heated public debate because Native Americans lived here long before Columbus *arrived* in 1492. Some history books still describe Euro-Americans as defending *their* homes against "Indian" attacks, rather than invading Native American lands. Words such as *primitive* and *backward* have been used to distort history and describe highly defined and complex Native American societies.

5. *Inactive listening.*   Poor listening skills can make it much harder to communicate across cultural boundaries. Listening intently and actively helps to overcome misunderstandings and maximize effective communication. Later in this chapter, we examine specific skills that promote active listening.

⚙ HOT BUTTONS

I was grocery shopping one day when an elderly woman called me a "nigger." All of the hate and venom was there. I didn't know what to do. I thought of going to the manager and demanding that he do something. But what could he do? I wanted the world to stop and pay attention to me because I had just been assaulted! I did my shopping in stunned, confused, and angry silence. Now I am sorry I didn't tell management in the store this happened while I was buying their groceries. I may not have gotten validation, but I would not have kept it quiet.

—Another perspective

Hot buttons refer to language that triggers negative reactions from people who view it as insulting and derogatory. Hot buttons are not the same for everyone. What is insulting and derogatory to one student might be perfectly acceptable to another. Similarly, a supervisor might consider a sexist joke "just playing around" or "part of the territory." An employee might view that same joke as threatening, serious, and possibly grounds for a lawsuit.

For some, the issue of hot buttons is a game of *political correctness*. There are those in the workplace who complain that they feel like they are "walking on eggshells" all the time. They maintain that they cannot be themselves. Others make the point we are simply talking about being respectful of others. Regardless of where you stand on this issue, it is important to understand just how powerful language can be. Saying something offensive can jeopardize communication, create mistrust and hostility, and damage a person's reputation.

Good intentions do not protect us from using hot buttons. A fellow teacher shared with me how his students became visibly upset in class when he referred to a few of them as "you people." He was completely taken aback by their reaction. After all, he did not mean anything negative by it. He explained "you people" was directed at certain students who did poorly on a test; it was meant to motivate them to do better. Only later did he find out the negative connotations of this hot button. Some students said it made them feel inferior and different. One student compared it to being called "you dog" or "you good-for-nothing."

Randall Kennedy, a professor of law at Harvard, examines the historical significance and political power of a single word in his book *Nigger: The Strange Career of a Troublesome Word*. "I have invested energy in this endeavor because *nigger* is a key word in the lexicon of race relations and thus an important term in American politics," Kennedy tells us. "To be ignorant of its meanings and effects is to make

JUNEAU JEWS · OREGON ORIENTALS · NIAGARA NEGROES · ARKANSAS ARABS · LOUISVILLE LATINOS · CLEVELAND INDIANS

FIGURE 5.4 Hot button or not? *(By permission from the Los Angeles Times Syndicate.)*

oneself vulnerable to all manner of perils, including the loss of a job, a reputation, a friend, even one's life."[22]

No matter how hard we try, periodically, each of us will use language that may take the form of a hot button. It is important to learn from our mistakes and accept responsibility for what we say and do.

Using appropriate language is not something we can easily turn on and off. It always helps to think things through before and after communicating. For instance, change a key word in a phrase and see if it still applies. Suppose that you read an article about "*the* gay lifestyle." Ask yourself, would it make sense to talk about "*the* heterosexual lifestyle?" Someone might consider the phrase "I don't think of you as Latino" a compliment. Change it. Would someone say "I don't think of you as White?"

Another point to consider is the history of a phrase or the context in which it is used. Comparing a hard-driving boss to a slave driver serves to trivialize a period of history that is very painful to some. This same kind of reasoning may apply to fans mimicking "tomahawk chops" and "war chants" at sports events. Whether these actions honor or slight Native Americans is currently the subject of much debate.

Another example is marketing. Sports teams have adopted names and mascots such as Redskins, Redmen, or Red Raiders (see Fig. 5.4). Because of efforts by Native American activists, many of these teams at the high school and college level have changed their names. Professional sports teams, such as the Washington Redskins, Atlanta Braves, and Cleveland Indians, insist on keeping their names. To support their position, they point to research that shows considerable disagreement among fans and Native Americans regarding the use of Indian nicknames, mascots, or symbols.[23]

Recently, students at the University of Northern Colorado named their intramural basketball team "The Fightin' Whites." A caricature of a white man appears on their jerseys along with the saying "Every thang's going to be all white." Made up of Native Americans, Hispanics, and Whites, the team chose its name after unsuccessful attempts to persuade a nearby high school to change its nickname, "the

Fightin' Reds," and the Native American caricature on its team logo. Although the team says it simply wants to use humor to encourage a community-wide discussion of this volatile issue, critics say this form of protest perpetuates yet another racial stereotype. Solomon Little Owl, a member of the team, says "We wanted, humorously, to make a point. 'Look at this from my point of view. See how it feels to be made fun of.'"[24]

The controversy over the volatile issue of culturally insensitive marketing is by no means limited to sports teams. A case in point is a company in New York that sells a malt liquor under the name Crazy Horse. The bottle features a Native American in headdress. While the makers of this product argue they are simply capitalizing on a clientele that identifies with the "Old West," others feel that it is one more example of how Native Americans have been dishonored and dehumanized throughout American history. One state lawmaker, who tried to ban Crazy Horse malt liquor in Minnesota, suggests that this debate illustrates a double standard. "Everybody would understand how insulting it would be to have, say, a Martin Luther King Jr. dark ale or a Golda Meir dark stout. But when it comes to Native Americans, somehow it's a different thing."[25]

THINKING THROUGH DIVERSITY

What are your personal hot buttons? How do you feel when someone triggers one of your hot buttons? Why? Do your encounters with hot buttons make it difficult for you to communicate effectively?

What Not to Say

In the early 1970s, Sheila Rush and Chris Clark authored the book *How to Get Along with Black People.* The authors cited a number of cliches that were extremely objectionable to Blacks. Interestingly, many of these cliches are still commonplace today.

- "What do you people want?. . ."
  Rush and Clark: "It assumes that Blacks must want something different from what white people want." When used in this context, the word *you* can be seen as degrading and dehumanizing."

- "A credit to his race. . . ."
  Rush and Clark: "The phrase assumes that Blacks need crediting or something to balance their dark doom. To become a 'credit', one must be compliant." It is also interesting to note when this phrase is or is

not used. Have you ever heard a white male referred to as a credit to his race?"

- "It's for your own good. . . ."
  Rush and Clark: "It implies that Blacks don't know their own best interests—and that's insulting." This comment is frequently directed at women, too.

- "But the Irish (Jews, Italians, Cubans) did it, why can't you?. . ."
  Rush and Clark: "The implication, of course, is that if Blacks had worked harder, their fate would have been different. . . . No group ever worked harder in the service of building America. (Remember slavery?) So why are Blacks still 'last'? For all but the fairest Blacks, the possibility of melting in the great American pot did not exist. Blacks could never get lost in the crowd. . . ."[26]

▣ DIFFICULT DIALOGUES

One day, I called a local radio station. A conservative talk show was on. The only thing I wanted to say was that until black people and white people, or just people in general, start talking there will always be racism. I was really upset and the talk show host made a fool out of me on the radio. For days after that, he made comments about me. . . like "her name's Utopia (he didn't think that was my real name); she must live in a utopia."

I cried that whole weekend. On Monday I went to school. I attended a predominantly white school. In most of my classes, I was the only Black. I remember walking into class and sharing with them what happened to me. I then said "I don't know if white people don't understand or they don't want to understand." I was just sitting there crying and that was the first time they all paid attention to me and listened to everything I had to say. That was the first day I felt I made a breakthrough with white people. I realized that it's possible that we can communicate, we can talk, and we can listen. Maybe not necessarily always agree but respect what each other has to say. That was the first year I even allowed myself to have white friends.

—Another perspective

Difficult dialogues are sometimes necessary. If we handle them well, these kinds of discussions can bring diversity issues out into the open and "clear the air." In one study, college students praised professors who know how to create a "comfort zone," and understand the importance of letting discussions continue even if they become heated. At the same time, these professors establish ground rules in advance, emphasize respect, and encourage students not to personalize issues.[27]

Another study cited earlier illustrates the importance of dealing with student concerns about intolerance, especially when it touches them personally. Of those minority students surveyed at five colleges in the eastern United States, one-fourth said that acts motivated by prejudice interfere with their ability to study.[28] If one considers co-victimization, the numbers are apt to be much higher. **Co-victimization** means that you can feel the pain of victimization even if people do not attack or victimize you directly. Anyone who has been through difficult times with a good friend knows how his or her life is affected as well.

Despite the importance of opening up and engaging in difficult dialogues, people rarely do it. This is the case in classrooms, offices, communities, and even on a national level. According to Cornel West, author of *Race Matters,* our society has never had an open and honest discussion about race.[29] The same can be said about other diversity issues. When a group of college students were asked to explain why these kinds of dialogues are so rare, they offered the following perspectives.

I don't want to be told that I'm the cause of someone else's pain and suffering.

⌘

Many people fear that if they open up and share their innermost feelings, they will be called racist, sexist, or homophobic.

⌘

People are afraid that they're going to say something that is really going to demoralize another person or demoralize themselves.

⌘

People fear being perceived as a complainer. They fear that their concerns won't be addressed, that people won't listen.

⌘

I don't want something I've said to be taken the wrong way.

—Other perspectives

Some of the reasons for the lack of dialogue may have more to do with the social setting than with the person. According to a report entitled *Racial Issues on Campus: How Students View Them,* many college students cite a lack of opportunity to voice their concerns. Many of these students, who attended 20 predominantly white and 20 predominantly black campuses, felt a sense of alienation and isolation. They had concerns about campus climate and personal experiences but few formal opportunities to address them.[30]

Often we reserve difficult dialogues for friends and family. This is because we feel that we know and trust them. In all likelihood, we will not risk opening up elsewhere unless we also feel a certain level of trust or a high degree of anonymity. "Y? The National Forum on People's Differences," one of the most innovative uses of technology in recent years, allows people to ask embarrassing, personal questions in a safe, anonymous setting on the Web. This low-tech site, *www.yforum.com*, relies on simple text with questions typed in by users worldwide. Interestingly, most of the questions revolve around small, everyday issues. Typical inquiries include: "Is there a way to tell the difference in Asian nationalities?" "Is it true that the direction the eyes slant is an indicator?" "Why do Jewish people eat Matzos?" "Why is it that Caucasians seem to spend so much time on lawn care?" "What would take place during a typical week night in a black family?"[31] Questions like these illustrate just how much we don't know about each other, and the critical need for honest dialogue.

In my classes, my students and I work very hard to get to the point where we can talk about race, gender, social class, and other issues related to sociology. This process starts on the first day of class with each of us sharing some of our personal background. Our comfort level with diversity increases as we discuss its relevance throughout the semester. Although students do not always agree, they learn to re-spect each other's opinions.

Prior to difficult dialogues, it helps to discuss and agree on certain ground rules. Some examples follow:

People don't get along because they fear each other. People fear each other because they don't know each other. They don't know each other because they have not properly communicated with each other.

—Martin Luther King, Jr.

Nine Ground Rules for Difficult Dialogues

1. If someone pushes a "hot button" of yours, it's okay to let the group know what it is and how it makes you feel.
2. Be as open and honest as you feel you can be. Try to move outside your comfort zone.
3. Respect each person's right to be heard.
4. Realize that we are all teachers and learners.
5. Be an active participant. Remember that we participate in different ways.
6. Listen even when you do not want to listen.
7. Do not judge another person's feelings.
8. Focus on the behavior rather than the person.
9. Do not ask people to be spokespersons for their groups.

COMMUNICATING INCLUSIVELY

There is a growing body of literature on multicultural or inclusive communication. As the world grows smaller and our society becomes more diverse, employers are more apt to view people who lack skills in this area as liabilities. Communicating in a way that makes people feel included rather than excluded is not a lesson that can be taught in a matter of minutes. It requires commitment and practice. The following 11 strategies provide a good starting point. Rather than focus on all of these at once, it might be helpful to focus on one or two strategies at a time.

1. *Address people the way they want to be addressed.* Many Native Americans identify with their tribal background. Consequently, they may prefer being called Navaho or Sioux rather than Native Americans. Do not judge a person's preference. Simply respect it. Also, keep in mind that different people within a group may want to be addressed differently.

Negative Messages Surround Adoption

Recently, a teacher e-mailed me regarding a "perspective" that appeared in the first edition of *Diversity Consciousness*. A student who is more light-skinned than the rest of her family had shared a perspective that caught the teacher's attention. Because of her skin color, the student explained how people constantly teased her, and joked about how she must have been adopted. The teacher, a parent of an adopted child, reacted strongly to this perspective. "As a parent, I feel angry at the implied message—that being adopted is always second class to being 'born into' a family. Being adopted means you don't really belong. That being 'adopted' was very hurtful to this student is indicative of a prevalent social attitude that those of us who formed our families by adoption frequently encounter. My son has been asked who his 'real' parents are, and I have been asked if I have any kids 'of my own.'

Upon finding out how our family was formed, some people express pity that we couldn't have children. Negative language around adoption abounds—we have been asked (within our son's hearing) why his 'real' mother didn't want him, or if we knew his 'father' (with my husband standing there)." By sharing her view of a significant but often disregarded dimension of diversity, the teacher made me more aware of gaps in my thinking.

2. *Keep an open mind.*   People can view the same thing differently. Be open to the "different lens" through which people view the world. Also, be willing to question your own assumptions and learn from the feedback you receive from others.

3. *Listen actively.*   Active listening skills require practice (see Diversity Box: Active Listening Skills Checklist). Often, we are so intent on getting our point across that we do not carefully listen to what people are saying and how they are saying it. For instance, we can learn something from inflections in a person's voice, and even from pauses. Remember to focus on body language. According to research, most of what we communicate during a conversation is nonverbal.

In part, effective listening hinges on our attunement and receptivity to other's feelings. *Mirroring,* commonly used in marital therapy, allows us to build rapport as we listen. When a person says something, we try to repeat or mirror what was said, attempting to capture the person's feelings and thoughts. Without being too obvious, we might start by aligning our body language and noticing the pace and tone of the individual's voice. As we do this, we check to make sure we are on target, and if not, we try again.

Active Listening Skills Checklist

- Do you listen intently even when you disagree with someone?
- Do you listen intently even when you have a difficult time understanding someone?
- Do you listen intently when someone talks very slowly and deliberately?
- Do you hear only what you want to hear?
- Are you aware of verbal and nonverbal messages?

- Do you restate, summarize, and question to promote understanding?
- Do you provide positive feedback through body language and "listening noises"?
- Do you give people time to respond?
- How do you make sure your biases do not interfere with your ability to listen?

4. *Check understanding.*   Instead of assuming that someone understands you, assume just the opposite. Ask questions that might pinpoint possible problems. "Is this clear?" "Do I need to explain further?" "What do you think I have been saying up to this point?" Repeat these questions continuously. When you are the receiver of information, ask questions, too. "Is that idea like. . . ?" "Are you suggesting that. . . ?" "Can you give me an example of. . . ?"

5. *Do some research.*   Businesspersons who are traveling abroad or venturing into unfamiliar markets at home often ignore this sort of preparation. The Internet can provide a wealth of current information. College libraries or ethnic organizations in your community may be other valuable resources.

General Motors is one company that did not do its homework. When the Chevy Nova was introduced in South America, the company could not explain the car's sluggish sales. Eventually, General Motors was forced to change the name of the model to Caribe after finding out that "No va" means "it doesn't go" in Spanish. Another company, Coors, discovered too late that its slogan "Turn It Loose," when translated into Spanish, meant the beer that would make you "Get the Runs."

6. *Think through what you are going to say before you say it.*   When you talk about others, do you refer to them by their race, ethnic background, social class, gender, or some other distinguishing characteristic? If so, ask yourself why.

7. *Avoid slang.*   Telling someone she has "phat" clothing can lead to misunderstanding. To my teenage daughter, it means awesome or good. To one of my colleagues at work, it might mean something insulting.

THINKING THROUGH DIVERSITY

If a fellow employee tells you a joke about gays during your lunch break, how would you react? Why?

8. *Do not share ethnic jokes.*   This is a serious matter, especially in the workplace and at school. To some, ethnic jokes or ethnic humor in general may be acceptable. This is particularly true of self-directed ethnic humor. However, you cannot assume or predict that people will interpret something the same way you do. Jokes are usually made at the expense of others. Think through how you should react if someone decides to tell an ethnic joke in your presence.

9. *Use as many different styles of communication as possible.*   Visual aids can help. You might want to write something down or spell difficult words if simply saying something does not seem to be working. Constantly question your assumptions about the right or preferred way to communicate. Be open to the existence of different cultural norms and their impact on communication styles. At the same time, remember that cultural norms may not apply to the behavior of any particular individual. Numerous factors, such as family background, schooling, and personalities, shape and alter the modes of communication we use and prefer.

10. *Do not assume that you can or should ignore differences.*   The problem lies in the value judgments we attach to individual or cultural differences, not in the differences themselves. For example, noticing someone's accent does not make you prejudiced. Having negative thoughts about the accent does.

The poem "For the White Person Who Wants to Know How to Be My Friend" suggests how we should and should not respond to cultural differences.

The first thing you do is to forget that I'm black.
Second, you must never forget that I'm black.
You should be able to dig Aretha,
but don't play her every time I come over.
And if you decide to play Beethoven—don't tell me
his life story. They make us take music appreciation too.

—Pat Parker[32]

11. *Be conscious of how fast you are talking.*   If you were raised in one region of the United States and now live in another, you may know how difficult it is to adjust to differences in pronunciation and terminology. Generally, it helps to slow down a little. Repeat yourself if necessary.

> *Acknowledge each other's differences and move past them; just don't move too fast.*
>
> —Another perspective

In this chapter we have addressed the importance of effective communication. Moreover, we have examined the interrelationship of diversity consciousness and communication. Communication is a diversity skill that we learn, develop, and refine throughout the course of our lives. As we become more conscious of diversity, our communication skills will improve. And as our communication skills improve, we become more diversity conscious.

CASE STUDIES

Case Study One

The student population at Ligua's college is predominantly White. In spite of her desire to be as inconspicuous as possible, Ligua often feels the urge to educate other students and even the teachers in her classes. These difficult dialogues often revolve around issues of social inequality. In her Cultural Diversity class, for instance, students were talking about the legal, economic, and political changes in the United States that have opened up all kinds of opportunities for minorities. Ligua interjected, "I hope no one here thinks that by earning a degree, and getting an education, that you're going to level the playing field." A heated discussion took place, and the class ended before there was any closure on this subject.

Because of her complexion and Spanish-sounding name, assumptions are made. Born in the United States, Ligua speaks English fluently but finds it difficult to communicate in Spanish. Last semester, in Intermediate Spanish, Ligua's teacher would make references about her knowledge of the language, assuming that the class was easy for her. In reality, Ligua had to work harder just so she wouldn't embarrass herself.

Ligua does not know how to handle these difficult dialogues. She doesn't want to bring attention to herself or alienate the teachers or students, but she feels she must say something.

Questions:

1. What advice might you offer Ligua to help her deal with the difficult dialogues she encounters in her classes?
2. If you were one of Ligua's classmates in Intermediate Spanish, what would you do, if anything? Why?

Case Study Two

Mary is currently doing a practicum at a children's mental hospital. In her role as a social worker, Mary often speaks to a family several times over the phone prior to meeting with them. With the background information she receives on each case, Mary is aware of the family's racial background before the family is aware of hers. In one instance, Mary had really connected with the mother of one of her patients. She and the patient's mother, Mrs. K, had talked on the phone several times. Mrs. K made a point of acknowledging Mary's competence and thanked her for how much help she had been.

When Mrs. K and Mary finally met, Mrs. K had a surprised look on her face. From the sound of Mary's voice over the phone and her ability to empathize and understand what the family was going through, Mrs. K had assumed that Mary was African American. She was shocked to see that Mary was White. The meeting was very uncomfortable. Mary could tell that Mrs. K was hesitant to share information and the working relationship they had formed seemed to disappear. When Mary came to work the next day, there was a message from Mrs. K stating that she wanted to work with a different social worker, someone who was not White. Mary was taken aback and did not know what she should do. All of the social workers at the hospital were White and she knew something had to be done so that the patient would continue to receive the best care possible.

Questions:

1. If you were Mary, how would you feel in this situation? Why do you think Mrs. K reacted the way she did to Mary?
2. If you were Mary, what would you do? Specifically, would you call Mrs. K and talk with her, or would you handle it some other way? Explain.

Case Study Three

Michael is constantly reminded that he is exceptional and deserving, unlike so many others. This can be uncomfortable, because the word *others* seems to apply to people who supposedly share his racial or cultural background.

A whole lot of stress in his life comes from his job as a consultant. For instance, there are people who are comfortable talking to him on the phone but are suddenly uncomfortable when they meet him. They might complain or question his competence by saying, "I don't feel comfortable working with Michael," or "I don't think Michael is the right person for this job." At times like this, he is left wondering, and angry.

Questions:

1. Michael is being confronted with a number of barriers to effective communication. Discuss two of these barriers.

2. What "hot buttons" does Michael encounter? If you were Michael, how would you respond to these hot buttons?

 EXERCISES

In-Class

Exercise 1: Active Listening

Directions for Instructor

Divide students into pairs. One student in each pair tells the other student about a problem at school or work that he or she is experiencing. The problem should not be too complex. The time limit is 1 minute. The listener may ask for clarification but cannot say anything else. In addition, the listener may use "listening noises" or body language. Notes may not be taken. After the speaker finishes, the listener gives feedback by "reflecting content," restating what was said without being judgmental. This reveals whether the listener heard and understood the speaker. Moreover, this type of feedback affirms the speaker and puts him or her at ease. When necessary, the speaker can correct and help the listener remember exactly what was said. Repeat this process with the listener and speaker exchanging parts.

Analysis. What did you learn from this experience? Were you more comfortable taking on the role of the speaker or the listener? Why? Did you have a difficult time tuning in and remembering what your partner said? If you did this again, what might you do differently to be a better listener?

Exercise 2: Responding to Hot Buttons

Directions for Instructor

Form groups of three to four students. Ask students to read the following five scenarios. Each group member should then pick one scenario and act out how he or she would respond. Afterward, the group discusses the appropriateness and effectiveness of each student's response, using the "Nine Ground Rules for Difficult Dialogues" (see page 170).

- You are at work. Your boss calls you "honey," but you prefer that he call you by your first name or as Ms. _____ (last name). You explain this to your boss as tactfully as possible, but he laughs it off. You don't want to offend your boss, but you don't feel that he understands how strongly you feel about this. How do you respond?

- You are a middle-aged male who works in an office. A coworker whose desk is next to yours makes a habit of cornering you one-on-one and sharing his latest joke. Most of the jokes are aimed at women and have sexual overtones.

Initially, you try to humor him but you are growing increasingly uncomfortable with this situation. You try to avoid this person, but it is not working. You feel that you must say something to him or your supervisor. How do you respond?

- You are at a party with a group of students that you do not know really well. You are watching a professional football game and one of the students makes a racist remark about one of the players. A number of people laugh but nothing is said. How do you respond?
- You and your friend are using the photocopying machine in the library. You accidentally copy the wrong material. Your friend, realizing the mistake that you just made, says: "You're such a retard." How do you respond?
- You and 40 coworkers are participating in a "diversity workshop." After lunch, the workshop facilitator divides the participants into smaller groups. She then asks group members to discuss any prejudices they might have. Midway through the exercise, one member of your group complains: "This discussion is a waste of my time. I don't see color. I'm colorblind." How do you respond?

Out-of-Class

Exercise 1: Ethnic Jokes

Imagine that you and other employees at work correspond by e-mail. You have just received the following message on your computer:

This one was priceless. . . I'm still laughing. Enjoy! This is a letter from a Cajun mother to her Cajun son:

Dear Son,

I'll try not to write too fast because I know you read kinda slow. After you got married and moved out of our home, we decided we had to do the same. Your pa read somewhere that most accidents happen within 20 miles of our home. We figured we didn't want to take a chance. I won't be able to send you our new address for a while. The Cajun family that used to live here took the numbers off the house when they moved. I guess they didn't want to have to change their address.

You know the coat we were going to send you. I still have it. Yesterday, I put it in a package, put some stamps on it, and took it to the Post Office. They told me that they couldn't send it because there was not enuff postage. They said it was too heavy. So I've decided to remove the heavy buttins on the coat so that the package won't weigh so much. I'll bring the buttins with me next time we visit you. And I'll try to remember to bring you some new shoes. I get worried about you walking around in bear feet all the time. You can save these shoes and use them if your feet wear out.

Just want to let you know that your Uncle Tom is no longer with us. He accidentally fell in a vat full of whiskey. Two men who saw what happened tried to pull him out but he couldn't bring himself to stop drinking. He wouldn't come up for air and ended up drowning. When the coroner cremated him, he ended up burning for days because of all that alcohol in him.

Say hi to your wife for me and pa.

Love, Ma

After reading this, you decide to respond by sending an e-mail message to the sender of this joke. Type your response.

Exercise 2: Creating an Action Plan

Imagine that you are the director of student affairs at a small liberal arts college in the Midwest. During a staff meeting, the president of the college shares a number of complaints from gay students. The complaints allege that many gay students encounter prejudice and discrimination both on campus and among townspeople. The students feel that these problems are college-wide and need to be addressed by the president and her staff as well as by community leaders.

The president asks you to create an action plan. She feels that the college needs to open the lines of communication and encourage inclusive, honest dialogue on this issue. Develop a two-page typewritten summary of what you propose. Include the rationale behind your action plan.

 ## INTERNET ASSIGNMENT

1. Go to an Internet job search Web site such as *www.careers.com* or *www. helpwanted.com*. Using the Web site's search feature, find jobs related to your present or future career. Then find job descriptions that specify communication skills you will need. Print at least three of these job descriptions.
2. Write a paragraph summarizing what you found.

 ## NOTES

[1] Roger E. Axtell, *Gestures: The Do's and Taboos of Body Language Around the World* (New York: Wiley, 1991), 10.

[2] Alice Reid, "Mosque's Children Await Playground," *The Washington Post,* Nov. 22, 1998, B4.

[3] Deborah Tannen, *You Just Don't Understand: Men and Women in Conversation* (New York: William Morrow, 1990); *Talking from 9 to 5: How Women's and Men's Conversational Styles Affect Who Gets Heard, Who Gets Credit, and What Gets Done at Work* (New York: William Morrow, 1994); *That's Not What I Meant* (New York: Ballantine Books, 1992).

[4] Oliver Sacks, *Seeing Voices: A Journey into the World of the Deaf* (Berkeley, CA: University of California Press, 1989), 127.

[5] E. Goffman, *Interaction Ritual: Essays on Face to Face Interaction* (Garden City, NY: Doubleday/ Anchor, 1967).

[6] Glenn McNatt, "Instant Communication Is Changing Our Very Form of Government," *The Sun,* Feb. 9, 1997, 5E.

[7] L. Sproull and S. Kiesler, *Connections: New Ways of Working in the Networked Organization* (Cambridge, MA: MIT Press, 1991), 61.

[8] Jennifer Rudick Zunikoff, conversation with the author, June 4, 2002.

[9] Emily Wax, "The Fabric of Their Faith," *The Washington Post,* May 19, 2002, C1.

[10] Shirley Brice Heath, *Ways with Words* (Cambridge: Cambridge University Press, 1983).

[11] Raymond Bingham, "Leaving Prejudice Behind," *The Washington Post Health Section,* Sept. 6, 1994, 9.

[12] D. Knox and C. Schacht, *Choices in Relationships* (Belmont, CA: Wadsworth, 1997), 134–135.

[13] Maya Angelou, *I Know Why the Caged Bird Sings* (New York: Bantam Books, 1993).

[14] Richard Beatty, *The Interview Kit* (New York: John Wiley & Sons, 2000).

[15] Countee Cullen (ed.), *Caroling Dusk* (Secaucus, NJ: Carol Publishing Group, 1993), 187.

[16] Kristin Downey Grimsley, "Training in the Theater of the Real," *The Washington Post Business Section,* Mar. 24, 1997, 12.

[17] Nancy Kolsti, "Accents Speak Louder Than Words," *North Texan Online,* Online, Winter 2000. Available: http://www.unt.edu/northtexan/archives/w00/accents.htmrl.

[18] George Henderson, *Cultural Diversity in the Workplace: Issues and Strategies* (Westport, CT: Praeger Publishers, 1994).

[19] Wilma Longstreet, *Aspects of Ethnicity: Understanding Differences in Pluralistic Classrooms* (Williston, VT: Teachers College Press, 1978).

[20] Charles Goldsmith, "Look See! Anyone Do Read This and It Will Make You Laughable," *The Wall Street Journal,* Nov. 19, 1992, B1.

[21] Anne Soukhanov, *Encarta World English Dictionary* (New York: St. Martin's Press, 1999).

[22] Randall Kennedy, *Nigger: The Strange Career of a Troublesome Word* (New York: Pantheon, 2002), 4.

[23] S. L. Price, "The Indian Wars," *Sports Illustrated,* March 4, 2002, 67–72.

[24] Julie Cart, "Irked by Mascot, Team Retaliates," *LOS ANGELES Times Online,* Online, March 15, 2002. Available: https://www.patrick.af.mil/deomi/Library/EOReadFile/Native%20Americans%20Issues/NAISpring02/Irked%20by%20Mascot.pdf.

[25] Michael Fletcher, "Crazy Horse Again Sounds Battle Cry," *The Washington Post,* Feb. 18, 1997, A03.

[26] Sheila Rush and Chris Clark, *How to Get Along with Black People,* copyright © 1972, Third Press, Joseph Okpaku Publishing Co., Inc., reprinted by permission of Okpaku Communications Corporation, New Rochelle, NY.

[27] Barbara Gold, "Diversifying the Curriculum: What Do Students Think?," *Diversity Digest,* Winter 2001, 12–14.

[28] Howard Ehrlich, *Campus Ethnoviolence: A Research Review,* Institute Report 5 (Baltimore: National Institute Against Prejudice and Violence, 1992), 8.

[29] Cornel West, *Race Matters* (New York: Vintage Books, 1993).

[30] Ansley Abraham, *Racial Issues on Campus: How Students View Them* (Atlanta, GA: Southern Regional Education Board, 1990).

[31] Philip Milano and Larry Lane, *Why Do White People Smell Like Wet Dogs When They Come Out of the Rain?* (Orlando Park, FL: Y Forum, 1999), 2, 3.

[32] Pat Parker, *Movement in Black* (Ithaca, NY: Firebrand Books, 1978), 68.

Teamwork

6

Chapter Objectives

Upon completion of this chapter, you will be able to:

- Explain the importance of teams today.
- Explain the relationship between teamwork and success.
- Discuss the meaning and challenges of virtual teaming.
- Define leadership.
- Describe Hofstede's four cultural dimensions and the relationship of each dimension to leadership.
- List strategies for building high-performance teams.
- List and give examples of obstacles to teamwork.
- Define conflict and conflict management.
- List and briefly explain the approaches to conflict management.

The scene: You are a surgeon in a hospital emergency room in a large city. A patient arrives by ambulance. He is a young child who appears to have a disability. The child's breathing is heavy and he has a fever of 104 degrees. Because he is so anxiety-ridden, he can hardly talk. He seems to be complaining about his stomach. His parents, who are recent immigrants from Cambodia, are unable to say more than a few words in English. The doctor who is the resident in charge is a Filipino woman born in the United States in 1940. The anesthesiologist is multiracial and hearing impaired. In a few minutes, the radiologist will arrive: a Cuban-American who plans on retiring in a few months. Also present is the registered nurse, a 29-year-old of German and French descent, and a nursing assistant, a young Nigerian man who just completed his education. You and other members of this team must deal with this emergency.

TEAMS TODAY

The multicultural setting described above requires people from vastly different backgrounds to work as a high-performing team in a pressure-packed situation. If each of these health professionals is not committed to the team and to the task at hand,

FIGURE 6.1 Surgical team at Johns Hopkins Hospital. Their ability to work together under pressure can mean the difference between life and death. *(Courtesy of the Office of Communications and Public Affairs, Johns Hopkins Medical Institutions, Baltimore, MD.)*

their effectiveness as a group will be severely undermined. Additionally, each professional needs to be able to relate effectively to people who have different beliefs, communication styles, learning styles, educational levels, and cultural backgrounds. Situations like this, which require working together in the midst of diversity, are commonplace today (see Fig. 6.1).

Because diversity can interfere with unity, teams often fall short of their goals. An abundance of research on teamwork, cited throughout this chapter, points to diversity consciousness as a critical variable. Studies show that different perspectives, talents, and experiences make some teams stronger and others weaker. The difference often lies in the ability of team members to appreciate the value of their differences and take advantage of them. In spite of the growing prevalence of diverse teams, this ability is all too rare. Consequently, teamwork is one of the most important diversity skills we must learn, practice, and continue to develop.

Most people think of sports when teams are mentioned. However, athletics is only one of many areas in which you find teams. A **team** is simply a number of people who are involved in a cooperative effort. Each of us belongs to many teams. Sometimes we are put on teams and have no choice in the matter. At other times, we may join voluntarily or even create new teams. Your teacher might put you on a team in class. As a college student, you may choose to form study groups or join support groups. These groups also constitute teams. You may be asked to join a variety of groups, such as those dealing with student government or your academic major. Additionally, there are numerous teams in the workplace and in the community. These teams might focus on your responsibilities at work, recreational interests, and community activities. The key thing to remember is that you cannot avoid teams—they are part of everyday life.

People have a tendency to want to work with people who are similar to them. However, most teams are made up of individuals who are different in any number of ways. As stated repeatedly in this book, diversity means more than differences in race and gender. When talking about teams in the workplace, the concept of diversity includes many other differences, such as age, personality, learning style, leadership style, job position, and tenure. Your success on any job-related team will depend in part on your ability to relate to all kinds of people. As a team player, you will be able to contribute more. You and your organization will reap the benefits.

Interest in teamwork has grown significantly in recent years. Organizations are becoming more team oriented, flexible, and collaborative. Businesses are using teams to improve marketing, customer service, and productivity. Employees who worked by themselves are now being organized into teams. The composition of these teams is also becoming more diverse. As businesses reorganize, restructure, and downsize, people increasingly find themselves on teams with others who differ markedly in terms of their employment and educational backgrounds. Because of demographic changes, cross-cultural work groups are becoming the norm rather than the exception.

Technology and globalization are also altering the composition of teams. Technological advances are making it possible for teams to overcome geographical barriers in an instant. The ability to communicate clearly and quickly and to work together from anywhere in the world at any time provides teams with a distinct competitive advantage.

> *One hand cannot applaud alone.*
>
> —Arabian proverb

Teamwork at School

Teamwork, the coordinated effort by a group of persons working toward a common goal, has been found to be an effective way of improving academic achievement. It has been shown that studying in teams can improve your grades. At the University of California, many freshmen, especially African-American and Latino students, were having difficulty with the calculus course for engineering, math, and physics majors. These students who were struggling with calculus were generally hard-working, highly motivated, and smart. A wide range of remedial programs and tutorial services were provided, but none of them worked.

Uri Treisman, a faculty member, identified the students who were having problems. He surveyed faculty and spent hundreds of hours interviewing students and their families. He discovered that these students were generally "academic loners," meaning that they struggled with calculus by themselves. However, groups with higher grades, such as the Cantonese speaking students, studied differently. They regularly studied two to three hours each day by themselves *and* then studied in groups to tackle more difficult problems.

Using this approach, a model program was created for all students, which was eventually adopted by many other colleges. Students in need of help were still given difficult problems to solve. They were instructed to solve as many problems as possible on their own. When they got stuck, they were expected to solve the problems in small groups. Also, they were asked to explain their solutions to other members of their study group so that everyone could understand.

The grades at the end of the semester indicate that students who study in groups do much better than those who do not. Those in study groups are more apt to stay in school and not drop out. Why? Working on teams enables students to spend more time practicing how to solve problems. Students also know that they need to understand the problems completely in order to teach other students. These students, working in small groups, could motivate and support each other, move at their own speed, and relate to each other.[1]

Besides increasing student achievement, numerous studies show that teamwork among students is one of the most effective ways of breaking down cultural barriers. In one research study, students were asked to name six of their friends at school. Those in traditional classes, which emphasized competition rather than cooperation among students, named 10 percent outside of their race. Those in classes that promoted cooperative learning, named 38 percent.[2] Another study by Elliot Aronson illustrates the benefits of a teaming technique called the jigsaw method.

Research findings that point to the educational and social benefits of teamwork begin to make sense when we think about the relationships we develop in school. Typi-

The Jigsaw Method

Elliot Aronson was asked to devise an educational plan that would reduce interracial tensions among students attending public schools in Austin, Texas. Aronson developed a cooperative learning technique, the jigsaw method. Classes were divided into teams of six students. Students in each group were racially and academically mixed. Each day, individuals in each group were assigned one of six subtopics. After learning about that segment of the lesson, each student taught the other group members. The results showed a decrease in prejudice and an increase in self-esteem among students in the jigsaw groups. The academic test scores of minority students in these groups also improved. Unlike before, these students had to work and fit together like pieces of a jigsaw puzzle. If they were going to do well on the tests, they had to pay attention and support each other. In the process, they learned not only the subject matter but also some valuable lessons about each other.

Carlos, one of the students in Aronson's study, had learned to be quiet in school because he was not very articulate in English. In his jigsaw group of five students, Carlos' experiences were different. "It began to dawn on the students that the only chance they had to learn about Carlos' segment was by paying attention to what he had to say. If they ignored Carlos or continued to ridicule him, his segment would be unavailable to them and the most they could hope for would be an 80 percent score on the exam—an unattractive prospect to most. . . . And with that realization, the kids began to develop into pretty good interviewers, learning to pay attention to Carlos, to draw him out, and to ask probing questions. Carlos, in turn, began to relax more and found it easier to explain out loud what was in his head. What they (students) came to learn about Carlos is even more important. . . . They began to like Carlos, and he began to enjoy school more . . . . After a few weeks, they noticed talents in him they had not seen before."[3]

cally, we learn more about each other in small group settings: an athletic team, a close circle of friends, or maybe a committee of some sort. Our learning increases when we depend on each other. We pay more attention to each person's talents and preoccupy ourselves less with differences that are irrelevant to the purpose of the team.

Research psychologist John Dovidio argues that getting people to cooperate, to work together as members of the same team, goes a long way toward reducing prejudice. In his experiments, he has put people of different races on the same team in order to examine group dynamics. When competing, the racial makeup of the team is not nearly as salient as the competition against another team. "We" versus "they" supersedes intragroup differences such as Black, White, Asian, and Latino. Furthermore, Dovidio's research reveals that when we categorize someone as belonging to another group, we tend to see that group as more homogenous than our own. These findings show the promise of dealing with prejudice indirectly, that is, getting people who normally would not work or socialize together to collaborate on some project at school or anywhere else for that matter.[4]

Social commentator Jack Kemp, who was the Republican Party's vice presidential candidate in 1996, often talks about the lessons in human relations that he learned playing quarterback for 13 years in the National Football League (NFL). John Mackey, who played against Kemp, remarked, "the huddle is colorblind." This was just another way of saying that when the quarterback gets in the huddle, the race of his teammates is the last thing on his mind. What matters is whether his offensive linemen, receivers, and running backs do their jobs and keep him from getting sacked or hurt.

Teamwork in the Workplace

At Ford Motor Company, different people with different ideas are included on teams to problem solve, innovate, and cater to new and emerging markets. A good example is the way Ford ensures that female perspectives are represented in the design of its vehicles. Female engineer and nonengineer workers create and evaluate concepts and features in the design of cars, vans, and trucks. As an example, the input of 30 female engineers known as the "Windstar Moms" helped make the Windstar minivan more appealing to its core customer base—women with children. Design features from the Windstar Moms include a rectangular cup holder for juice boxes, a larger gas tank so mothers can do more of their daily chores without having to stop as often for fuel, and a drop-down "conversation mirror" for checking small children in the rear seats. Other family-friendly features include a row of hooks across the back of the rear for plastic shopping bags and "sleeping baby lights" that permit parents to see their sleeping children.

Teams, particularly those made up of people from diverse backgrounds, are proliferating in the workplace. The accent on teamwork in the workplace is a surprise to many students. In college, the focus is typically on individual success and competition. According to Judy Blair, vice president of Recruitment and Career Development for American Management Systems, the teamwork focus "is often an adjustment from school where achievement tends to be individual and aimed at getting the best grade. . . . Although individual contribution matters in the workplace, the teamwork element is also key. Someone may be responsible for a particular aspect of work on a project, but collaboration and cooperation with others on the project is key."[5]

Teamwork is not sold as a technique for promoting human relations. Rather, it is viewed as good business. Many companies utilize **total quality management (TQM),** an approach for continuously improving the performance of every member of an organization. The idea behind TQM is that for organizations to compete effectively, employees must commit to and participate in the continual effort to improve quality. This includes employees at every level and in all areas of responsibility. One of the principal components of TQM is teamwork and the role it plays in the continuous improvement of a company's product or service. As more and more companies expand globally, teamwork is being sold as a means to increase productivity and profits. The idea of bringing the world closer together through teamwork is an effective marketing strategy. For example, Ford's home page for its Web site champions its worldwide connections, and Boeing refers to itself as "people working together as one global company for aerospace leadership."

Research findings point to the benefits of teamwork, especially when it involves people from diverse backgrounds. A number of academic studies show that diverse teams are more creative and innovative. At the University of North Texas, business students were divided into teams for a period of 17 weeks. Teams made up of students who were culturally and racially diverse were pitted without their knowledge against teams who were all White and much less diverse. During the first few weeks, the all-white teams sprinted ahead. But by the end of the competition, the more diverse teams were being more creative and flexible in the way they attacked and solved work-related problems. Larry K. Michaelsen, one of the three professors who conducted the experiment, commented: "Cultural diversity in the U.S. workforce has sometimes been viewed as a dark cloud. Our results suggest that it has a silver lining."[6]

Teams are not always necessary or desirable. Some tasks lend themselves to individuals. It may not make sense to form a team if time is a concern and the task is clear-cut and relatively simple. However, many tasks in the workplace are too complex and too demanding for one person. Moreover, some jobs require more cooperation than others. The same is true of sports and other activities. A long-distance truck driver does not need to possess the same teaming skills as a police officer, an airline pilot, or a member of the surgical team mentioned earlier in the chapter.

Employees who hoard information and are unwilling or unable to work together waste time and money. However, employees who thrive in a work environment of teamwork and information sharing are highly valued. From top management to workers in offices and factories, people who are adept at working in teams can pool their talents and be more productive. This is called **synergy,** the concept that members of a team interacting cooperatively will accomplish much more than if they act alone (see Fig. 6.2). In his book *The Seven Habits of Highly Effective People,* Stephen Covey uses this word to describe a problem-solving approach that is better than compromise. According to Covey, synergy makes it possible for one plus one to equal more than two.[7] Think of a time when you and other people were able to brainstorm about an issue or problem. What you came up with as a group was in all probability more creative and useful than anything originally proposed by a single person.

FIGURE 6.2   The power of synergy. Each year, more than 1,000 plebes (freshmen) at the U.S. Naval Academy team up to retrieve a cap placed at the top of the 22-foot Herndon Monument. Since the monument is covered with 200 pounds of lard, it often takes hours for the plebes to scale it. *(Courtesy of the Office of Media Relations, U.S. Naval Academy, Annapolis, MD.)*

Teaming Up for Taurus

For years, Ford Motor Company used a straight-forward process to design, build, and sell cars. The designers submitted their sketches to the manufacturing departments. The cars were then built and sent on to the sales department. Ford decided that it needed to take a different approach to create a new and competitive midsized car. They put the designers, manufacturers, and salespeople on one team. Each person was asked to describe his or her ideal car and submit a "wish list". The end product of this team effort was the Taurus, one of Ford's best-selling models.

Virtual Teaming

Computer technology is revolutionizing the concept of teaming. In today's world, virtual teams are enabling more people to link together at an accelerating rate. In their book *Virtual Teams*, Jessica Lipnack and Jeffrey Stamps contrast conventional and virtual teams. The authors describe a **virtual team** as a group of people that work "across space, time, and organizational boundaries with links strengthened by webs of communication technologies."[8] Virtual teaming allows our individual and group creativity to flourish by enhancing our ability to express ourselves. It can also significantly increase our ability to draw on the talents of a culturally diverse and geographically dispersed group of people. At the same time, the diversity of the group is often difficult to gauge unless it comes out in the course of communication or face-to-face interaction. When we communicate on the Internet, individual characteristics such as appearance, religion, and social class may be kept invisible.

According to research in the field of communications, the physical distance of team members and their use of electronic media can affect relationships. L. Sproull and K. Kiesler found that relationships via computers tend to be more democratic.[9] This is particularly true when people communicate anonymously. The message, rather than who is sending it, becomes the focal point. This encourages more input from people with diverse backgrounds and positions. One drawback of virtual teaming is that members tend to ignore each other's individual needs. When communicating from geographically disperse locations, desensitization to the values, goals, and competencies of individuals can occur easily.

Teamwork on a virtual team poses a number of challenges. Everything that can go wrong in a face-to-face team can also be a problem in a virtual team. A lack of trust, miscommunication, and conflict are even more problematic. Unfortunately, a good deal of training dealing with computer technology ignores the interpersonal dynamics of virtual teaming. This reinforces the idea that computers are tools for individuals, not groups. For members of a virtual team to be successful, they need to learn how to share their beliefs, knowledge, and skills. When communicating across distances, keep in mind the following strategies:

1. Share and clarify your group's mission and goals.
2. Openly discuss the challenges of virtual teaming and communication.
3. Be aware of the value of communication with other locations and invite feedback.
4. Identify and discuss differences. These differences may be cultural, organizational, or geographic.
5. Take advantage of any opportunities to meet face to face. This will personalize and reinforce relationships.
6. Seek and share knowledge. Do not hoard it. Hoarding delays results and works against synergy.

A Virtual Water Cooler

American Management Systems (AMS) describes itself as an international business and information technology consulting firm. It has thousands of people working on hundreds of projects in more than 50 offices worldwide. One of the ways in which AMS encourages the sharing of knowledge, experiences, and ideas is through *knowledge centers.* Throughout Europe and North America, there are knowledge centers or virtual AMS communities connected by interest and expertise. Each of these communities has a home page that serves as a "virtual water cooler." As with face-to-face interaction around a water cooler in a traditional at office setting, this home page provides the opportunity to chat and exchange knowledge about almost anything. Access to the knowledge centers may begin with a call to the "AMS-Know" hotline. The hotline can answer questions eight times faster than consultants do by themselves. According to the director of the knowledge centers, the hotline handled about 6,000 calls in its first year of operation and saved the company $500,000 in research expenses.[10]

AMS bases its high-tech approach to teamwork on the premise that their collective intellectual capital is more powerful than any one person's knowledge. Technology and communities allow AMS to communicate without regard to geographical boundaries. Consequently, the firm is able to "leverage the knowledge of a diverse population, people who have interests and expertise in common, but who are often otherwise dissimilar in terms of culture, industry expertise and often language."[11]

DEVELOPING TEAMWORK SKILLS

As part of your education, have you been taught how to work with people who commit themselves to a common purpose? Is your education providing you with opportunities to develop and practice teaming skills? Many employers believe that there is a mismatch between the skills that students need

THINKING THROUGH DIVERSITY

Given your plans for the future, how will developing teamwork skills benefit you?

when they enter the workforce and those they learn in college. This is particularly true in the area of interpersonal skills. Teaming, teaching others, negotiating, and managing people with diverse backgrounds are essential in today's workplace, although they are not always emphasized in the college classroom.

Interest in training related to teamwork has grown with the realization that working together does not necessarily mean working *together*. Good intentions or even a common purpose are not enough. Nor can we assume that people understand teaming is a process that requires education and experience. A variety of educational and training programs exist to help people learn and develop teamwork skills. Some examples follow:

1. One college program forms teams of engineering and business students to work in the classroom and at job sites on real-life problems. The program is based on the idea that students will be collaborating on teams in the workplace. Many of these teams will be cross-functional, meaning that people with different areas of expertise, backgrounds, and job functions will be working together.

2. Marines, from raw recruits to senior officers, go through a three-day test. The test emphasizes values, morality, and above all, teamwork. Marines are evaluated on their ability to work continuously as a team for 54 hours; they stand or fall as a group.

FIGURE 6.3 Students in the Colorado Rockies practice teamwork skills en route to their campsite. *(© Ken Krehbiel, Courtesy of Colorado Outward Bound School.)*

3. Companies are spending more time and money on team-building exercises outside the workplace. In business, programs such as Outward Bound teach the importance of teamwork and communication through physical challenges such as rock climbing and white-water rafting. These experiences help employees see each other without their titles. They also make it necessary to work as a single unit. For example, employees who might not trust each other have to help each other and work together in a rock-climbing exercise. If they do not, someone will get hurt. Ideally, this kind of teamwork will carry over into the workplace. Since programs of this nature are aimed at personal as well as professional growth, their appeal extends to people of all ages and interests including families, schools, and community groups (see Fig. 6.3).

4. Airlines have crew resource management (CRM) training programs. CRM focuses on promoting teamwork among cockpit crew members by improving their communication. Crews are put through various flight exercises in aircraft simulators. The trainers videotape and analyze the interaction of crew members and their ability to respond to emergency situations. The possibility that a number of airline crashes have resulted from certain commands being misinterpreted or ignored by the captain or the rest of the crew has provided the impetus for such training.

5. Sports psychology has become a big-time industry in recent years. Sports psychologists are in demand, in large part, because of their expertise in the area of team building. Dr. Colleen Hacker, a "mental skills coach" with a degree in sports psychology, works with the U.S. women's national soccer team to improve their team chemistry, focus, and confidence in each other. Hacker challenges people's assumption that "team chemistry" is a noun, a quality that simply exists. She sees it as a verb, as something you do. Therefore, her team-building activities provide action-based learning environments to help individuals and groups develop "the intricate web of connections that exist among any group of diverse people, talents, roles and abilities."[12] In one of her team-building drills, the U.S. team drove to the top of a cliff in Portland, Oregon. Hacker blindfolded half of the team, and instructed the remaining teammates to lead them down a steep, narrow ledge. Their biggest weapon, according to the players, is "their uncommon bond as teammates and friends."[13] Like other sports psychologists, Hacker tailors team-building activities to the age, maturity, and conflict tolerance of the group.

DIVERSITY CONSCIOUSNESS AND TEAMING

Diversity consciousness develops over time. As it grows, we become better able to deal with team members, who in all likelihood will have a wide variety of values, personalities, behaviors, and abilities. Therefore, we are in a position to contribute more to a team.

> *None of us are as smart as all of us.*
>
> —Japanese proverb

Every team is diverse. In any team, group members vary in background, knowledge, and attitudes to some degree at least. People may even view the concept of team building differently. What is the role of an effective team member? Does it mean being assertive and outspoken or agreeable and a good listener? Is it necessary to build trusting relationships among members before any action can be taken? Is it OK to "rock the boat" or is maintaining harmony of utmost importance? How you answer these questions may depend on your personality or cultural background or even the setting.

Picture yourself in a class of students. You are put in groups at the beginning of the semester. Prior to each test, time is set aside in class so that each group can review the material. Although some students may prefer to defer to other group members, your instructor has made it clear that she wants everybody to be part of the discussion.

Some students may find this experience very traumatic because they are not comfortable in small group settings. A young female, raised to believe that women should be seen but not heard, may struggle with her role in the group. A group member from Japan or Laos might stress the importance of being courteous and cooperative. However, team members who were born and raised in the United States may be more apt to speak their minds, even if it results in conflict and confrontation.

Cooperative Learning Among Hmong Adults

The Hmong are the largest ethnic minority in Laos. Many Hmong refugees resettle in the United States. When Hmong adults participate in American basic education, their cultural background affects their classroom behavior. Through participant observation, a researcher from the University of Wisconsin was able to study a class for nonliterate and low-literate Hmong adults.

According to the researcher, these Hmong students view classroom work as a cooperative activity. They are constantly in touch with each

continued

Cooperative Learning Among Hmong Adults (continued)

other and are hesitant to be singled out as being more able than their peers. The stronger students help the weaker students. Students check each other's books, papers, and worksheets. Interestingly, there is no competition. The researcher observed. "When Mee Hang has difficulty with an alphabetization lesson, Pang Lor explains, in Hmong, how to proceed. Chia Ying listens in to Pang's explanation and nods her head. Pang goes back to work on her own paper, keeping an eye on Mee Hang. When she sees Mee looking confused, Pang leaves her seat and leans over Mee's shoulder. She writes the first letter of each word on the line, indicating to Mee that these letters are in alphabetical order and that Mee should fill in the rest of each word. This gives Mee the help she needs and she is able to finish on her own. Mee, in turn, writes the first letter of each word on the line for Chia Yang, passing on Pang Lor's explanation".[14]

THINKING THROUGH DIVERSITY

Consider the times you have participated on teams. When was diversity within these teams an asset? Why? And when was it a liability? Why?

Group differences are only an asset when members develop the competencies needed to utilize the assets and meet the challenges of diversity. By becoming more conscious of diversity, you will improve those skills that are essential for true teamwork; these include communication, conflict management, empathy, self-evaluation, and leadership. In turn, developing these skills will expand your diversity consciousness.

1. *Communication.* Since people process information in different ways, it is important to utilize a variety of communication styles (see Chapter 5). For example, team members may be more productive and creative if they constantly combine visual, verbal, and experiential modes of communication.

2. *Conflict management.* Dealing effectively with conflict requires fundamental skills in interpersonal relations. These skills, which include showing empathy and listening actively, can help team members work through and benefit from conflict. Conflict in groups is discussed in more detail toward the end of this chapter.

3. *Empathy.* Author Stephen Covey views empathy as the most important skill we need for teamwork. He argues that all members of a team must really listen and "put themselves in other people's shoes."[15] This skill creates the openness that allows creativity to flourish. It also helps us to realize that there is more than one way to accomplish a task.

4. *Self-evaluation.* As a team member, you need to evaluate your performance continually. This is particularly important in self-managed work teams. To use Langer's terminology, replace mindlessness with mindfulness. *Mindlessness* blots out intuition and much of the world around us. *Mindfulness* raises our consciousness and awareness.[16] Although total self-awareness is virtually impossible, ask yourself questions that focus on how you see yourself and others. Such questions might include:

- Are there parts of myself that I do not share with others?
- Am I comfortable with myself and other team members?

- What do I know, think, and feel about team members?
- How do my emotions, values, and experiences affect my ability to work *with* other team members?
- How do I handle conflict and change?

5. *Leadership.*   **Leadership** is the ability to influence group members and enable them to work together to achieve their goals. Leaders succeed through the efforts of others. By inspiring a "team culture," leaders help group members sacrifice individual goals and agendas for the common good. By moving with ease across personal and cultural boundaries, leaders unify, empower, and, if necessary, heal. Increasingly, leadership is expected of all group members rather than a select few. When we learn to accept and share leadership, we are able to bring out the best in everyone. For example, you may show leadership when you fill a particular role in a group. Perhaps you take on an assignment that no one wants. Or maybe you help other members work through conflict that threatens your ability to function as a team.

TEAM LEADERSHIP

As work teams become more global and heterogeneous, leaders will need to develop their diversity consciousness. Moreover, leadership skills are becoming increasingly important for everyone. Employers typically expect workers with widely different job functions and levels of authority to assume leadership roles. As an example, it is not unusual for management to delegate responsibilities to workers, who then organize teams and get the job done with little if any supervision. These are sometimes referred to as *self-managed work teams*.

Many companies have found that self-managed work teams raise product quality and lower employee absenteeism. Suarez Electric Company, one of the fastest-growing Latino-owned companies in the United States, illustrates this kind of shared, team leadership. The owner, David Suarez, divides his workforce into teams. Each team is delegated the responsibility of doing their jobs and *not* accepting mediocrity. At each job site, there are usually one or two leaders. Although Suarez provides minimal supervision, he is always accessible through his pager and cellular phone.

Like other skills related to diversity consciousness, we can learn and develop leadership skills. John Kotter's *The General Managers* is based on his study of the traits of top executives. The author, a professor at Harvard Business School, found that effective leaders are trained and learn to develop their own potential. According to Kotter, the careers of effective general managers are distinguished by almost constant growth in their interpersonal and intellectual skills and in their relationships with "relevant others."[17]

What qualities do you think make a leader effective? This question was asked of a wide cross section of employees in public, private, and academic institutions. Their answers point to specific attitudes and behaviors each of us can develop over time. Based on responses from these employees, a model of effective leadership emerges.

In this study, effective leaders are described as "pluralistic" because they are adept at working with many diverse populations. As pluralistic leaders, they:

- *Are open to change based on input and feedback from the team.*   In particular, they are open to diverse views and encourage others to disagree. They value feedback and are not defensive when their opinions are challenged.
- *Empower others.*   They have a coaching style that is encouraging rather than conforming. Moreover, they give timely, constructive, and honest feedback.
- *Have a broad knowledge and awareness of diversity issues.*   They do not wait for others to educate them, rather, they seek out information from a variety of sources. Those surveyed often point to a leader's language and communication skills as a gauge of personal understanding. Specifically, pluralistic leaders use inclusive language, adapt to different communication styles, and quote diverse resources.
- *"Walk the talk" when it comes to diversity.*   It is not enough just to say the right thing, they lead by example. A pluralistic leader shows that he or she values diversity by taking a stand and being a catalyst for change.[18]

Pluralistic leaders such as William Pagonis combine expertise and empathy. Pagonis learned to be a leader in places like Vietnam and Saudi Arabia. As head of the U.S. Army's 22nd Support Command fighting in the 1991 Persian Gulf War, he came to understand the vital importance of empathy. He says, "We asked ourselves constantly: What do the other people on our team need? Why do they think they need it, and how can we give it to them?"[19] Empathy, according to Pagonis, helped him learn when and when not to adapt.

In one instance, for example, troops were unloading supplies into a building that was situated next to a particularly devout Muslim community. The sight of female soldiers with uncovered hair and rolled-up sleeves offended these Muslims. Before the situation developed into a crisis, it was decided that U.S. military personnel would wear long-sleeved shirts and female soldiers would wear hats. Another point of contention had to do with female soldiers driving vehicles and carrying weapons, activities that were prohibited for Saudi women. This time Pagonis stood firm—making it clear that all soldiers, including females, need to be able to use the tools of their trade.

There is more than one way to be an effective team leader. **Instrumental leaders** tend to focus more on the task at hand and less on how group members get along. **Expressive leaders** take a different approach. Their primary concern is the well-being of group members and their ability to work as a unit. Some leaders are both instrumental and expressive or find that different situations require different approaches.

For example, imagine that you are asked to lead a task force at work. You are given a relatively short period of time to gather information, analyze it, and submit a report to your supervisor. Seven other employees whom you hardly know have also been appointed to work with you. Which type of leader are you going to be in this situation? Given the fact that you need to produce a report quickly, you might prefer to focus on making sure that your team completes its job. However, what if the people on the task force find it difficult to get along with each other? Is this something you can afford to ignore? What about your own personality? Do you feel equally comfortable as an instrumental or an expressive leader?

Leadership in a Cultural Context

In different cultures, there are different views regarding what a leader should do. For instance, people in the United States do not expect leaders to be infallible; but people in many other cultures are much more unforgiving when one of their leaders admits a mistake. Geert Hofstede, an international management scholar, surveyed more than 116,000 workers in 40 countries, all of whom were employees of International Business Machines (IBM). Not surprisingly, he found that a country's culture had a profound effect on workers' attitudes and values. Hofstede's framework for understanding cultural differences helps us understand that principles of sound management, or effective leadership strategies, are not universal.

The data show that these cultures differ along four dimensions. Hofstede emphasizes that within a culture there is considerable variability; therefore, each dimension represents an average pattern of beliefs and values found in a particular country. Different countries show greater or lesser amounts of each dimension. The dimensions include individualism versus collectivism, power distance, uncertainty avoidance, and masculinity-femininity.[20]

Individualism versus Collectivism

This dimension refers to the degree to which cultures emphasize the importance of individuals (individualism) as opposed to groups, such as the extended family or an organization (collectivism). Individualism reinforces people's reliance on self, and encourages a greater concern with one's own interests. Collectivism reinforces a greater reliance on others, and a greater concern for the welfare of others.

- *Examples of highly individualist countries.*   United States, Australia, the Netherlands, Great Britain.
- *Examples of highly collectivist countries.*   Colombia, Singapore, Pakistan, Japan.
- *Leadership.*   Leadership in collectivist societies is more of a group phenomenon. Workers bring considerable loyalty to their jobs and place their utmost faith in leaders. In return, workers expect leaders to show loyalty as well by looking out for the workers' best interests. Leaders in the United States, found to be highest on the dimension of individualism, tend to prioritize an individual's needs. The self-interests of leaders and followers tend to be more important than the group.

Large or Small Power Distance

This dimension refers to the degree to which power is distributed unequally. In large power distance cultures, significant inequalities among people are both accepted and expected. Small power distance cultures, however, play down inequalities in power and wealth as much as possible.

- *Examples of large power distance countries.* The Philippines, Colombia, India, Singapore.
- *Examples of small power distance countries.* Denmark, Israel, Australia, United States.
- *Leadership.* In a large power distance society, leaders lead autocratically. Employees show a great deal of respect for those in authority. A person's title and rank is socially significant, and impacts greatly on interpersonal relationships. Students, for example, are expected to treat an authority figure such as a teacher with a great deal of respect and deference. In the United States, the relationship between those in authority and subordinates tends to be more egalitarian, but the power still remains with the leader. For instance, teachers in the United States often seek more input from and delegate more authority to students. Nevertheless, the relationship between students and teachers remains hierarchal.

Strong or Weak Uncertainty Avoidance

This dimension refers to the degree to which ambiguity and uncertainty are tolerated, and absolute truths are avoided. In societies characterized by strong uncertainty avoidance, risk and uncertainty are avoided if at all possible. People in weak uncertainty avoidance societies do not feel nearly as threatened by behavior and opinions different from their own.

- *Examples of strong uncertainty avoidance countries.* Greece, Turkey, Japan.
- *Examples of weak uncertainty avoidance countries.* Sweden, Great Britain, Ireland.
- *Leadership.* In strong uncertainty avoidance societies, followers create a feeling of security by relying heavily on leaders. Business leaders and organizations in a strong uncertainty avoidance society are people whose word is accepted as a kind of law. These leaders are apt to have more rules and tolerate less deviance from those rules. In the United States (weak uncertainty avoidance), leaders are more inclined to take risks, tolerate deviance, and encourage employees not to back down but to speak their mind. This type of leadership strategy is seen as a way to promote new ideas.

Masculinity versus Femininity

This dimension refers to the degree to which gender roles are differentiated and valued. Some societies allow males and females to assume many different roles, whereas others make a sharp distinction regarding what males and females should and should not do. Hofstede refers to "masculine cultures" as those that sharply delineate gender roles and attach more importance to roles associated with males, such as assertiveness and independence. "Feminine cultures," as defined by Hofstede, are those that distinguish among gender roles to a lesser degree and attach more importance to roles associated with females, such as relationship-oriented activities and interpersonal sensitivity.

- *Examples of feminine cultures.*   Sweden, Norway, the Netherlands.
- *Examples of masculine cultures.*   Japan, Austria, Germany.
- *Leadership.*   Of the countries he surveyed, Hofstede found Japan to be the most masculine country, with very strong sex role differentiation in leadership. In contrast, leaders in the United States were found to view these traditional sex role divisions as outdated and stereotypical, but expectations based on traditional roles remain nonetheless.

Hofstede's model forces us to expand our view of leadership. Traditionally, leadership has been evaluated from a narrow, ethnocentric perspective. Theories on leadership usually reflect a *micro-level orientation,* a viewpoint that focuses on interaction among individuals in specific settings. A *macro-level orientation* focuses on large-scale patterns of behavior in organizations, societies, and the world as a whole. By viewing leadership from a broader perspective, Hofstede shows the importance of evaluating leadership in a cultural context. Given the gap between countries on the four cultural dimensions, there is a strong likelihood that the leadership styles will be dissimilar and, in some cases, markedly so. As an example, leaders from Australia or the United States (highly individualistic, small power distance) will probably have to radically modify their leadership styles if they find themselves in a country such as Colombia or Singapore (highly collectivist, large power distance). If they are not prepared for this degree of adjustment, the result could very well be **culture shock,** feelings of disorientation and stress due to experiencing an unfamiliar cultural environment.

Leadership Strategies

One of the major challenges that team leaders face today is how to manage and utilize the creative power of diverse work teams. Leaders, including those in business, government, education, healthcare, and the entertainment industry, adopt a variety of techniques to cope with this challenge.

1. A top-ranking government official manages her team by hiring "top-notch" people from all walks of life. She then gives them a great deal of freedom and support. By discussing issues and problems one-on-one with as many people as possible, she gets more input. The result is that she can choose from more varied and creative solutions. Additionally, more people buy into the solutions since they are part of the decision-making process.

2. Leaders of one large corporation now refer to employees as associates. This new terminology was partly in response to data collected from a survey of its employees. Findings from the survey indicated that many employees did not feel they were part of any group. Consequently, they were not inclined to think in terms of the company's welfare. Both employees and management view the term *associate* positively because it makes titles unimportant. Treating each other as associates symbolizes a willingness to work together as equals.

3. A few years ago, a multicultural executive team was assembled to build a record company. With most record labels, white and black employees have traditionally been segregated into different music departments. At this company, the leadership seeks to diversify the racial and cultural composition of work teams. These teams market and promote pop, rock, rap, and rhythm and blues records. The result is phenomenal. Not long ago, this company had a greater market share than such established labels as Capitol and Motown Records.

4. One of the first actions taken by the president of a newly formed multinational organization was to restructure the organizational chart. He now refers to it as a "pizza chart" because it resembles a pizza covered with many pieces of pepperoni. The circular shape of the pizza shows the sharing of leadership in this organization as well as the inclusiveness. Pepperoni represents self-directed work teams and the role they play in carrying out key business functions. According to the president of this organization, the pizza chart "makes people take off their organizational hats and put on their team hats. It gives people a much broader perspective and forces decision making down at least another level."[21]

To summarize, leadership has become a necessary skill for everyone. Our diversity consciousness enhances our ability to lead all types of people in all kinds of situations. We are better able to relate to others, build cohesive relationships, and if necessary, mobilize people in order to get things done. Similarly, we are much more likely to be successful if we look to others to challenge and complement our thinking and come up with new ideas. Conversely, we severely compromise our effectiveness if we can relate only to people who think and act like us. Research shows that one of the primary reasons that managers and executives fail is their inability to build teams with colleagues. Regardless of our job function and position, our ability to lead and work with others will be tested.

▣ HIGH-PERFORMANCE TEAMS

> **Working Together Works**
> Working together can never be a policy.
> It can only be an idea.
> It can never be a code of rules.
> It can only be a way of looking at the world.
> We can say, "This is mine," and be good,
> or we can add, "This is ours" and become better.
> We can think, "I do my share," and be satisfied,
> or we can ask, "Can I do more?" and become prosperous.
> We can work along side each other and function,
> or we can work with each other and grow.
>
> —Author Unknown[22]

High-performance teams do not just happen. They evolve over time and require people who possess certain talents, a wide range of diversity skills, a common vision, and a strong commitment to the team. They develop something Albert Bandura refers to as **collective efficacy,** people's shared belief that they are capable of effecting change and making a difference.[23] Reflect on the teams to which you belong in school, at work, or in your community. On which teams do people work well together? Which teams do the best job of making people feel included? Which teams accomplish the most? High-performance teams are not necessarily made up of the most talented individuals. In sports, it is not uncommon for a team of superstars to get beaten by a team with much less individual talent. Things such as team togetherness, commitment, and communication can be as, if not more, important than raw talent (see Fig. 6.4).

THINKING THROUGH DIVERSITY

More often than not, teams operate at less than peak efficiency. Why?

Research has shown that it is not enough simply to include diverse and capable people on a team. High-performance and low-performance teams differ in how they manage diversity. "When well-managed, diversity becomes a productive resource to the team. . . . When ignored, diversity causes process problems that diminish the team's productivity."[24] For a moment, think of the storyline from *The Wizard of Oz*. In a training video for business, a management expert analyzes the team that Dorothy built. Her team consists of a scarecrow, a lion, and a tin man. Each character has a different talent. Together they delegate tasks, take risks, establish trust among themselves, and pursue a common goal. When managed effectively over a period of time, their diversity allows them to empower each other.

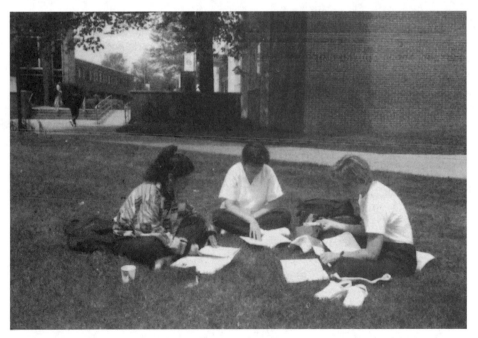

FIGURE 6.4 A study group of students can develop into a high-performance team over time.

In real life, team members need to come together, coalesce, and realize their common purpose in much the same way. According to B. W. Tuchman, periods of conflict (called *storming*) will occur. Often, it will take considerable time and effort to develop a sense of trust and cohesiveness, as well as a common understanding regarding the norms or rules of the team and its mission (called *norming*).[25] Although the development of each high-performance team is unique, there are ten proven strategies to keep in mind.

Ten Proven Strategies for Building High-Performance Teams

1. Get to know each other first.
2. Make sure that you understand your role and the team's goal(s).
3. Respect the ideas and feelings of other team members.
4. Manage conflict effectively.
5. Continue to build relations with other members of the team.
6. Think and act like a team.
7. Decenter and recenter.
8. Avoid groupthink.
9. Be flexible.
10. Periodically assess the team's performance.

With each of these strategies, what is involved, and why is it important? A brief explanation follows.

1. *Get to know each other first.*   Before you start focusing on the task at hand, take some time to learn about group members. What are your interests at home and at work? What special talents do each of you have? What is distinctive about your personal and professional backgrounds? Sharing a part of yourself with the group initiates the process of establishing and nourishing a comfort zone in which to operate. It brings out individual differences and similarities and uncovers team members' skills. Although becoming acquainted takes time, it is worth it. If you ignore this step, there is a good chance that you will encounter problems later.

2. *Make sure that you understand your role and the team's goal(s).*   High-performance teams unite around a common vision. Team goals, team knowledge, team skills, and even team problems should be your focus. Also, everybody needs to understand what part they play and how every part is vital to their success as a group. If certain people feel that others do not want or value their input, commitment to the group is likely to be weak.

3. *Respect the ideas and feelings of other team members.*   This helps to create an open, supportive environment that allows team members to feel comfortable and express themselves uniquely. Building diversity consciousness in yourself enhances your ability to value what each member brings to the team.

4. *Manage conflict effectively.*   By doing this, different agendas and competitive struggles do not drain the energy of the group or threaten group cohesion and morale. Conflict management strategies are discussed later in this chapter.

5. *Continue to build relations with other team members.*   Sometimes, high-functioning teams are described as having the right "chemistry." Typically, this is something that evolves over time. To complement others, you need to know something about them. Over time, for example, my wife and I have learned to work as a team. When it comes to computer technology and anything of a mechanical nature, I tend to look to her for help. If we need groceries, she invariably seeks my advice. I cut out the coupons, read the ads, and buy virtually all of the food for our family. With other tasks, our skills are more similar than complementary. It is important to remember that utilizing our respective strengths does not just happen magically. It requires hard work, mutual respect, and continual learning about each other and ourselves.

6. *Think and act like a team.*   Put your attitudes and individual egos aside. Bill Russell, one of the greatest basketball players in the history of the sport, explains that he was extremely egotistical. "But my ego always was a team ego," he adds. "My ego was totally linked with the success of my team. It wasn't linked to personal achievement. It was linked to team achievement."[26]

7. *Decenter and recenter.*   As discussed earlier, synergy occurs when the sum total of a group is greater than its parts. Decentering and recentering represent two techniques for achieving synergy in a diverse team. When you decenter, you and other team members shift your perspective and adopt multiple points of view. Recentering allows each member to identify and construct a common vision. Both are critically important and interconnected.

8. *Avoid groupthink.*   As mentioned earlier, groupthink is the tendency to go along with a group and discourage differences of opinion. When this happens, every voice is not heard and teamwork suffers. Part of the lure of groupthink is that decisions can be made quickly. This often becomes an overriding concern in a society such as ours which revolves around deadlines and emphasizes immediate results. In a high-performance team, the mindset of the group does not constrain or stifle you. Rather, you are comfortable raising issues, challenging others, and being yourself.

9. *Be flexible.*   Exercise "give and take" as needed. For example, be willing to give help and receive help. When necessary, assume the role of a leader in order to mobilize the team for high performance. Similarly, there are situations that require you to be a good follower. This might mean taking directions and accepting criticism from someone who thinks differently than you.

10. *Periodically assess the team's performance.*   High-performance teams evaluate their strengths as well as their weaknesses. By making this a group priority, you can examine group processes with more precision and confidence. In turn, the team not only builds on its successes, but also learns from its failures.

Realize the process of building a high-performance team is not linear. It has its ups and downs. Reaching decisions may take longer. You can do your part to construct a high-performance team by keeping track of where you are and where you are going. Are you helping to create a climate of trust, commitment, cooperation, and flexibility? When you assume leadership, is it empowering or conforming? Finally, do you really believe in the value of diversity and what each member brings to the group?

> *When spider webs unite, they can tie up a lion.*
>
> —Ethiopian proverb

⚙ OBSTACLES TO TEAMWORK

Numerous obstacles can detract from the synergy of a team. Some can be traced to the thinking and behaviors of individual members; others originate outside the team. Obstacles, such as those that follow, compromise a team's potential.

1. *Social values.*   Teamwork can be difficult in a society that stresses the importance of individualism and competition. Common sayings in the United States, such as "make your own breaks" and "look out for number one," support values that may undermine teamwork. As an example, U.S. workers are sometimes reluctant to share their ideas because they fear that someone else might get the credit. Contrast this kind of thinking with the African saying: "One finger cannot pick up a grain."

Musical Chairs

Susan Takata, a professor at the University of Wisconsin, uses the game of musical chairs to teach students the value of cooperation. The game, as it is traditionally played, teaches the value of competition and "going for yourself." Participants walk around a number of empty chairs while music is being played. When the music stops, they scramble to find a seat. Because there are not enough chairs for everyone, one person is left standing. It is a win–lose situation.

After playing this game by the traditional rules, Takata introduces a twist. The chairs are reset, the music begins, and Takata tells the students to find either a lap or a chair to sit on. As she gradually removes chairs one by one, students must become more creative and cooperative. Afterward, students analyze how they feel about the two games and why they reacted the way they did.

2. *Stereotypes.*   One popular exercise used in diversity training illustrates the negative effect of stereotypical images on teamwork. A label is placed on each person in a small group, such as leader, secretary, newcomer, rebel, and idealist. Participants are instructed to treat each other according to his or her label. Then they are assigned a task. What evolves during this role-playing is typical of what takes place in teams on a daily basis. If we let stereotypes cloud our thinking, it becomes difficult to move beyond these labels and interact with each other as individuals.

3. *Unequal distribution of power.*   In the context of teamwork, power affords you the opportunity to participate in decision making, access resources, make yourself heard, and make things happen. In some cases, an imbalance of power or a disagreement regarding the implications of power can sabotage team goals. As an example, it may be difficult for supervisors and their subordinates to work together as a team. A subordinate may be afraid to talk openly and honestly to his supervisors because of the power they hold. A supervisor may perceive her subordinates as rebellious or militant when they speak out or resist going along with the group. Because of their relative lack of power, subordinates may be expected to keep a lower profile.

4. *Disagreement over the roles of team members or the team's mission.*   Think of a team as an interlocking set of gears on a machine. Each gear needs to do its part and work together in order for the machine to run smoothly and efficiently. This same set of dynamics governs a team. Team members need to agree and be clear regarding their individual responsibilities and collective goal or goals. If not, roles will overlap and time as well as effort will be wasted.

5. *Unequal treatment or the perception of unequal treatment.*   Discrimination is one of the surest, quickest ways to sabotage teamwork. It undermines trust and cohesiveness. It arouses anger and makes it more difficult to focus on the task at hand. Excessive avoidance or acquiescence replaces genuine interaction. Psychologically speaking, the group mentality shifts to "us" versus "them."

6. *Lack of communication or miscommunication.*   Communication is the "glue" that holds a team together. It is the vehicle by which people come together, share, and learn from each other. Unfortunately, open, honest, and clear communication is a rarity on many teams. As teams get larger and more heterogeneous, communication styles and skills tend to become more numerous and differentiated. This makes it difficult for a team to develop a common language.

7. *Lack of outside support.*   Teams do not operate in a vacuum. They connect to other teams, organizations, and the larger community. External support can take many forms, including funding, volunteer help, and commitments from organizational and community leaders. A team that feels cut off from the outside world will probably find it difficult to sustain any amount of synergy.

As we develop diversity consciousness, these obstacles to teamwork will become more visible. Furthermore, we will have a vast array of skills at our disposal to possibly prevent, minimize, or overcome such obstacles.

CONFLICT

Conflict is the struggle that results when two or more parties perceive a difference or incompatibility in their interests, values, or goals. It can occur between individuals as well as among and within groups, communities, and societies. Every time we interact with someone, there is the potential for conflict.

A variety of individual, group, and cultural differences may give rise to conflict. More specifically, it may stem from misunderstandings as well as different interests, values, and needs. Within a team, potential sources of conflict include stereotypical assumptions, discriminatory behavior, and disagreements regarding the roles of team members and the team's mission.

> *Absolute calm is not the law of the ocean. And it is the same with the ocean of life.*
>
> —Gandhi

What comes to your mind when you hear the word *conflict?* When I pose this question to college students, the answers I get typically portray conflict as problematic or negative. Some of the terms that students use are *disagreement, "attitude," problems, trouble, fighting, frustration, anger,* and *tension.*

Traditionally, conflict has been viewed as a negative in the United States. It is seen as something that stands in the way of communication and teamwork. Therefore,

FIGURE 6.5   Chinese characters for the word *crisis.*

some people assume that we should avoid conflict at all costs. Although conflict can have negative consequences, it can have positive outcomes as well. At school, conflict can increase your achievement by motivating you to work harder. It can also be a learning experience that deepens your understanding of a problem. Conflict in your personal life can make you stronger and strengthen your relationships with others. In the workplace, conflict can bring certain issues out into the open and in some cases bring people closer together. It can stimulate creativity and signal a need for change.

Richard Tanner Pascale, author of *Managing on the Edge: How the Smartest Companies Use Conflict to Stay Ahead,* examines a number of innovative organizations that actually embrace tension. He cites Honda as an example. With its "contention-management system," Honda seeks to find the proper balance between debate and harmony. Subordinates openly, but politely, challenge their bosses. Takeo Fujisawa, the cofounder of Honda, compared the challenge of fostering openness and questioning to conducting an orchestra. "As president, you must orchestrate the discordant sounds into a kind of harmony. But you never want too much harmony. One must cultivate a taste for finding harmony within discord, or you will drift away from the forces that keep a company alive."[27]

> *In my marriage, I am often the one who is wrong in the conflict. It hurts, it's not pretty, but that is where the real growth starts and I am better for it. Even with all the affirming, it still is an uncomfortable experience.*
>
> —Another perspective

> *Without struggle there is no progress.*
>
> —Frederick Douglass

In Chinese, the word *crisis* is created by using two characters, representing both danger and opportunity (see Fig. 6.5). Without a crisis or conflict of some sort, personal growth is often impossible. For example, take the smallest and most intimate of all teams—a marriage. Many of us grow up with the belief that a perfect relationship is one in which conflict is avoided or absent. However, that kind of relationship is not realistic or productive. Two people have different needs, values, and priorities. These differences often result in conflict. Although conflict may be emotionally difficult and painful, it needs to be addressed for growth to occur.

Conflict Management

The effect that conflict has on us depends largely on how well we manage it. **Conflict management,** the process by which conflict is dealt with in an effective and constructive manner, is a key diversity skill. To develop this skill and understand the causes and consequences of conflict, we need some knowledge of subjects such as history, sociology, economics, and psychology. Of equal importance are basic interpersonal skills. In some cases the management of conflict results in resolving or eliminating conflict by changing how we relate to an issue and/or each other. There are other circumstances when it makes sense to avoid or smooth over conflict. Although this does not necessarily make the conflict go away, it might very well be the prudent thing to do in a particular situation. A variety of approaches to managing conflict are discussed later.

People who manage conflict well at school, work, and home have an advantage. The issue is not whether people experience conflict but how they experience it. While conflict frustrates and stymies some people, others seem to take it in stride and even thrive on it. The difference in how people react has a lot to do with their upbringing, cultural background, and people skills. In his book *Conflict: Resolution and Prevention,* John Burton argues that it is important to take a proactive approach to conflict.[28] Dealing with conflict proactively means that we prepare ourselves for conflict in advance. In other words, it is important to develop our conflict management skills continuously.

Learning to deal effectively with conflict is a skill that expands both your diversity consciousness and your chances for success. It builds your self-respect and increases your confidence in yourself. Your interpersonal relationship skills benefit as well. These include your ability to communicate, cooperate, negotiate, manage your anger, and exercise self-control. In addition, working through conflict in a constructive way helps you to develop your cognitive skills. You will become a better problem solver by developing your understanding of the sources, dynamics, and effects of conflict.

THINKING THROUGH DIVERSITY

Think back to a situation in which there was conflict that you needed to manage. How did you deal with the conflict? What was the outcome? What did this experience teach you about conflict management?

Approaches to Conflict Management

Different situations may require different approaches. Flexibility is key. Sometimes, situations call for strong responses, and sometimes the response needs to be more gentle. The setting, as well as the people and their relationships to each other, need to be taken into consideration. If your boss at work comments "You're so articulate for a foreigner," you might feel rage, hurt, or a mix of positive and negative feelings. Depending on how you feel, you might want to hit her or him over the head, ignore it, or explain why you find this "compliment" offensive. Your ability to control your feelings, consider the consequences of your actions, and act accordingly will be pivotal to your success on the job.

Cultural differences need to be taken into consideration. Although we should not jump to conclusions about people because of their cultural backgrounds, it is important to be sensitive to the impact that culture might have on managing conflict. For example, what do you assume about people who disagree on important issues? Can they work through their differences and interact effectively? When confronted with an argument, do you look at all sides or presume automatically that there are only two sides? Do you assume that if people think differently, they must be opposed to each other? People's responses to these questions have a lot to do with their cultural backgrounds. For example, in many Native American and Asian cultures, people view differences or opposites existing in harmony. Humans or things are not either this *or* that; rather, they overlap and interconnect. The ancient Chinese concepts of yin and yang illustrate this kind of thinking. Differences can be interactive and even complementary. Instead of simply focusing on differences, the concept of yin–yang reminds us to search for common ground.

Yin and Yang

The dark and light halves of the yin–yang symbol represent the two sides of a hill, one shadowy and one sunny. Although the outer circle of the symbol shows that yin and yang are not two separate things, the small black and white dots in the symbol show that yin and yang contain the seed of its opposite. Like day and night, one cannot exist without the other. Viewing conflict in terms of yin and yang helps us realize that sometimes there are more than two sides to an issue. Similarly, differences do not necessarily have to result in opposition.

According to Deborah Tannen, author of *The Argument Culture*, Americans traditionally assume that opposition is the best way to get things done. As a result, people are inclined to settle their differences by resorting to debate, fighting, and lawsuits. There is an emphasis on finding fault rather than solving a problem, having an argument rather than making an argument, and winning the argument rather than understanding another point of view.[29] We can find evidence of this emphasis in the metaphors we use. Examples include phrases such as the "battle of the sexes" and the "war on drugs." The power of words to shape perceptions has been substantiated by research. Phrasing a conflict as "Black" versus "White," "rich" versus "poor," or "old" versus "young" is counterproductive. It not only forces people into two artificial, opposing camps, but it may also alienate or exclude many people.

THINKING THROUGH DIVERSITY

What is one issue that elicits considerable disagreement among college students? Can you think of more than two sides to this issue?

Approaches to Conflict Management: The 6 C's

When you encounter conflict, you may choose to communicate, circumvent, confront, conform, compromise, or collaborate.

Approach 1: Communicate. With dialogue, people who hold conflicting views on divisive and emotional issues are brought together to talk, listen, and learn. Unlike a debate, the goal is not to score points. As an example, the Public Conversations Project is an initiative that has brought people with strong differences together to converse on such potentially volatile topics as sexual orientation, abortion, and the environment. The project team establishes certain guidelines to ensure that conversations are respectful and constructive. Project leaders encourage participants to avoid name-calling, stay on task, and give everyone "a home in the conversation." Dialogues do not necessarily resolve the conflict or significantly change positions on an issue. However, they can open up lines of communication and help people see each other as people rather than enemies. When this happens, people's views can shift ever so slightly and new options may emerge.

Conflict and Communication

Conflict can make person-to-person communication particularly difficult. Anger and ill feelings can easily get in the way of meaningful dialogue. One way to work through conflict is to view communication as a building process. Breaking the process down into steps can help you take advantage of the opportunities conflict affords.

1. Share information. Use the "I feel" formula. Each person should state the problem clearly. Try not to blame. Rather, focus on how you feel as a result of what happened. For example, I feel _____ when you _____ because _____. In stating how you feel, try to avoid words such as *angry* or *mad*. Be more specific, such as I feel "left out" or "embarrassed."
2. Explore differences and similarities in your assumptions.
3. Try to understand the perspectives of others through deliberate, active listening. Chinese distinguish between listening or *ting* (attending to the other person with your ears, eyes, and heart) and simply hearing.
4. Brainstorm possible solutions. Determine the advantages and disadvantages of each.
5. Try to agree on a solution that is fair to all.

Approach 2: Circumvent.   There are times when it is necessary to avoid or get around conflict in some way. Sometimes, you may feel as though you want to "fight the world." Everything seems to be a source of potential conflict. To keep from being overwhelmed, you may find it necessary to "pick your battles." In other words, choose what to fight and what to avoid. Sometimes the situation might be too volatile. Maybe the timing is bad and people need to "cool off." After thinking it through for a while, you may even discover that you are at fault or overreacting.

Some students encounter the possibility of conflict on an everyday basis. A gay woman comments: "I unfortunately very often feel different from my fellow students and instructors. Working in the dental hygiene clinic, I have heard negative comments regarding gay people. They come from department coordinators, instructors, and students. The interesting aspect of it is they include me in these discussions, never thinking for a moment that I might be gay. It is funny how people just assume that sometimes. I know in these situations I just have to play the game. There are too many people to deal with, and I know it would not be in my best interest to come out. I have also been warned by other gay women who have graduated from this program to remain discrete. The program is tough enough as it is. I think it is better in this case to avoid unnecessary emotional turmoil."

Approach 3: Confront.   In some instances it is necessary to be assertive and take action immediately. Maybe it is a matter of speaking up for yourself or someone else. A person's safety may be an issue. Certain conflicts may result in people being denied respect or even basic human rights. For example, what if a coworker or your boss tells you the latest "Polish joke"? You might respond by informing the coworker that you find this joke offensive. With your boss, you might simply not laugh and walk away. Remember: Confrontation need not be overtly challenging to be effective.

Confrontation may also be necessary when people show a lack of respect for certain cultural traditions. Put yourself in the position of a person who has to take time off from work or school to observe a religious holiday. If you are denied this opportunity or penalized in some way because of your religious beliefs, you have the right to take whatever action is necessary to ensure that your rights are not being violated.

Approach 4: Conform.   There may be times when you feel that you have to smooth over conflict or simply "give in" because you do not want to upset or jeopardize your relationship with others. The people may be more important than the issue. In some instances, conformity is a short-term solution. For example, you may find yourself in a no-win situation with your parents. They make it clear to you that they do not approve of the fact that you are unmarried and living in a co-ed apartment. Consequently, they have asked you to avoid talking about your living arrangement when other people are present. Although you may disagree with your parents and even think of them as old-fashioned, you respect their strong feelings on this issue and conform to their expectations.

Approach 5: Compromise.   With this approach, all the parties feel they can give a little. A typical example is what happens when students reside in a college living unit. Students living in close quarters are likely to prefer different kinds of music. Chances are they will play it softly or loudly at different times of the day and night. Given these differences, compromise is often necessary.

A widely used program that teaches students the need for compromise is the "Model United Nations." Using a realistic simulation of the actual United Nations, its purpose is to bring students together to discuss real-world issues. During these discussions, conflicts arise that students need to resolve. A student UN delegate comments: "My experiences as a delegate allow me to see the world through others' eyes. Passing substantive resolutions is extremely difficult. Many end up being watered down to make them agreeable to countries."

Approach 6: Collaborate.   Rather than taking sides or compromising, we may reach agreement by finding some common ground. Collaboration requires creativity and "buy in" from everyone. Maybe you remember a time when you were part of a group that was trying to solve a problem of some sort. No one could agree on a solution. Each person felt strongly that his or her approach was right. Nevertheless, all of you were determined to find a solution that was satisfactory to everyone. After brainstorming for a while, someone came up with a great idea that was surprisingly simple. Everyone immediately felt a collective sense of relief.

There is no one correct approach to conflict management. An approach that works for you in one situation might backfire on someone else. Sometimes, we can use a combination of approaches. As an example, confrontation may lead to communication and even collaboration. The situation as well as your own comfort level with various approaches are factors you need to consider. You may feel more at ease being confrontational at times, while someone else may prefer to avoid this approach at all costs. Remember that you will make mistakes. You might not control your anger, or perhaps you will avoid a situation you need to confront. Simply learn from your mistakes. Like team building, conflict management is a continual growth process.

Multicultural Mediation Team

Mediation is a give-and-take process in which a neutral third person (the mediator) helps disputing parties reach an agreement. Since mediators lack authority or power, their decision is not binding. This distinguishes it from **arbitration,** in that an arbitrator has the power to render a binding decision. Mediation is used in a wide variety of settings, including international conflicts, workplace and public policy disputes, and divorce proceedings. A skilled mediator may employ one or more approaches to conflict.

In recent years, a growing number of programs at all levels of schooling have initiated peer mediation. One such example is the Multicultural Mediation Team at the University of Massachusetts. The team hears disputes that revolve around such issues as race, gender, sexual orientation, and disabilities. The team is made up of 24 undergraduate and graduate students from extremely diverse backgrounds. As part of their training, they study mediation techniques, engage in case discussions, and role-play. The emphasis is on student mediators being able to understand themselves and others from a variety of perspectives.

The Ten Principles of Conflict Management

Regardless of your approach to conflict management, you may not always be able to control your emotions. This makes it more difficult to compromise, collaborate, or even communicate. The following principles of conflict management will help you manage your emotions, relate to others, and maintain your focus.

1. *Manage conflict in the early stages.*   Do not wait for it to explode. Conflict that we allow to build up, especially when communicating across a distance, is more difficult to resolve.
2. *Think through conflict.*   In other words, what is the conflict about, why does it concern you, and what would be a satisfactory solution for you and the other parties involved? Additionally, what do I need to learn and do to deal more effectively with conflict of this nature?
3. *Take enough time to get your emotions under control and gather your thoughts.* When you are angry, it is difficult to evaluate the situation from different perspectives. Ask yourself "Is this the best time and place to resolve this?" "Are my feelings under control?" "Is there enough privacy?" As you deal with conflict, try to be constantly aware of your own thoughts and feelings. This can help you avoid a destructive power struggle.

> *As a child, people picked on me because I was the quiet one, the "nerd." I took martial arts. It gave me discipline, self-motivation. It taught me not to resort to violence every time a problem arises. It taught me to tone down my temper, keep it under control.*
>
> —Another perspective

4. *Listen actively.*   Pay careful attention to what you and others are saying and feeling. Listen to the total message rather than what you want to hear. Try restating what you think the other person is saying before responding. Active listening coupled with good feedback promotes understanding.

5. *Watch your body language.*   Most certainly, there are times when you share something very personal and important to you. If the person with whom you are talking appears disinterested, how does that make you feel? How does it affect your communication? As you interact, be aware of your body language. For instance, nodding your head and leaning forward while seated in a chair shows your interest. Leaning back, crossing your arms, pointing your finger, or smiling during a heated discussion might put others on the defensive. Keep your non-verbal language consistent with your verbal message.

6. *Keep an open mind.*   Realize that your view is just one way of looking at things. Instead of asking yourself how you can win, ask yourself what you can learn. Also, be alert to the influence of cultural differences. You might discover that because of a person's cultural background, dealing with conflict face-to-face is not as effective as a written exchange. Or perhaps because of different cultural beliefs, questions that seem only natural to you might be at odds with someone else's attitudes toward disclosure. For example, "What was the conflict about?" "What was your role?" "How do you feel about the conflict?" may come across as intrusive and inappropriate. Therefore, a lack of cross-cultural sensitivity may lead to inaccurate conclusions.

7. *Criticize ideas, not people.*   Keep your focus on the issue or issues. Insulting or blaming people blocks communication and results in destructive conflict.

8. *Ask questions rather than assume.*   You can only guess what another person is thinking. Keep checking out your assumptions. Accept and respect corrections from others.

9. *Try to put yourself in the other person's place.*   Bernard Guerney states: "Once you have placed yourself 'inside' the other person, 'walk around' in there. Ask yourself: If I were this person, what would I be thinking?. . . How would I be feeling? What would I be wishing for?"[30] This does two things. First, it helps you get a better idea of someone else's perceptions, beliefs, and wishes. Second, it helps you react in a way that is respectful and caring.

10. *Be willing to change.*   You are at a severe disadvantage if you are extremely rigid in your thinking and locked into your approaches or solutions to conflict. A willingness to change allows you to turn conflict into opportunity.

Like many other diversity skills, the management of conflict is a critical component of teamwork. Although teamwork is not necessarily one long-drawn-out battle, there will be times when conflict occurs. Conflict can tear a team apart and waste human potential. As a team member, you can help make conflict a growth experience. This is clearly not easy. It takes knowledge, skills, and commitment on your part. How well you and your team work together in the face of conflict will have a significant impact on your individual and collective success.

Throughout this chapter we have explored a variety of issues and concepts related to teamwork. We examined how teams are changing and why employers attach so much importance to teamwork. Additionally, we focused on the relationship between teamwork and diversity consciousness. Finally, we addressed a variety of obstacles that can make teamwork difficult, if not impossible. Developing and refining diversity skills, such as communication, conflict management, and leadership, makes it possible to recognize and overcome these obstacles.

 CASE STUDIES

Case Study One

Usually in meetings on her job, Ligua is very passive. She doesn't speak up. She thinks this might have something to do with her upbringing. Ligua was raised not to push, not to be aggressive. If she has something to contribute at meetings, she hesitates. If somebody else receives credit for work she does, she finds it difficult to open her mouth and say, "That was my work. I did that."

Ligua has been working at her present job for the past five years. Recently, three individuals with less experience than Ligua were promoted to positions with some managerial responsibilities. She has begun to wonder why she hasn't been offered a similar promotion, especially since her evaluations have been excellent. When she arranged for a meeting to discuss this matter, her supervisor initially was taken aback. She was under the impression that Ligua was content with her position. As they talked, it became apparent that Ligua's supervisor thought she needed to be more outspoken, and assume more of a leadership role. Also, the supervisor made the comment that some of Ligua's coworkers perceive her to be too "soft," someone who needs to be less concerned with people's feelings and more concerned with holding people accountable. However, her supervisor could not be any more specific and refused to mention names.

Questions:

1. When Ligua asks for feedback regarding her prospects for promotion, what might her supervisor do differently?
2. Specifically, what teamwork skills does Ligua need to work on and why?
3. Considering that Ligua is planning on teaching in the future, what leadership skills might Ligua seek to develop? Why?

Case Study Two

At the children's mental hospital where Mary is doing her practicum, a multidisciplinary team is used to treat the child. Mary is part of a team that includes a social worker, psychiatrist, psychologist, psychology intern, psychiatric resident, nurse, and direct service associate. The members of the team are very diverse in terms of ethnicity, race, age, and experience levels. Mary's experience with the team has been great. Although a variety of disciplines are represented, everyone is treated equally and all ideas are heard and critiqued. As a result, the patient receives a high level of care.

Mary has heard from other social workers that at some hospitals all disciplines are not equally valued. Hospitals that operate out of the medical model may have doctors "running" the teams—doctors who do not place much importance on the opinions of professionals in other disciplines such as social workers. Katie, one of Mary's friends, is also completing a social work practicum at a local medical hospital. She often feels that the doctors do not listen to her ideas, as she is "just a social worker." Out of frustration, Katie is debating whether to continue working at this hospital since she does not feel valued. Additionally, she is beginning to have second thoughts about social work as her chosen profession.

Questions:

1. If you were Mary, what advice would you give Katie?
2. If you were Katie, what could you do to try to make the situation better?
3. What are the benefits of the multidisciplinary team approach at the children's mental hospital? What are the implications of this approach for the patients?

Case Study Three

Michael is a brilliant loner. As a student, he made a habit of avoiding group assignments and group work whenever possible. At work, he prefers to stay to himself. If he has to work with others, he prefers projects in which everyone has individual responsibilities. Teaming with coworkers, he feels, slows him down and lessens the quality of his work. Michael readily points to examples of his work on groups. In some instances, the final product, he thinks, is not nearly as good as what Michael feels he is capable of creating alone. When he is not the group leader, Michael feels as though his talents are underutilized. Invariably, he gets assigned tasks that do not challenge him.

In addition, Michael largely avoids interacting with other employees after work. He does not dislike other employees; rather, he feels somewhat uncomfortable. At company picnics and parties, he has a difficult time finding common ground in his conversations with coworkers. His taste in music, food, and entertainment is clearly not the norm. Since he is often one of only a few African-Americans at these functions, he feels "under the spotlight." Consequently, he relishes his time away from work, where he can be himself, play with his son, and relax.

Questions:

1. Michael's experiences at work illustrate obstacles to teamwork. What are these obstacles, and how do they interfere with teamwork?
2. What might Michael do to become more of a team player? What might his coworkers do to facilitate teamwork and help Michael feel more included?

 # EXERCISES

In-Class

Exercise 1: Obstacles to Teamwork

Directions for Instructor

Arrange five chairs in a semicircle at the front of the classroom. Ask five students to be *role-players*. Instruct them to sit in the chairs. Randomly, put a label on each one. Instruct the five students *not* to read their own labels. (*Note:* You might place the label on a hat or hang it around the person's neck.) The labels might read "smart and helpful," "knows a lot," "asks stupid questions," "idealistic," and "talks too much." Remember to position the label so that it can be seen by everybody except for the student wearing it. Position the other students in class so that they can see and hear the students in the semicircle. These other students will act as *observers*.

Role-Playing. Next, the five students will create and act out a scenario that takes place at school or in the workplace. For instance, students might imagine that they are members of a student committee discussing an issue of concern to the student body. Another possible situation might relate to work. Perhaps they are members of a task force looking into some aspect of employer–employee relations. The role-players have approximately 5 to 10 minutes to perform the scenario, treating each other according to her or his label. During this time, the observers will closely examine how the role-players interact. In particular, observers should focus on any obstacles that get in the way of teamwork. Observers should not interrupt.

Analysis. Finally, provide time to analyze what took place.

1. Ask each of the five role-players to try to figure out what is written on his or her label.
2. Ask the role-players:
   - How did it feel to be treated according to your label?
   - How did your label influence the reactions of others toward you? How did it influence your behavior? How did it affect the team's ability to work together and accomplish its goal?
3. Ask the observers:
   - Do you see this kind of thing happening at school or at work?
   - How can we create teams where labels like these do not operate?

Exercise 2: Teamwork in Motion

Directions for Instructor

You will need a number of sheets (or blankets) for this exercise depending on the size of the class. Mark one side of each sheet with "SIDE ONE." Throughout the classroom, place the sheets on the floor with side one facing up. Divide students into groups of at least six. Have each group stand on a sheet. Tell them they must flip the sheet over without touching the floor or stepping off the sheet. Specify the time for completing this task.

Analysis

1. Ask members of each group to explain how teamwork was/was not evident during this exercise.
2. Ask groups what they might have done differently to make better use of the talents of *all* group members.

Exercise 3: Cooperative Controversy

This group exercise is modeled after "cooperative controversy," a cooperative learning method that we can use to study an issue that generates a lot of disagreement.[31] When using this method, there are seven rules to follow.

1. I am critical of ideas, not people.
2. I remember that we are all in this together.
3. I encourage everyone to participate.
4. I listen to everyone's ideas even if I do not agree with them.
5. I restate what someone says if it is not clear to me.
6. I try to understand both (all) sides of the issue.
7. We first bring out all the ideas, then we put them together.

Directions for Instructor

Divide the class into groups of four. Each group will examine the following statement: "Students who dine solely with members of their own ethnic group and participate in ethnic student organizations and activities contribute to a decline of ethnic relations on campus." In each group, students should follow these steps:

1. Two students should argue in support of this statement and two students should disagree.
2. Switch sides and argue the opposite position.
3. Try to reach some consensus regarding the statement.
4. Have groups share their conclusions with the class.

Out-of-Class

Exercise 1: Conflict Management

1. Describe one example of conflict you encounter at work or school.
2. Explain how you manage the conflict.

3. Which of the 6 C's of conflict management (communicate, circumvent, confront, conform, compromise, collaborate) do you use, and why? Do you feel that you manage the conflict effectively? Why?

Exercise 2: High-Performance Teams

Form a team with other students in your class. Team members agree to use the "Ten Proven Strategies for Building High-Performance Teams" (see page 198). You will use these strategies throughout this exercise.

Task.   Find a high-performance team in your community. Write a report on this team that addresses the following:

1. Briefly describe the team: who they are and what they do.
2. Explain why you think members of this team work so well together and utilize everybody's talents.
3. Explain how members of this team promote teamwork. In other words, what things do they do to make sure that everyone is working together toward a common goal? What obstacles to teamwork do they encounter? How do they deal with these obstacles?
4. The last section of your report should focus on *your* team of students. How effectively did you work together? Of the ten strategies, which seemed to help the most?

Exercise 3: Team Journal

Select a team to which you currently belong. Keep a journal of this team for a week or more during the semester. Record your thoughts about any of the following:

- Conflict and how you as well as other team members manage it
- Assignment of tasks and roles
- Ability of the team to think and act as one
- Team leadership
- Communication among team members
- Ability of the team to utilize its diversity

Note: You may want to bring your team journal to class. As you discuss communication, diversity consciousness, and other concepts related to teamwork, refer to your team journal entries.

 INTERNET ASSIGNMENT

Find Web sites that address the concept of teamwork *or* virtual teaming. In particular, search until you find at least three sites that discuss the relationship between one of these concepts (teamwork, virtual teaming) and diversity. Write a one-page paper that summarizes what you found. Include the Web addresses in your paper.

NOTES

[1] Jerome Dancis, "Group Learning Helps Minority Students Excel at University," *Cooperative Learning,* 12(1), Oct. 1991, 26–27.

[2] Abby Karp, "Working Together: Innovative Programs Promote Tolerance in Schools," *The Sun,* Oct. 17, 1989, 1C.

[3] Elliot Aronson and Neal Osherow, "Cooperation, Prosocial Behavior, and Academic Performance: Experiments in the Desegregated Classroom," *Applied Social Psychology Annual,* 1, 1980, 174–175.

[4] Ellis Cose, *Color Blind* (New York: HarperPerennial), 226.

[5] Sherry Silver, "Advice for Adjusting to the World of Work," *Washington Post Advertising Supplement,* Oct. 19, 1997, 60, 65.

[6] Faye Rice, "How to Make Diversity Pay," *Fortune,* Aug. 8, 1994, 79.

[7] Stephen Covey, *The Seven Habits of Highly Effective People* (New York: Simon & Schuster, 1989).

[8] Jessica Lipnack and Jeffrey Stamps, *Virtual Teams* (New York: Wiley, 1997).

[9] L. Sproull and S. Kiesler, *Connections: New Ways of Working in the Networked Organization* (Cambridge, MA: MIT Press, 1991).

[10] Mark Mehler, "AMS Centers Deliver Global Information Access," *Integration Management: The Newspaper for Global Integrators,* 1(8), Sept. 18, 1997, 1.

[11] Sue Hanley, letter to the author, Dec. 22, 1997.

[12] "Team Building 101." Online, May 10, 2002. Available: http://www.eateamz.com/baseball/instruction/psych/article.cfm?article = tb101rl.

[13] Amy Shipley, "A Successful Science Project," *The Washington Post,* June 29, 1999, D1+.

[14] Christina Hvitfeldt, "Traditional Culture, Perceptual Style, and Learning: The Classroom Behavior of Hmong Adults," *Adult Education Quarterly,* 36(2), Winter 1986, 70.

[15] Stephen Covey, "How to Succeed in Today's Workplace," *USA Weekend,* Aug. 29–31, 1997, 5.

[16] E. J. Langer, *Mindfulness* (Reading, MA: Addison-Wesley, 1989).

[17] John Kotter, *The General Managers* (New York: Free Press, 1982).

[18] Marilyn Loden and Judy Rosener, *Workforce America: Managing Employee Diversity as a Vital Resource* (Homewood, IL: Business One Irwin, 1991), 180–195.

[19] William Pagonis, "Leadership in a Combat Zone," *Harvard Business Review,* Dec. 2001, 107–116.

[20] G. Hofstede, *Culture's Consequences: International Differences in Work-Related Values* (Beverly Hills, CA: Sage Publications, 1980).

[21] D. Sullivan, "Organization Structure in Multinational Corporations," in *International Encyclopedia of Business and Management,* M. Warner (ed.) (London: Routledge, 1996), 3595.

[22] "Working Together Works," Online, World Wide Web, Nov. 28, 1998. Available: http://www.diversitydtg.com/thoughts/thought_mnu.html.

[23] Albert Bandura, "Exercise of Human Agency Through Collective Efficacy," *Current Directions in Psychological Science,* 9, 2000, 75–78.

[24] N. Adler, *International Dimensions of Organization Behavior* (Boston: Kent, 1986), 111.

[25] B. W. Tuchman, "Developmental Sequences in Small Groups," *Psychological Bulletin,* 63, 1965, 384–399.

[26] Rick Pitino and Bill Reynolds, *Learn to Succeed* (New York: Broadway Books, 2000), 39.

[27] R. T. Pascale, *Managing on the Edge: How the Smartest Companies Use Conflict to Stay Ahead* (New York: Simon & Schuster, 1990), 26.

[28] John Burton, *Conflict: Resolution and Provention* (New York: St. Martin's Press, 1990).

[29] Deborah Tannen, *The Argument Culture: Moving from Debate to Dialogue* (New York: Random House, 1998).

[30] Bernard Guerney, *Relationship Enhancement Program,* 2nd ed. (Bethesda, MD: Ideals, 1997), 4.

[31] K. A. Smith, D. W. Johnson, and R. T. Johnson, "Can Conflict Be Constructive? Controversy versus Concurrence Seeking in Learning Groups," *Journal of Educational Psychology,* 75, 1983, 654.

7 Conclusion

Chapter Objectives

Upon completion of this chapter, you will be able to:

- Explain the value of diversity education.
- Explain why diversity consciousness will expand your opportunities for success in the future.
- Discuss three future challenges that will test your diversity skills.

The scene: As you walk down the halls, you hear many different languages. Flags hang in the front lobby of the school designating each student's country of origin. The principal can say "welcome" in a dozen languages. In her office, she makes a habit of displaying and rotating dolls and other cultural gifts she has received from students over the years. The school's philosophy is simply "the best way to learn about diversity is to live it." Thirty-nine countries are represented at Wellwood International Elementary School.

Teaching these youngsters, says one Wellwood teacher, means helping them adjust to a new way of life, including new customs and behaviors, even new foods. "There's a lot of acclimation that has to go on."[1] For example, some students have never eaten in a school cafeteria or seen a slice of pizza.

Wellwood International School provides us with one effective form of diversity education. In the process of working and learning together, Wellwood students develop diversity awareness and skills at an early age. They learn that people look different and may act different . . . and that is "OK." Students learn to help each other. For example, children who do not speak English are assigned a buddy. This type of buddy system challenges children to be creative. They have to figure out a way to communicate. At a very young age, these students are gaining skills that many adults lack.

FIGURE 7.1 Dance workshop. The arts provide us with a basis for engaging and communicating with each other, as well as the opportunity to discover "common ground." *(Courtesy of the Office of Communications, Colgate University, Hamilton, NY.)*

> *The best education for this world is one that gives students first-hand experience of diversity during their college years and includes multicultural fluency as a skill graduates are expected to acquire.*
>
> —Karen Kennelly, President, Mt. St. Mary's College

Diversity education extends over a lifetime. It involves much more than books, workshops, and dialogues about diversity issues. Indeed, some argue that one of the best ways to learn about diversity is through life experiences that *involve* diversity but are not *about* diversity (see Fig. 7.1). Former U.S. Senator Bill Bradley wrote: "Only through doing things together that have nothing to do with race will people break down the racial barriers . . . in a way that conversation cannot."[2]

Although Bradley focuses on the issue of race, what he says applies to all facets of diversity. One highly effective diversity education program cited by Bradley is Common Ground, held annually at Western Maryland College. This community program for people of all ages offers a wide variety of hands-on activities with master musicians, artists, and craftspeople. The thinking behind Common Ground is that the arts allow us to experience each other as artists, as human beings. Walt Michael, Director of Common Ground, expands on this idea. "You learn about yourself when you paint, play music or engage in some other art form. In the process of self discovery, a lot of stereotypes go out the window. As an example, our expectations about who prefers what kind of music might be reversed . . . maybe a black student becomes fascinated by blue grass music while a white student gets into the blues."[3]

OPENING OUR MINDS TO OPPORTUNITIES

Through perpetual learning, we increase our diversity consciousness. As previously stated, too often, we think learning about diversity is a single learning experience rather than something that is ongoing and lifelong. Building consciousness of this nature is a multifaceted process that requires our commitment, time, and energy. It reaches far beyond what takes place in a formal educational setting. Moreover, there is no optimal level at which we can stop. The greater our diversity consciousness, the more we realize how much more we have to learn and grow.

Education is our passport to the future, for tomorrow belongs to the people who prepare for it today.

—Malcolm X

The skills we acquire through this process, such as communication, teamwork, flexible thinking, and conflict management, will become even more important in the future. As change in our lives becomes even more rapid, we will need skills such as these to adjust. Viewing each new situation as one more opportunity to expand our diversity consciousness will ensure that we will not get left behind.

In the future, diversity consciousness will open your mind to new and exciting opportunities for a number of reasons.

1. *Diversity consciousness prepares you for life.* The more prepared you are for life, the greater your opportunities. The benefits of diversity consciousness extend far beyond a particular job or field of employment. By developing diversity consciousness, you have fundamental skills you need for *any* job. Furthermore, the value of these skills extends to one's relationships at home, at school, in the community, and elsewhere. As your consciousness builds within you in each of these settings, you are better able to meet the growing demands of your many roles.

It is very important for students to become not only knowledgeable in diversity but skilled as well. Valuing and understanding diversity allows students to handle themselves adeptly in a heterogeneous society.

—Andrea-Teresa "Tess" Arenas, Assistant to the President for Multicultural Affairs, University of Wisconsin System Administration

2. *Diversity consciousness empowers you and others.* It gives you skills that enable you to capitalize on your own potential and the potential of others. By way of illustration, learning about sociocultural theory (see Chapter 2) helps you recognize that which you can or cannot change in your life. A case in point is a heated discussion about social inequality that took place in one of my classes. Samuel, a student who has served time in prison, laments the lack of opportunities "out there." "All I see is negative," he says. "I see brothers on the corner selling drugs. I see prostitutes. I go back to my old neighborhood in L.A. Some of my friends went to jail, some got shot, and some are incoherent." From his point of view, he has few if any choices.

Other students take issue with what Samuel is saying. They argue that despite all the barriers—where he was born, who his friends are, his criminal background—he does have important choices to make. One student, who describes herself as a poor single parent, feels that Samuel is confusing "insurmountable barriers" with "stumbling blocks." She elaborates: "People who tell me I cannot do it or I am crazy for going to school and raising a child are stumbling blocks. They are easy to overcome because I do not let them mentally become a barrier. If I let these same people mentally debilitate me, then they become a barrier. They make me unable to use the one thing that could help me overcome them. That is my mind." This student was clearly empowered by her ability to make sense of the relationship between her environment and her choices in life.

If you can't see the top, how are you going to make it to the top?

⌘

Each person, whatever their diversity, needs to accept themselves and feel proud even in the face of oppression. Change takes time. But with education and understanding, piece by piece, the world can become a better place.

—Other perspectives

---

3. *Diversity consciousness changes the way you view differences.* Throughout this book, we examine how people view and react to diversity. Diversity consciousness gives us the awareness and understanding we need to embrace, value, and enjoy differences. If we only learned to appreciate one type of food, one type of music, or one type of recreational activity, think of all we would miss. American Express Financial Advisors, one of the largest financial planning companies in the United States, expands on this idea. "Our differences are what make us strong. . . . How dull to live in a world where everyone is the same. After all, it's our differences that make us learn and grow. It's our differences that shape who we are, who

Often we look so long at the closed door that we do not see the one which has been opened for us.

—Helen Keller

FIGURE 7.2 During the 2001 Super Bowl, Cingular Wireless ran an ad featuring Dan Keplinger. In the ad, Keplinger talks about the importance of self-expression. He concludes by saying, "I am so lucky." By highlighting his artistic ability and not his disability, the ad conveys a very positive message about diversity. Keplinger adds, the ad "is about me as an artist and that's who I am." *(Courtesy of Cingular Wireless.)*

we love, and what we believe. At American Express Financial Advisors, we encourage diversity in our workplace and we celebrate it wherever we find it."[4]

Recently, my youngest daughter shared her thoughts about people with disabilities. During the course of talking with her about her brother, who is autistic, she observed, "People see disability as a disadvantage, as something you're stuck with. But I see it as more of a gift." To me, that comment represents the promise of diversity consciousness. Because of this attitude, she sees things in her brother and in other people who appear different, things that others may not see. At times, the beauty of diversity is hidden from view because of our cultural lens, values, and assumptions. A disability, for example, does not hide the promise of diversity. Our culturally bound views do. When we learn to acknowledge, accept, and respect diversity, when we develop the realization that diversity is a gift, then we change who we are, our relationships with others, and our view of what is possible (see Fig. 7.2).

4. *Diversity consciousness prepares us for the future.* Donna Britt of *The Washington Post* writes, "There have never been so many nations within our nation, linked and separate, distant and rub-up against intimate. Never so many restaurants, markets, hair salons, doctor's offices and small businesses where English is barely spoken. So many enclaves where entire worlds exist, hidden or in plain view."[5] In the future, these trends will become more pervasive. The world's religions, languages, customs, and ethics will continue to find their way into our schools, workplaces, and neighborhoods regardless of where we live.

Embracing this diversity is imperative, according to Martha Barnett, former President of the American Bar Association. "People from various ethnic, racial and cultural backgrounds provide a wealth of talent, perspective, insight, and innovative thinking that we would not otherwise have. Our society can only become richer and healthier for the contributions that our diverse population brings."[6] Embracing and benefiting from diversity, however, is not a given. Nor is it linear. Rather, we will make advances, regress, and struggle with doubts about the value of diversity. But if we develop our diversity consciousness, we will learn to adapt to these changes and hopefully come to see diversity as a gift that enriches our lives in a multitude of ways.

FUTURE CHALLENGES

The relevance of diversity consciousness takes on additional significance when we examine future challenges. Because we do not anticipate or react quickly enough to change, many of us are not in a position to compete in the twenty-first century. Therefore, it is important to assess whether a gap exists between the skills we have now and those we need in the years ahead.

> *The day on which one starts out is not the time to start one's preparations.*
>
> —A Nigerian proverb

Our changing cultural landscape, discussed in the first chapter, is causing us to reevaluate how we view diversity. The elasticity of the term *diversity* makes it possible to constantly redefine and broaden what we know about human differences. Gradually, the term has become more inclusive and multidimensional. Our differences extend far beyond race, ethnicity, and gender. We are single and multiple jobholders, computer whizzes and phobics, auditory and visual learners, and so much more. Indeed, when we consider our inner dimensions of diversity, there are an infinite variety of possibilities. This is important to remember, especially as we learn more and more about ourselves and others.

Organizations have traditionally invested most of their time and money in training directed at technical skills rather than what has been termed "soft stuff" such as interpersonal skills. Nevertheless, in many cases it will be the breadth and depth of one's diversity skills that can either create problems or lead to success. Consider the advice given by Yvonne Chang, the Director of Corporate Affairs for American Telephone and Telegraph (AT&T) in Basking Ridge, New Jersey. She emphasizes that you have to "be flexible and have many different skills" to succeed in corporate America. "You can't be very good at one thing; you have to be good at a lot of different things. The most important things to have are diversity of knowledge, interpersonal skills, and an understanding of technology."[7]

The indispensability of diversity skills becomes even more apparent when we examine the social, technological, and economic changes that are occurring all around us. In the United States, knowledge workers and service workers continue to replace laborers. Consequently, different skills are necessary. For most jobs, skills that enable us to absorb and share information are more important than mechanical or physical abilities. The frequency of interpersonal, intergroup, and cross-cultural interactions is increasing as well. These changes, along with growing global competition, make diversity consciousness a business issue.

The days of people staying and working within a few miles of where they grew up is long gone. The norm is becoming two or three jobs in ten years with significant geographic moves to secure those jobs. And country boundaries are no longer a barrier as well. I looked around a recent meeting in our corporate headquarters and saw our female IT [information technology] specialist, executive vice president, a programmer from India, a division head from Italy, and a marketing manager from Ohio. It's people who are comfortable in this type of environment that will be successful. The stars of this new workforce will be those who can mediate these widely different working styles and get the most out of a broadly diverse group of people.

—Carl T. Camden, Executive Vice President for Field Operations, Sales, and Marketing, Kelly Services, a Fortune 500 staffing services company

A number of notable challenges lie ahead. Three in particular will test our diversity skills: technological change and globalization, changing demographics, and the potential for divisiveness. These challenges will have implications for each of us.

Technological Change and Globalization

According to *Workforce 2020,* technological advances will be one of the major forces shaping our lives in the early twenty-first century.[8] This report states that the pace of technological change has never been greater, and it will only accelerate in the future. The best jobs in the Innovation Age will be filled by those who possess the necessary skills. These skills will increasingly rely on brains rather than brawn. As "knowledge organizations" continue to proliferate, workers will have to keep pace with the need for continual learning and growth. If workers with a certain skill level cannot be found in the United States, companies will continue to look elsewhere.

Due to this change, the rest of the world will become more fused with our immediate world in the years ahead. James Becker, senior consultant at the Social Studies Development Center at Indiana University, states: "We don't look at the world as separate pieces of real estate, but as a society in which people interact in different ways."[9] The increased flow of communications, goods, and people is making distance less important. However, cultural barriers are much more difficult to overcome than geographical barriers. With globalization a reality today, it is becoming increasingly necessary to look at the "big picture" (see Fig. 7.3).

For those innovative, flexible thinkers who can adopt a multicultural perspective, globalization will open up opportunities. Conversely, ethnocentric thinking will be a liability to an even greater degree than it has been in the past. In a booklet titled *Transforming Higher Education: A Vision for Learning in the 21st Century,* Donald Norris and Michael Dolence state that tomorrow's student, teacher, and worker need to move beyond thinking "out of the box." Rather, they will need to see "around the curvature of the earth."[10]

FIGURE 7.3   Students, representing different regions of the world, work in teams to solve complex problems. This global simulation requires them to see across geographical and cultural boundaries. *(Courtesy of the Office of Communications, Colgate University, Hamilton, NY.)*

> *It is imperative that I develop a global perspective in order to attain a more definitive and unbiased perception of who I am, and not just who they say I am. If given the choice between the fish bowl and the ocean, I for one choose the ocean. To first understand it will make it easier for me to embrace it.*
>
> —Another perspective

As technology grows, globalization envelopes our lives. As one business consultant points out, the global marketplace is not only the Pacific Rim or faraway places. It includes downtown Toronto, Phoenix, Spokane, and lesser known places. In short, "the global marketplace is wherever organizations do business."[11] According to experts, U.S. companies that cannot understand what is going on around the world will not be successful at home or abroad. Consider a company such as Bank of America. Their employees work in 37 countries. Staff at their California customer service center can communicate in at least 13 different languages. This allows them to accommodate millions of customers who speak a language other than English.

THINKING THROUGH DIVERSITY

In what ways will an increasingly global environment alter the skills required by your chosen career?

In an environment becoming more global each day, it is absolutely essential to think and act inclusively. If our thoughts and actions are too restricted, we waste precious human resources and miss opportunities. Coopers and Lybrand, a professional services firm, captures this idea in one of its advertisements. The advertisement poses the question: "Who would you exclude from the future? Your choices include 730,000,000 people in the world with ideas to share; 4,000 languages in which to communicate; 255 nationalities with different perspectives and goals; 20 major religions with unique beliefs and customs; and 1 belief that everyone has something to contribute." The advertisement ends by stating: "You never know from where the next great idea will come."

Learning to Manage Globally

Do today's leaders have the skills they need in a global marketplace? According to a survey of 108 executives, 75 percent feel that their companies do not have nearly enough global leaders. Moreover, only a handful (8 percent) have programs in place to address this shortage. Data from the survey, which appear in the book *Global Explorers: The Next Generation of Leaders,* show about 80 percent of the executives feel overseas assignments are critically important.[12]

One example of diversity education that incorporates experiences overseas is the Fluor program. Participants in this program spend 12 to 18 months "living out of their suitcase" overseas. Their work on consulting teams assigned to operations worldwide means that they have to deal with numerous languages and complex cultural issues. They learn to think flexibly, process a large amount of information, and do their homework. Laws, government regulations, currency, transportation, credit systems, and political conditions are just some of the issues they must study.

One corporate leader, with multiple assignments throughout Asia, spends an inordinate amount of time learning how to conduct business in "Thailand versus Malaysia, or in the Philippines versus Japan." He adds that his overseas experiences sharpen his listening skills. By learning to ask more questions, he ensures that he and colleagues from other countries will understand each other.[13]

Changing Demographics in the United States

At present, we are in the midst of a rapid demographic shift. As the U.S. population grows more diverse and inclusive, a number of trends are increasingly evident:

- People of color are a growing percentage of the workforce.
- Whites are a decreasing percentage of the workforce.
- More women are working.
- People with disabilities are gaining more access to the workplace.
- Workers are increasingly from "nontraditional" families (single parents, dual wage earners).

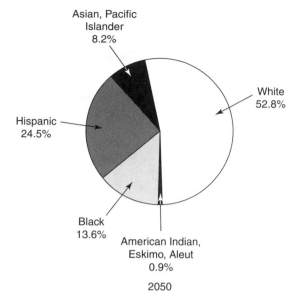

Asian, Pacific
Islander
8.2%

Hispanic
24.5%

White
52.8%

Black
13.6%

American Indian,
Eskimo, Aleut
0.9%

2050

FIGURE 7.4 U.S. population distribution: 2050 (projected; total population = 393.9 million). Data from the U.S. Census Bureau makes it possible to project the racial and ethnic distribution for the year 2050. Projections are based on estimates of future birthrate and immigration trends. *(From U.S. Bureau of the Census,* Current Population Reports, Series P25-1092, *U.S. Government Printing Office, Washington, D.C., 1992, and* Statistical Abstract of the United States, *1994, U.S. Government Printing Office, Washington, D.C., 1994.)*

- The average age of workers is increasing.
- The religious diversity of workers is increasing.

Within the lifetime of today's teens, population changes will significantly alter how we conceptualize age, race, and ethnicity in this country. According to the authors of *Workforce 2020,* "the American labor force will become somewhat more brown and black in the next 20 years, but its most pervasive new tint will be gray."[14] People over 85 are presently the fastest-growing segment of the U.S. population. America's aging baby boomers, those born between 1945 and 1965, will stay on the job longer and seek more flexible work options. Social institutions, such as the family, economy, education, and medicine, will have to adapt.

With regard to racial and ethnic diversification, Census data indicate a much greater percentage of the U.S. population (approximately 33 percent) will be Hispanic, Asian/Pacific American, and Native American by the year 2050 (see Fig. 7.4). The steady growth of intermarriage will continue to make the racial and cultural mix that much more blurred and complex. Many of today's youth will see the day when no one ethnic group—including Whites of European descent—makes up more than 50 percent of the nation's population.

If Census Bureau projections are on target, religious diversity will become even more noticeable. At present, Protestants account for roughly 56 percent of the total population, followed by Catholics (26 percent), Jews (2 percent), and Muslims (slightly less than 2 percent). If projections hold true, by the year 2050 no religious faith will constitute a majority. Two religious groups, Catholics and Muslims, are likely to experience the most growth during the next 50 years.[15]

My family looks like the U.N. It ranges from Jews to Buddhists. We have East Indians. We have a couple of American Indians, a couple of Europeans. My husband is from Lima, Peru. And it's great . . . . The fights we have in our family are not about color. They're about religion.

—Another perspective

Immigration will continue to drive population growth according to Census Bureau experts. Census 2000 figures show that foreign-born residents account for 11.1 percent of the nation's population, or about one in nine residents.[16] That percentage is expected to continue to grow, with the bulk of new immigrants not coming from Europe, but from other regions of the world.

Migration within the United States will continue to affect specific regions. For instance, in 1940, nearly 90 percent of Asian-Americans lived in the western United States. A study by Sharon Lee based on U.S. Census data and published by the Population Reference Bureau reveals only about 54 percent live in this region today.[17]

Developing our diversity consciousness will become even more critical as we attempt to meet the challenges posed by these demographic changes. Earlier, we examined how this process begins with an examination of our worlds and ourselves. We may, however, avoid self-examination by focusing on others. For example, a recent nationwide poll by *The New York Times* examined people's views of the present and future challenges posed by these demographic shifts. One of the more revealing findings from this poll relates to people's views of themselves and their neighborhoods versus the larger community and the country as a whole. In general, people believe that race relations are generally good in their neighborhoods, where they work, and at their children's schools. They depict themselves and their neighbors as open-minded, but are less positive about the rest of the country. As their attention moved away from home, respondents saw much more room for improvement.[18]

While it is tempting to focus on the shortcomings of others, the development of our diversity consciousness requires us to begin with ourselves. Throughout this book, one of the major themes has been personal growth. Our vision of the need for collective change becomes clearer when we acknowledge our own need to understand, learn more about others, and take action. For example, what are our innermost feelings about diversity? When does it nourish and sustain us, and when does it drain and paralyze us? Do we feel that everyone has something to learn? Have we come to the realization that our lives and futures are interconnected? Should we spend less time worrying about the intolerance of others and devote more time toward educating ourselves? Most importantly, where does this kind of questioning lead? How can we make a difference through our actions? And do we?

No matter what occupations or activities students pursue in the future, individual interaction will be more diverse than ever before in the history of this country. Most dramatic is skin color, culture/background and gender, but it will include many other differences and attributes.

—Frank Blethen, CEO of the Seattle Times Company

Continuing Potential for Divisiveness and Hope

Numerous surveys in recent years reveal that the growing diversity in the United States is giving rise to a sense of pessimism about the future. This pessimism is fueled by what many perceive as the downside of diversity and change. People are skeptical about whether the motto *e pluribus unum* (out of many one) can become a reality. Does the emphasis on diversity weaken our sense of oneness?

Initiatives aimed at recognizing diversity can have unintended effects. For example, misunderstanding and intolerance can become more of a problem if we do not handle diversity education with care. Some well-intentioned programs actually teach people to stereotype by ignoring the diversity within groups. Also, programs that focus exclusively on human differences may reinforce ignorance of our many similarities.

I have learned pain has no color; disappointment has no color; abuse has no color; caring, joy, hope, and happiness have no color; and above all, love has no color.

—Arnette Scott Ward, President, Chandler-Gilbert Community College

In all likelihood, hatred and hostility will continue to be a major social problem as our world changes. W. E. B. Dubois, civil rights leader and author as well as the first African-American to earn a doctorate from Harvard University, foresaw the potential divisiveness of diversity years ago. Dubois stated that the problem of the twentieth century would be the problem of the color line. In the 1960s, the historic Kerner Commission provided a similar warning. The Commission warned: "Our nation is moving toward two societies, one black, one white—separate and unequal."[19] Since that time, the lines or divides have been transformed. There are more divisions and inequality is more complex. While the race divide is still a central issue, it is one of many. A growing number of divides are economic as well as cultural.

THINKING THROUGH DIVERSITY

Where is the hostility in your life? Where is the hope?

A Shift in Attitudes Among Youth?

While some assume that divisiveness is on the increase, recent surveys of youth show a willingness to bridge at least some of our differences. One poll by *USA Weekend* magazine examines the attitudes of nearly a quarter of a million teenagers. Of those teens surveyed, nearly three out of four say that they have a close friend of another race.[20] Another *USA Today*/Gallup

continued

A Shift in Attitudes Among Youth? (continued)

survey of teens throughout the country reveals a similar trend. A majority of teens who report going out on dates say that they have been out with someone of another race or ethnic group.[21] Findings such as these may signal an important shift in attitudes and behavior in the future. Other surveys conducted in 1997 by MTV[22] and *Time*/CNN[23] show that young people tend to be more optimistic than adults. They generally see less divisiveness, fewer barriers, and more tolerance.

As we examine the negatives associated with diversity, it is important to remember how far we have come, both individually and collectively. William Raspberry, the noted journalist, says: "All of us are capable of getting so caught up in the distance that remains to be run that we forget to give ourselves full credit for the distance we've come."[24] It is all too easy to focus solely on our shortcomings and the social problems that have seemingly become a permanent fixture in our communities. We tend to do this because much of the change in the area of diversity is incremental and hardly noticeable. Additionally, what we read and see in the media often emphasizes the negative.

To focus only on the progress we have *not* made is to ignore reality. In your own life, think of the times when somebody was "hurting" and people helped. The fact that they did not share the same skin color, background, or values did not matter. What about the great relationships that you see among your friends and coworkers of various races and cultures?

On a broader level, it is important to remember the barriers of discrimination, segregation, and bigotry that have fallen. Alice Moy keeps her perspective by remembering her past. "It's like fifth heaven today I would say, for people who come over now. Opportunities galore. It wasn't available to us at that time, even though we were born here and we went to school here. Now I remember I had friends who attended and graduated from MIT, attended and graduated from Harvard—no one would hire them. Where did they end up? They ended up working for Chinese restaurants. No American firm would hire them."[25]

Change is one of the few things we can count on as we peer into the future. Technology, globalization, changing demographics, and the continuing potential for divisiveness will challenge our adaptability and our ability to get along with each other. If we can develop diversity consciousness in ourselves, we will be much better prepared to meet these challenges and open our minds to many more people, cultures, and opportunities.

The need for developing diversity skills on the part of our students extends well beyond their success in school and in the workplace. If our increasingly diverse society is to achieve its fullest potential, it will be because we collectively have made a deep and personal commitment to understanding "the other," to caring about "the other," and to having the skills to work together to shape a just and effective society.

—Lou Albert, Vice Chancellor of Educational Services,
San Jose Evergreen Community College District

CASE STUDIES

Case Study One

Periodically, Ligua thinks back to her childhood and wonders how much things have changed since then. In middle school, she had Anglo teachers that were surprised that she was Latina *and* smart. Some of them seemed to think that she could not fully grasp what was being said, and should not be considered for advanced placement classes. Ligua noticed that when white teachers worked one-on-one with white students, it was hands on. The teachers would lean toward the students and touch their hands or shoulders. But when working with her and other students of color, there was no leaning and no touching. She wonders if this kind of thing still goes on today. And if so, is it prevalent?

Ligua's educational experiences and those of her children provide her with the motivation to go to school, be a teacher, and make a difference. In one of her education classes, the teacher asked students to outline their *"sphere of influence,"* that is, those lives that they have the power to change. Ligua thought about this long and hard. Given her future as a teacher, she sees her sphere of influence growing and extending well beyond her family.

Case Study Two

According to Mary, her ultimate goal in life has a spiritual foundation. By spiritual, she does not actually mean religion, like going to church or some religious ritual. Spiritual success to Mary is how connected she is with herself, how much time she spends with herself, and how at peace she is with herself.

Deep down, Mary wants to do everything she can to change people's lives for the better. She wants to start in her community, by giving something back because she has been given so much by so many. Although she is not exactly sure of her career plans, Mary knows she wants to do something to motivate others, to give others a second and a third chance. Working at a food bank helped her realize this.

Mary has never experienced what it is like to go to bed hungry. Ever since she can remember, she always had the luxury of a well-stocked refrigerator and pantry to satisfy her appetite. When she was full at dinnertime, she threw away food that she didn't want. Untouched, forgotten food in the refrigerator was discarded without a second thought. She has always taken food for granted, including the fresh fish and poultry, fresh fruits and vegetables, and other foods she buys to keep healthy.

At the food bank, she remembers standing in an assembly line of volunteers like herself. For hours at a time, Mary performed the monotonous task of combining one tablespoon minced onion, six bouillon cubes, one scoop navy beans, and one scoop kidney beans. She mixed the seasonings in a small plastic bag, tapcd it shut, and then repeated this process. Initially, she did not find this experience particularly fulfilling. Mary did not really stop to think about what she was doing or for whom she was doing it. But when she was through, she saw the hundreds of plastic bags of soup. She knew that even though she wouldn't be there to witness it, those children and adults who do not have enough food or enough healthy food would appreciate her efforts. While not solving the world's hunger problem, Mary's efforts perhaps would help others in some small way. It opened up her eyes to a world that was invisible to her up to that point.

Case Study Three

Michael can still hear his wealthy grandfather, Grandpa Joe, refer to poor Whites as "white trash" and poor Blacks as "niggers." The forceful tone in Joe's voice when he uttered those words was something Michael always hated. Michael also remembers being scared when the two of them would drive through the "poor" part of town. Joe would go on and on about how "those people" lived and how they were too lazy to work.

Michael loves his grandfather because Joe is fundamentally a good man to his wife and his family, but Michael doesn't *respect* him. It bothers Michael that certain coworkers, with whom he shares an office, may be just as biased and ignorant as his grandfather, only they are more adept at hiding it.

Even though he is ashamed to admit it, Michael sometimes feels compelled to judge people the same way. "It's really easy to judge or exclude people based on their social class," he says, "But it seems to be much more admirable to recognize what people of all social classes have to offer." How to do that, he thinks, is one of his biggest challenges.

 EXERCISES

In-Class

Exercise 1: Checking Up on Yourself

Directions for Instructor

Randomly assign students to groups. Ask students in each group to:

1. Explain how their diversity skills (i.e., communication, teamwork, conflict management, flexible thinking) will affect their plans for the future.
2. Discuss how their perceptions of diversity have changed during the course of the semester, and what might have precipitated this change.

Exercise 2: A Look Back

Directions for Instructor

Ask students to:

1. Write down *one* thing they will remember most about this class in the future. It can be anything—an important concept, a funny story, someone's comment, an assignment, discussion, or something else that relates to the class.
2. Share what they wrote with the entire class. Consider forming a circle and using a pencil or some other object as a "talking stick." Traditionally, in decision-making meetings, Native Americans sometimes pass around such a stick to show

whose turn it is to talk. Only the person holding the stick can talk. All others should actively listen and express their desire to participate nonverbally.

Out-of-Class

Exercise 1: The Transformation of Barbie

The Barbie doll is the world's best-selling toy. Three Barbies are sold every second. Sales each year exceed $2 billion. In recent years, Barbie has undergone significant changes in order to broaden her appeal. According to one toy analyst, Barbie is like Betty Crocker. Her looks get updated to keep up with the times. Answer the following questions regarding Barbie and her transformation.

1. Find someone who remembers what Barbie dolls looked like 20 to 30 years ago. Ask this person the following questions. How did Barbie look years ago? Describe her physical appearance. What about her occupations? Could you choose the race or ethnicity of Barbie? Was it different from today's Barbies?
2. Visit a local toy store and see what kinds of Barbie dolls are for sale. Do you think the image of Barbie has been altered? Why? Is the change driven by financial and/or social concerns? Explain. Finally, what do you think of the changes?

Exercise 2: Stretch Targets

Situation: You are a city employee. As one of five employees in the Department of Tourism, you are responsible for finding new and innovative ways of increasing the number of tourists visiting your city. Recently, the mayor attended a conference in which he learned about using *stretch targets* to increase worker productivity. Stretch targets are "gigantic, seemingly unreachable milestones . . . which require big, athletic leaps of progress."[26] The mayor has sent out a memo asking all employees to establish one stretch target in the area of diversity.

Directive: Specifically, you are to write a memo to the mayor and clearly explain (a) your chosen stretch target, (b) how it relates to your job, and (c) how you will evaluate your progress in reaching the goal or target. The memo states that your response to the mayor should be no more than one typewritten page.

Exercise 3: A Classroom for All

Situation: You have been appointed to serve on a statewide task force on higher education. Your work on the task force requires you to create an orientation course at the college level for incoming freshmen. The purpose of this course is to acquaint students with the skills they need to be successful. Your responsibility focuses on the part of the course that deals with diversity skills.

Directive: Submit an outline of the diversity skills to be taught. Briefly describe:

- Each skill.
- The connection between the skill and student success.
- Ten specific resources that students will use. These may include videos, books, journal articles, and Web sites. List the skill or skills *each* resource addresses.

INTERNET ASSIGNMENT

Using the Internet, find two diversity training programs. These programs should approach diversity training differently. What are the major differences and similarities in the programs? Based on the information available, which of the two do you think would be more effective? Why? Support your answer and be as specific as possible. Include the URL for each Web site.

 NOTES

[1] Carol Sorgen, "Wellwood School Teaches Diversity Every Day," *The Sun: A Special Advertising Section,* Mar. 3, 2002, 6.

[2] Bill Bradley, "How America Can Make Brotherhood Work," *Reader's Digest 75th Anniversary Issue,* 1997, 96–101.

[3] Walt Michael, letter to the author, Jan. 9, 1998.

[4] Richard Gaskins, letter to the author (attachment), Nov. 9, 1997.

[5] Donna Britt, "Relishing Region's Many Hues," *The Washington Post,* Oct. 15, 1999, B1.

[6] Martha Barnett, letter to the author, July 2, 2002.

[7] Jerry Berrios, "A Balancing Act," *LATINA Style,* 3(2), 1997, 24–28.

[8] Richard W. Judy and Carol D'Amico, *Workforce 2020: Executive Summary* (Indianapolis, IN: Hudson Institute, 1997).

[9] Karen Rasmussen, "Gaining Perspective on Global Education," *ASCD (Association for Supervision and Curriculum Development) Curriculum Update,* Summer 1998, 3.

[10] Donald Norris and Michael Dolence, *Transforming Higher Education: A Vision for Learning in the 21st Century* (Ann Arbor, MI: Society for College and University Planning, 1995), 3.

[11] Trevor Hitner, letter to the author, Mar. 15, 1998.

[12] Hal Lancaster, "Learning to Manage in a Global Workplace," *The Wall Street Journal,* June 2, 1998, B1.

[13] Ibid.

[14] Frank Swoboda, "Study: Many in Graying Work Force May Not Have the Green to Retire," *The Washington Post,* Apr. 18, 1997, G3.

[15] U.S. Bureau of the Census, *Statistical Abstract of the United States,* 1994 (Washington, DC: U.S. Government Printing Office, 1994).

[16] Stephen Dinan, "Immigration Growth at Highest Rate in 150 Years." Online, June 5, 2002. Available: http://www.washtimes.com/national/20020605-76931088.html.

[17] Nicole Koch, "Asian-Americans Have Become Fastest-Growing Ethnic Group," *The Dallas Morning News,* June 9, 1998, 4A.

[18] Kevin Sack and Janet Elder, "Poll Finds Optimistic Outlook But Enduring Racial Division," *The New York Times on the Web.* Online, July 11, 2000. Available: http://www.nytimes.com/library/national/race/071100sack-poll.html.

[19] National Advisory Commission on Civil Disorders, *Report of the National Advisory Commission on Civil Disorders* (New York: Bantam, 1968) 1.

[20] William Raspberry, "What Actions Are Affirmative?" *The Washington Post,* Aug. 21, 1995, A21.

[21] Karen Peterson, "Teenage Dating Shows Racial Barriers Falling," *USA Today,* Nov. 3, 1997.

[22] Entertainment Editors, "Young People More Hopeful About Race Relations than Six Years Ago," *Entertainment Wire,* Dec. 3, 1997.

[23] Christopher John Farley, "Kids and Race," *Time* 150 (22), Nov. 24, 1997, 88–91.

[24] William Raspberry, from a lecture at Kansas State University, *Vital Speeches of the Day,* June 1, 1995, 493–496.

[25] Alice Moy, as found in Balch Institute of Ethnic Studies, "The Bachelor Society," *Perspective,* Spring/Summer 1998, 4.

[26] Sharon Tully, "Why to Go for Stretch Targets," *Fortune,* Nov. 14, 1994, 145–158.

Diversity Links

American Folklife Center

The American Folklife Center preserves and presents American folk life. Established by Congress in 1976, the Center and its collections have grown to encompass all aspects of folklore and folk life from this country and around the world. (http://www.loc.gov/folklife)

American Memory

Developed by the Library of Congress, American Memory is a gateway to rich primary source materials relating to the history and culture of the United States. The site offers more than 7 million digital items from more than 100 historical collections. (http://www.memory.loc.gov/ammem)

Balch Institute for Ethnic Studies

The Balch Institute is a multicultural library, archive, museum, and education center. With education as its primary focus, the Institute's mission is to promote greater inter-group understanding by documenting and presenting America's ethnic and racial experiences. This site includes links to descriptions of diversity awareness workshops and public education programs. (http://www.balchinstitute.org)

Center for Applied Linguistics

This is a good place to start for information on the practical application of linguistic knowledge to social and educational problems. (http://www.cal.org)

Center for Research on Education, Diversity, and Excellence (CREDE)

CREDE is a federally funded research and development program focused on improving the education of students whose ability to reach their potential is challenged by language or cultural barriers, race, geographic location, or poverty. (http://www.crede.ucsc.edu)

Conflict Research Consortium

The Conflict Research Consortium is a multidisciplinary program of research, teaching, and application, focused on finding more constructive ways of addressing conflict. The Consortium unites researchers, educators, and practitioners from many fields for the purposes of theory building, testing, disseminating, and applying new conflict management techniques. (http://www.colorado.edu/conflict)

Diversity Database

The American Association of Colleges and Universities (AAC&U) and the University of Maryland maintain this site. It provides a comprehensive index of multicultural and diversity resources. (http://www.inform.umd.edu/EdRes/Topic/Diversity)

Diversity University, Inc.

DU Inc. is a nonprofit organization dedicated to promoting education through online services. This Web site provides literature, classes, and consulting services for teachers, students, and administrators, as well as maintaining Diversity University MOO, an Internet-accessible virtual campus. DU MOO is a freely accessible virtual reality teaching and learning environment used by thousands of teachers and students around the world. (http://moo.du.org)

Ethnologue

This site offers reference information on the world's more than 6,000 oral languages, many of which face probable extinction in this century. (http://www.ethnologue.com)

National Clearinghouse for English Language Composition (NCELA)

NCELA is funded by the U.S. Department of Education to collect, analyze, and disseminate information concerning the education of linguistically and culturally diverse (LCD) learners. It provides information regarding exemplary practices and research as they relate to the effective education of LCD students in the United States. (http://www.ncela.gwu.edu)

News Watch

News Watch is a project of the Center for Integration and Improvement of Journalism of the San Francisco State University Journalism Department. The project promotes candid dialogue regarding coverage of people of color, lesbians and gays, and other communities that have been the victim of biased reporting. News Watch examines both good and bad coverage in ways that help us learn lessons. (http://newswatch.sfsu.edu)

Public Conversations Project

Promotes constructive conversations and relationships among those who have differing values, worldviews, and positions related to divisive public issues. (http://www.publicconversations.org)

Southern Poverty Law Center

The Southern Poverty Law Center combats hate, intolerance, and discrimination through education and litigation. Its programs include Teaching Tolerance, a national education project dedicated to helping teachers at all grade levels foster equity, respect, and understanding in the classroom and beyond. (http://www.splcenter.org)

WKCD (What Kids Can Do)

WKCD is a national nonprofit organization founded in 2001. WKCD documents the value of young people working with teachers and other adults on projects that combine powerful learning with public purpose. The site is for an audience of educators and policymakers, journalists, community members, and students. (http://www.wkcd.org)

WWWomen

WWWomen is a directory of more than 5,000 women's sites. Links include "Diversity Among Women," "The Education of Women," and "Women's Resources." (http://wwwomen.com)

For further up-to-date links, go to the author's Web site

(http://www.diversityconsciousness.com)

Bibliography

ABC News. *The Eye of the Storm* (video). Mount Kisco, NY: Guidance Associates, 1981.

Abraham, Ansley. *Racial Issues on Campus: How Students View Them*. Atlanta, GA: Southern Regional Education Board, 1990.

Adler, N. *International Dimensions of Organization Behavior*. Boston: Kent, 1986.

Aguilar-San Juan, Karen (ed.). *The State of Asian America*. Cambridge, MA: South End Press, 1994.

Allport, Gordon. *The Nature of Prejudice*. Reading, MA: Addison Wesley, 1954.

Alvarez, Rafael, and Dan Thanh Dang. "Embracing the New, Preserving the Old," *The Sun,* Apr. 27, 1995, 1A+.

American Association of Colleges of Teacher Education. *Teacher Education Pipeline IV: Schools, Colleges, and Department of Education*. Washington, DC: AACTE, 1999.

American Management Association. "What Do Organizations Really Want?" *AMA Catalog of Seminars,* Oct. 1997.

Angelou, Maya. *I Know Why The Caged Bird Sings*. New York: Bantam Books, 1993.

Appel, Morgan, David Cartwright, Daryl Smith, and Lisa Wolf. *The Impact of Diversity on Students*. Washington, DC: Association of American Colleges and Universities, 1996.

Aronson, Elliot, and Neal Osherow. "Cooperation, Prosocial Behavior, and Academic Performance: Experiments in the Desegregated Classroom," *Applied Social Psychology Annual,* 1, 1980, 174–175.

Ashe, Arthur. *Days of Grace*. New York: Ballantine Books, 1993.

Associated Press. "Number Living in Poverty Drops for 3rd Year in a Row, U.S. Says," *The Sun,* Sept. 25, 1998, 3A.

Association of American Colleges and Universities. "The Educational Value of Diversity: Research from Louisville High Schools," *Diversity Digest,* Winter 2001, 10, 11.

Astin, Alexander. "Diversity and Multiculturalism on the Campus: How Are Students Affected?" *Change,* Mar./Apr., 1993, 44–49.

Astin, Alexander. *What Matters in College? Four Critical Years Revisited*. San Francisco: Jossey-Bass, 1993.

Axtell, Roger E. *Gestures. The Do's and Taboos of Body Language around the World*. New York: Wiley, 1991.

Balch Institute of Ethnic Studies. "The Bachelor Society," *Perspective,* Spring/Summer 1998.

Bandura, Albert. "Exercise of Human Agency Through Collective Efficicacy," *Current Directions in Psychological Science* 9, 2000, 75–78.

Barnett, Martha. Letter to the author, July 2, 2002.

Bates, Karen G., and Karen E. Hudson. *Basic Black: Home Training for Modern Times*. New York: Doubleday, 1996.

Beatty, Richard. *The Interview Kit*. New York: John Wiley & Sons, 2000.

Belenky, Mary, Blythe Clinchy, Nancy Goldberger, and Jill Tarule. *Women's Ways of Knowing.* New York: Basic Books, 1996.

Bellarosa, James M. *A Problem of Plumbing and Other Stories.* Santa Barbara, CA: J. Daniel, 1989.

Berrios, Jerry. "A Balancing Act," *LATINA Style* 3(2), 1997, 24–28.

Berscheid, E., and E. Walster. "Beauty and the Beast," *Psychology Today,* Mar. 1972, 42–46, 74.

Bingham, Raymond. "Leaving Prejudice Behind," *The Washington Post Health Section,* Sept. 6, 1994, 9.

Black, J. Stewart, Allen Morrison, and Hal Gregersen. *Global Explorers: The Next Generation of Leaders.* New York: Routledge, 1999.

Blanchard, Fletcher et al. "Reducing the Expression of Racial Prejudice," *Psychological Science* 2, 1991, 101–105.

Blauner, Bob. *Black Lives, White Lives.* Berkeley, CA: University of California Press, 1989.

Block, J. Richard, and Harold Yuker. *Can You Believe Your Eyes?* New York: Brunner/Mazel, 1992.

Bodenhausen, Galen V. "Stereotypic Biases in Social Decision Making and Memory: Testing Process Models of Stereotype Use," *Journal of Personality and Social Psychology,* 55, 1988, 726–737.

Bogardus, Emory. "Measuring Social Distance," *Journal of Applied Sociology,* 9, Mar./Apr. 1925, 299–308.

Bradley, Bill. "How America Can Make Brotherhood Work," *Reader's Digest 75th Anniversary Issue,* 1997, 96–101.

Branigin, William. "Immigrants Question Idea of Assimilation," *The Washington Post,* May 25, 1998, A1.

Bridge, M. Junior. "Marginalizing Women," *Women, Men, and Media.* Unabridged Communications, 1996.

Britt, Donna. "Relishing Region's Many Hues," *The Washington Post,* Oct. 15, 1999, B1.

Brown, David (ed.). *Higher Education Exchange.* Dayton, OH: Kettering Foundation, 1995.

Bureau of Labor Statistics. *Projections from Current Population Survey,* 1988–1998.

Burton, John. *Conflict: Resolution and Provention.* New York: St. Martin's Press, 1990.

Butterfield, Bruce. "Xerox Makes It Work," *Boston Globe,* Oct. 20, 1991, 33–37.

Cannedy, Dana. "Back at the Office. . . ," *Essence* 23, 11, Mar. 1998, 80, 140.

Carson, Benjamin. "Carson Philosophy Is 'Think Big,'" *The Sun,* Aug. 24, 1997, 6H.

Carson, Benjamin. *Gifted Hands.* Washington, DC: Review and Herald Publishing Association, 1990.

Cart, Julie. "Irked by Mascot, Team Retaliates," *LOS ANGELES Times Online.* Online, Mar. 15, 2002. Available: https://www.patrick.af.mil/deomi/Library/EOReadFile/Native%20Americans%20Issues/NAI_Spring02/Irked%20by%20Mascot.pdf.

Carter, Carol, Joyce Bishop, and Sarah Lyman Kravits. *Keys to Success.* Upper Saddle River, NJ: Prentice Hall, 1998.

Chansanchai, Athima. "She Walks the Line of Poverty, Incognito," *The Sun,* Sept. 16, 2001, 1N+.

Checkley, Kathy. "The First Seven. . . and the Eighth: A Conversation with Howard Gardner," *Educational Leadership,* 55(1), Sept. 1997, 8–13.

Chemers, Martin M., Stuart Oskamp, and Mark A. Costanzo (eds.). *Diversity in Organizations.* Thousand Oaks, CA: Sage, 1995.

Clemens, Lynda P., and Andrea T. Dolph. *How to Hit the Ground Running in Your New Job.* Lincolnwood, IL: VGM Career Horizons, 1995.

Cohen, Sarah, and D'Vera Cohn. "Racial Integration's Shifting Patterns," *The Washington Post,* Feb. 1, 2001, A1.

Cohn, D'Vera, and Darryl Fears. "Multiracial Growth Seen in Census," *The Washington Post,* Mar. 13, 2001, A1.

The Color of Fear (video). Oakland, CA: Stir Fry Productions, 1994.

Connolly, Ceci. "Report Says Minorities Get Lower-Quality Health Care," *The Washington Post,* Mar. 21, 2002, A2.

Cortés, Carlos E. "The Societal Curriculum: Implications for Multiethnic Education," in *Education in the 80's: Multiethnic Education,* James Banks (ed.). Washington, DC: National Education Association, 1981.

Cose, Ellis. *The Rage of a Privileged Class.* New York: HarperCollins, 1993.

Cose, Ellis. *Color Blind.* New York: HarperPerennial.

Covey, Stephen. "How to Succeed in Today's Workplace," *USA Weekend,* Aug. 29–31, 1997, 4–5.

Covey, Stephen. *The Seven Habits of Highly Effective People.* New York: Simon & Schuster, 1989.

Cox, T. *Cultural Diversity in Organizations: Theory, Research, and Practice.* San Francisco: Berrett-Koehler Publishers, 1993.

Cox, T., and S. Blake. "Managing Cultural Diversity: Implications for Organizational Competitiveness," *The Executive,* 5(3), 1991, 45–56.

Critchell, Samantha. "Silent Since September and Learning a Lot," *The Washington Post,* May 15, 2001, C4.

Crozier-Hogle, Louis, and Darryl Babe Wilson. *Surviving in Two Worlds: Contemporary Native American Voices.* Austin, TX: University of Texas Press, 1997.

Cullen, Countee (ed.). *Caroling Dusk.* Secaucus, NJ: Carol Publishing Group, 1993.

Dancis, Jerome. "Group Learning Helps Minority Students Excel at University," *Cooperative Learning,* 12(1), Oct. 1991, 26–27.

DeSantis, Andrea, and Wesley Kayson. "Defendants' Characteristics of Attractiveness, Race, and Sex and Sentencing Decisions," *Psychological Reports,* 81, 1997, 679–683.

Digest of Education Statistics. U.S. Department of Education, 2000.

Dinan, Stephen. "Immigration Growth at Highest Rate in 150 Years." Online, June 5, 2002. Available: http://www.washtimes.com/national/20020605-76931088.html.

Disch, Estelle. *Reconstructing Gender: A Multicultural Anthology.* Mountain View, CA: Mayfield Publishing, 1997.

"Diversity: Making the Business Case," *Business Week Special Advertising Section,* Dec. 9, 1996, 83+.

Dowd, Karen, and Jeanne Liedtka. "What Corporations Seek in MBA Hires: A Survey," *The Magazine of the Graduate Management Admission Council,* Winter, 1994, 34–39.

Dubois, W. E. B. *The Souls of Black Folk.* New York: Fawcett, 1961.

Edsall, Thomas B. "Anti-Muslim Violence Assailed," *The Washington Post,* Sept. 15, 2001, A9.

Ehrlich, Howard J. *Campus Ethnoviolence: A Research Review,* Institute Report 5. Baltimore: National Institute Against Prejudice and Violence, 1992.

Enayati, Amanda. "Not Black, Not White," *The Washington Post,* July 13, 1997, C1.

Enos, Lori. "Report: English-Only A Mistake for U.S. Sites," *E-Commerce Times.* Online, May 17, 2001. Available: http://www.ecommercetimes.com/perl/story/9812.html.

Entertainment Editors. "Young People More Hopeful About Race Relations than Six Years Ago," *Entertainment Wire,* Dec. 3, 1997.

Farley, Christopher John. "Kids and Race," *Time* 150 (22), Nov. 24, 1997, 88–91.

Feagin, Joe. "The Continuing Significance of Race: Anti-Black Discrimination in Public Places," *American Sociological Review,* 56, 1991, 101–116.

Feagin, Joe, and Melvin Sikes. *Living with Racism: The Black Middle Class Experience.* Boston: Beacon Press, 1994.

Feagin, Joe, and Hernan Vera. *White Racism.* New York: Routledge, 1995.

Federal Glass Ceiling Commission. *A Solid Investment: Making Full Use of the Nation's Human Capital.* Washington, DC: U.S. Department of Labor, 1995.

Fernandez, John P. *Managing a Diverse Work Force: Regaining the Competitive Edge.* Lexington, MA: Lexington Books, 1991.

Fine, Marlene G. *Building Successful Multicultural Organizations: Challenges and Opportunities.* Westport, CT: Quorum Books, 1995.

Fine, Michelle, and Adrienne Asch (eds.). *Women with Disabilities: Essays in Psychology, Culture, and Politics.* Philadelphia: Temple University Press, 1988.

Fletcher, Michael. "Crazy Horse Again Sounds Battle Cry," *The Washington Post,* Feb. 18, 1997, A03.

Fong, Timothy, and Larry Shinagawa. *Asian Americans: Experiences and Perspectives.* Upper Saddle River, NJ: Prentice Hall, 2000.

Ford, Clyde W. *We Can All Get Along.* New York: Dell Publishing, 1994.

Frankenburg, Ruth. *White Women, Race Matters: The Social Construction of Whiteness.* Minneapolis, MN: University of Minnesota Press, 1993.

Fraser, Barbara. "U.S. Colleges Step Up Recruiting in Latin America," *Chronicle of Higher Education,* XLIV(10), Oct. 31, 1997, A58–A59.

Frey, William. "The Diversity Myth," *American Demographics,* June 1998, 38–43.

Gallagher, Carol. *Going to the Top.* New York: Viking Press, 2000.

Gallagher, Charles. "White Reconstruction in the University," *Socialist Review,* 24, 1994, 165.

Gang, Philip. *Rethinking Education.* Atlanta, GA: Dagaz Press, 1989.

Gannett News Service. "Muslim Nations, U.S. Have Opposite Views," *Carroll County Times,* Mar. 5, 2002, A11.

Gardner, Howard. *Frames of Mind: The Theory of Multiple Intelligences.* New York: Basic Books, 1983.

Gaskins, Richard. Letter to the author (attachment), Nov. 9, 1997.

Gibson, M. A. "Parental Support for Schooling." Paper presented at the annual meeting of the American Anthropological Association, Dec. 1986.

Gilens, Martin. "Race and Poverty in America: Public Misperceptions and the American News Media," *Public Opinion Quarterly,* 60, 1996, 515–541.

Goffman, E. *Interaction Ritual: Essays on Face to Face Interaction.* Garden City, NY: Doubleday/Anchor, 1967.

Gold, Barbara. "Diversifying the Curriculum: What Do Students Think," *Diversity Digest,* Winter 2001, 12–14.

Goldsmith, Charles. "Look See! Anyone Do Read This and It Will Make You Laughable," *The Wall Street Journal,* Nov. 19, 1992, B1.

Goleman, Daniel. *Working with Emotional Intelligence.* New York: Bantam Books, 1998.

Gonzales, Juan L., Jr. *The Lives of Ethnic Americans,* 2nd ed. Dubuque, IA: Kendall/Hunt, 1994.

Granrose, Cherlyn S., and Stuart Oskamp (eds.). *Cross-Cultural Work Groups.* Thousand Oaks, CA: Sage Publications, 1997.

Graves, Earl. "On Financial Hurdles Facing African Americans," *The Washington Post,* May 4, 1997, H4.

Greissman, Eugene. *Diversity: Challenges and Opportunities.* New York: HarperCollins, 1993.

Griffin, John H. *Black Like Me.* New York: NAL/Dutton, 1999.

Griggs, Lewis Brown, and Lente-Louise Louw (eds.). *Valuing Diversity: New Tools for a New Reality.* New York: McGraw-Hill, 1995.

Grimsley, Kristen Downey. "Training in the Theater of the Real," *The Washington Post Business Section,* Mar. 24, 1997, 12–14.

Guerney, Bernard, Jr. *Relationship Enhancement Program,* 2nd ed. Bethesda, MD: Ideals, 1997.

Hacker, Andrew. *Two Nations.* New York: Ballantine Books, 1995.

Hall, Roberta M., and Bernice Sandler. *Out of the Classroom: A Chilly Campus Climate for Women?* Washington, DC: Project on the Status and Education of Women, Association of American Colleges, 1984.

Hall, Roberta M., and Bernice Sandler. *The Classroom Climate: A Chilly One for Women.* Washington, DC: Association of American Colleges, 1982.

Hanley, Sue. Letter to the author, Dec. 22, 1997.

Harvey, Carol, and M. June Allard. *Understanding Diversity: Readings, Cases, and Exercises.* New York: HarperCollins, 1995.

Heath, Shirley Brice. *Ways with Words.* Cambridge: Cambridge University Press, 1983.

Hegi, Ursula. *Tearing the Silence.* New York: Simon & Schuster, 1997.

Henderson, George. *Cultural Diversity in the Workplace: Issues and Strategies.* Westport, CT: Praeger Publishers, 1994.

Heredia, Al. "Cultural Learning Styles," *Eric Clearinghouse on Teaching and Teacher Education,* Dec., 1999.

Higginbotham, E. *Integrating All Women into the Curriculum.* Memphis, TN: Memphis State University Center for Research on Women, 1988.

Hitner, Trevor. Letter to the author, Mar. 15, 1998.

Hofstede, Geert. *Culture's Consequences: International Differences in Work-Related Values.* Beverly Hills, CA: Sage Publications, 1980.

Horowitz, Irving Louis. *The Decomposition of Sociology.* New York: Oxford University Press, 1993.

Huffman, Terry. "The Transculturation of Native American College Students," in *American Mosaic: Selected Readings on America's Multicultural Heritage,* Young I. Song and Eugene C. Kim (eds.). Englewood Cliffs, NJ: Prentice Hall, 1993, 211–219.

Huffman, Terry, Maurice Sill, and Martin Brokenleg. "College Achievement among Sioux and White South Dakota Students," *Journal of American Indian Education,* Jan. 1986, 32–38.

Hvitfeldt, Christina. "Traditional Culture, Perceptual Style, and Learning: The Classroom Behavior of Hmong Adults," *Adult Education Quarterly,* 36(2) Winter 1986, 65–77.

IBM, "Directory of Diversity Programs." Online August 28, 2002. Available: http://www-3.ibm.com/employment/us/diverse/programs_ibm.shtml.

"Inclusion," *Book and Video Catalog.* Manhattan, KS: The MASTER Teacher, 1999.

"Inclusion, Not Rejection Will Spur Racial Harmony," *USA Today,* June 16, 1997, 18A.

Irvine, Jacqueline, and Darlene York. "Learning Styles and Culturally Diverse Students: A Literature Review," in *Handbook of Research on Multicultural Education,* James Banks (ed.). New York: Simon & Schuster, 1995, 484–497.

Jackson, Susan, and Marian Ruderman (eds.). *Diversity in Work Teams; Research Paradigms for a Changing Workplace.* Washington, DC: American Psychological Association, 1996.

Jamieson, Daniel, and Julie O'Mara. *Managing Workforce 2000.* San Francisco: Jossey-Bass, 1991.

Janis, Irving L. *Victims of Groupthink.* Boston: Houghton Mifflin, 1972.

Johnston, William B., and Arnold Parker. *Workforce 2000: Work and Workers for the 21st Century.* Indianapolis, IN: Hudson Institute, 1987.

Judy, Richard W., and Carol D'Amico. *Workforce 2020: Executive Summary*. Indianapolis, IN: Hudson Institute, 1997.

Kabagarama, Daisy. *Breaking the Ice: A Guide to Understanding People from Other Cultures*. Boston: Allyn & Bacon, 1997.

Karp, Abby. "Working Together: Innovative Programs Promote Tolerance in Schools," *The Sun*, Oct. 17, 1989, 1C.

Katz, Neil H., and John Lawyer. *Communication and Conflict Resolution Skills*. Dubuque, IA: Kendall/Hunt, 1992.

Kauffman, L. A. "The Diversity Game," *Voice*, Aug. 31, 1993, 29–33.

Kendall, Diana. *Race, Class, and Gender in a Diverse Society*. Boston: Allyn & Bacon, 1997.

Kennedy, Randall. *Nigger: The Strange Career of a Troublesome Word*. New York: Pantheon, 2002.

Kenton, Sherron, and Deborah Valentine. *CrossTalk: Communicating in a Multicultural Workplace*. Upper Saddle River, NJ: Prentice Hall, 1997.

King, Martin Luther, Jr. *Where Do We Go from Here: Chaos or Community?* Boston: Beacon Press, 1968.

Knox, D., and C. Schacht. *Choices in Relationships*. Belmont, CA: Wadsworth, 1997.

Koch, Nicole. "Asian-Americans Have Become Fastest-Growing Ethnic Group," *The Dallas Morning News*, June 9, 1998, 4A.

Kochman, Thomas. *Black and White Styles in Conflict*. Chicago: The University of Chicago Press, 1981.

Kolsti, Nancy. "Accents Speak Louder Than Words," *North Texan online*. Online, Winter 2000. Available: http://www.unt.edu/northtexan/archives/w00/accents.html.

Kotter, John. *The General Managers*. New York: Free Press, 1982.

Kramer, Martin, and Stephen Weiner. *The Project on Campus Community and Diversity*. Phoenix, AZ: Oryx Press, 1994.

Kuntz, Gabriela. "My Spanish Standoff," *Newsweek*, May 4, 1998, 22.

Labaton, Stephen. "Denny's Gets a Bill for the Side Orders of Bigotry," *The New York Times*, May 29, 1994, E4.

Lahr, John. "Speaking across the Divide," *The New Yorker*, Jan. 27, 1997, 41–42.

Lancaster, Hal. "Learning to Manage in a Global Workplace," *The Wall Street Journal*, June 2, 1998, B1.

Langer, E. J. *Mindfulness*. Reading, MA: Addison-Wesley, 1989.

Larcom, Barbara, and Allyson George. "First Glimpse of New Workplace Research," *National Institute Against Prejudice and Violence Forum*, Mar. 1992, 1+.

LeBeau, Christina. "Attitude Adjustment," *Rochester Democrat and Chronicle*, Oct. 19, 1997, 1e+.

Levinson, Wendy, Debra Roter, John Mullooly, Valerie Dull, and Richard Frankel. "Physician-Patient Communication: The Relationship with Malpractice Claims Among Primary Care Physicians and Surgeons," *Journal of the American Medical Association*, February 19, 1997, 553–559.

Levy, Becca. "Improving Memory in Old Age Through Implicit Self-Stereotyping," *Journal of Personality and Social Psychology*, 71(6), 1996, 1092–1107.

Levy, Becca, and Ellen Langer. "Aging Free from Negative Stereotypes: Successful Memory in China and Among the American Deaf," *Journal of Personality and Social Psychology*, 66(6), 1994, 989–997.

Lipnack, Jessica, and Jeffrey Stamps. *Virtual Teams*. New York: Wiley, 1997.

Loden, Marilyn, and Judy Rosener. *Workforce America: Managing Employee Diversity as a Vital Resource*. Homewood, IL: Business One Irwin, 1991.

Longstreet, Wilma. *Aspects of Ethnicity: Understanding Differences in Pluralistic Classrooms.* Williston, VT: Teacher's College Press, 1978.

Maddox, Amy. "Underneath We're All the Same," *Teaching Tolerance,* Spring 1995, 65.

Massachusetts Commission Against Discrimination, as reported on "Age and Attitudes," *ABC News Primetime Live* June 9, 1994.

Massey, Douglas. "Latino Poverty Research: An Agenda for the 1990s," *Social Science Research Council Newsletter,* 47, Mar. 1993, 7–8.

McIntosh, Peggy. *White Privilege and Male Privilege.* Wellesley, MA: Wellesley College Center for Research on Women, 1988.

McLaughlin, Barry, and Beverly McLeod. "Educating All Our Students: Improving Education for Children from Culturally and Linguistically Diverse Backgrounds." Online, World Wide Web, June 1996. Available: http://www.ncbe.gwu.edu/miscpubs/ncrcdsll/edall.htm.

McLuhan, Marshall. *The Mechanical Bride: Folklore of Industrial Man.* Boston: Beacon Press, 1967.

McNatt, Glenn. "Instant Communication Is Changing Our Very Form of Government," *The Sun,* Feb. 9, 1997, 5E.

Mehler, Mark. "AMS Centers Deliver Global Information Access," *Integration Management: The Newspaper for Global Integrators,* 1(8), Sept. 18, 1997.

Merton, Robert. "Discrimination and the American Creed," in *Sociological Ambivalence and Other Essays.* New York: Free Press, 1976, 189–216.

Michael, Walt. Letter to the author, Jan. 9, 1998.

Milano, Philip, and Larry Lane. *Why Do White People Smell Like Wet Dogs When They Come Out of the Rain?* Orlando Park, FL: Y Forum, 1999.

Montagu, Ashley. *Man's Most Dangerous Myth: The Fallacy of Race.* Cleveland, OH: World Publishing, 1964.

Moremen, Robin. "A Multicultural Framework: Transforming Curriculum, Transforming Students," *Teaching Sociology,* 25(2), Apr. 1997, 107–119.

Morgan, Appel, David Cartwright, Daryl Smith, and Lisa Wolf. *The Impact of Diversity on Students: A Preliminary Review of the Research Literature.* Washington, DC: Association of American Colleges and Universities, 1996.

Morin, Richard. "Needed: A Hillbilly Anti-Defamation League," *The Washington Post,* May 4, 1997, C5.

Morin, Richard, and Michael Cottman. "Most Black Men Profiled by Police, Poll Says," washingtonpost.com. Online, June 21, 2001. Available: http://www.washingtonpost.com/ac2/wp-dyn?pagename–article&node–&contentId=A30338-2001Jun21&notFound=true

Morrison, Toni. *Playing in the Dark.* Cambridge, MA: Harvard University Press, 1992.

Murphy, Mark. "Rocker a 'Prisoner,' At Least When It Comes to Treatment." Online, Jan. 11, 2000. Available: http://cbs.sportsline.com/u/ce/multi/0,1329,1878900_52,00.html.

"The Nation: Students," *The Chronicle of Higher Education Almanac,* Sept. 1, 2000, 24+.

National Advisory Commission on Civil Disorders. *Report of the National Advisory Commission on Civil Disorders.* New York: Bantam, 1968.

National Center for Education Statistics. *Digest of Education Statistics 2000.* Washington, DC: U.S. Department of Education, 2000.

National Council of La Raza. *Don't Blink: Hispanics in Television Entertainment.* Washington, DC: Center for Media and Public Affairs, 1996.

National Institute of Education. "Involvement in Learning: Realizing the Potential of American Higher Education," *Report of the Study Group on the Conditions of Excellence in American Higher Education.* Washington, DC: U.S. Department of Education, 1984.

National Opinion Research Center. *General Social Science Survey.* Chicago, IL: University of Chicago, 1996.

Nelton, Sharon. "Meet Your New Workforce," *Nation's Business,* July 1988, 15.

Nieto, Sonia. *Affirming Diversity: The Sociopolitical Context of Multicultural Education.* White Plains, NY: Longman, 1996.

Norris, Donald, and Michael Dolence. *Transforming Higher Education: A Vision for Learning in the 21st Century.* Ann Arbor, MI: Society for College and University Planning, 1995.

Northeast and Islands Regional Educational Laboratory at Brown University. *Student Voices: English Language Learners,* 2000.

Olson, C. B. "The Influence of Context on Gender Differences in Performance Attributions: Further Evidence of a 'Feminine Modesty' Effect." Paper presented at the annual meeting of the Western Psychological Association, San Francisco, CA, 1988.

Olsson, Karen. "Bad Old Boys," *The Washington Post Book World,* Feb. 10, 2002, 4.

Pagonis, William. "Leadership in a Combat Zone" *Harvard Business Review,* December, 2001, 107–116.

Parillo, Vincent. *Diversity in America.* Thousand Oaks, CA: Pine Forge Press, 1996.

Parker, Pat. *Movement in Black.* Ithaca, NY: Firebrand Books, 1978.

Pascale, R. T. *Managing on the Edge: How the Smartest Companies Use Conflict to Stay Ahead.* New York: Simon & Schuster, 1990.

Peterson, Karen. "Teenage Dating Shows Racial Barriers Falling," *USA Today,* Nov. 3, 1997.

Pettigrew, T. F., and J. Martin. "Shaping the Organizational Context for Black American Inclusion," *Journal of Social Issues,* 43(1), 1987, 41–78.

Pinchin, Jane. "Let Them Go—Because 60 Seconds of World News Is Not Enough," *The Colgate Scene,* March 2002.

Pitino, Rick, and Bill Reynolds. *Learn to Succeed.* New York: Broadway Books, 2000.

Pitts, Leonard. "It's Time for Men to Act Like Men," *The Sun,* July 16, 2001, 7A.

Pitts, Leonard. "Watching Whites Struggle to Understand Their Whiteness," *The Sun,* Apr. 21, 1997, 9A.

Price, S. L. "The Indian Wars," *Sports Illustrated,* Mar. 4, 2002, 67–72.

Proctor, Samuel D., and William Watley. *Sermons from the Black Pulpit.* Valley Forge, PA: Judson Press, 1984.

Rasmussen, Karen. "Gaining Perspective on Global Education," *ASCD (Association for Supervision and Curriculum Development) Curriculum Update,* Summer 1998.

Raspberry, William. Quote from a lecture at Kansas State University, *Vital Speeches of the Day,* 61(16), June 1, 1995, 493–496.

Raspberry, William. "What Actions Are Affirmative?" *The Washington Post,* Aug. 21, 1995, A21.

Reid, Alice. "Mosque's Children Await Playground," *The Washington Post,* Nov. 22, 1998, B4.

Reuters. "Victims by Country." Online, Sept. 20, 2001. Available: http://www.cnn.com/SPECIALS/2001/trade.center/interactive/victims.map/mpa.exclude.htmlrlUntitled.

Rice, Fay. "How to Make Diversity Pay," *Fortune,* Aug. 8, 1994, 79–86.

Riley, Dorothy Winbush (ed.). *My Soul Looks Back, 'Less I Forget: A Collection of Quotations by People of Color.* New York: HarperCollins, 1995.

Ritzer, George. *The McDonaldization of Society.* Thousand Oaks, CA: Pine Forge Press, 2000.

Robins, Lynne, Joseph Fantone, Julica Hermann, Gwen Alexander, and Andrew Zweifler. "Improving Cultural Awareness and Sensitivity Training in Medical School," *Academic Medicine,* 73(10), Oct. Supplement, 1998.

Rodríguez, Cindy. "Latina America," *Latina,* July 2001, 87.

Rodriguez, Clara. *Changing Race: Latinos, the Census, and the History of Ethnicity in the United States.* New York: New York University Press, 2000.

Rodriguez, Richard. *Hunger of Memory: The Education of Richard Rodriguez.* Boston: David R. Godine, 1982.

Rubinstein, Moshe. *Patterns of Problem Solving.* Englewood Cliffs, NJ: Prentice Hall, 1975.

Ruderman, Marian, Martha Hughes-James, and Susan Jackson. *Selected Research on Work Team Diversity.* Washington, DC: American Psychological Association, 1996.

Rush, Sheila, and Chris Clark. *How to Get Along with Black People.* New Rochelle, NY: Third Press-Joseph Okpaku Publishing Co., Inc., 1972.

Ryan, Michael. "If You Can't Teach Me, Don't Criticize Me," *Parade Magazine,* May 11, 1997, 6–7.

Sack, Kevin, with Janet Elder. "Poll Finds Optimistic Outlook But Enduring Racial Division," *The New York Times on the Web.* Online, July 11, 2000. Available: http://www.nytimes. com/library/national/race/071100sack-poll.html.

Sacks, Oliver. *Seeing Voices: A Journey into the World of the Deaf.* Berkeley, CA: University of California Press, 1989.

Schuman, David, and Dick Olufs. *Diversity on Campus.* Boston: Allyn & Bacon, 1995.

Schwartz, Howard. "Further Thoughts on a 'Sociology of Acceptance' for Disabled People," *Social Policy,* Fall 1988, 36–39.

Scripps Howard News Service, "White Men Still at Top of the Business Heap, Study Finds," *Carroll County Times,* Mar. 16, 1995, A7.

Sedgwick, John. *Rich Kids.* New York: William Morrow, 1985.

Servaes, J. "Cultural Identity in East and West," *Howard Journal of Communications,* 1(2), 1988, 58–71.

Shapiro, Bill. "Speakers Call for Greater Effort in Combating Racism," *American Psychological Association Monitor,* 28(10), Oct. 1997, 39.

Shipler, David. *A Country of Strangers.* New York: Alfred A. Knopf, 1997.

Shipley, Amy. "A Successful Science Project," *The Washington Post,* June 29, 1999, D1+.

Silver, Sheryl. "Advice for Adjusting to the World of Work," *Washington Post Advertising Supplement,* Oct. 19, 1997, 60, 65.

Silver, Sheryl. "New Grads: Make the Most of Your First Job," *The Washington Post High Tech Horizons,* Aug. 3, 1997, M19.

Simpson, Ian. "U.S. Race Bias Suits on the Rise, Putting Companies on the Defensive." Online, July 14, 2000. Available: http://news.excite.com/news/r/000714/13/economy-race-suits2.

Singh, Ravjot. "Stop the Hate." Online, September 19, 2001. Available: http://www. doubleedge.net.

Slavin, Robert. "Synthesis of Research on Cooperative Learning," *Educational Leadership,* 48, 1991, 71–82.

Slepper, Jim. "Liberal Racism," *The New Democrat,* July/Aug. 1997, 8–12.

Smedley, Brian, Adrienne Stith, and Alan Nelson (eds.). *Unequal Treatment: Confronting Racial and Ethnic Disparities in Health Care.* Washington, DC: National Academies Press, 2002.

Smith, K. A., D. W. Johnson, and R. T. Johnson. "Can Conflict Be Constructive? Controversy versus Concurrence Seeking in Learning Groups," *Journal of Educational Psychology,* 75, 1983, 651–663.

Smith, Robert, and Richard Seltzer. *Contemporary Controversies and the American Racial Divide.* Lanham, MD: Rowman and Littlefield, 2000.

Snyder, T. (ed.). *Digest of Education Statistics, 1998*. U.S. Department of Education National Center for Education Statistics, 1998.

Solomon, Joshua. "Skin Deep: Reliving *Black Like Me:* My Own Journey into the Heart of Race Conscious America," *The Washington Post,* Oct. 30, 1994, C01.

Sorgen, Carol. "Wellwood School Teaches Diversity Every Day," *The Sun: A Special Advertising Section,* Mar. 3, 2002, 6.

Soukhanov, Anne. *Encarta World English Dictionary*. New York: St. Martin's Press, 1999.

Southern Poverty Law Center. "E-mail on Trial," *Intelligence Report,* Winter 1998, 5.

Southern Poverty Law Center. *Intelligence Report,* Spring, 2002.

Southern Poverty Law Center. "163 and Counting . . . Hate Groups Find Home on the Net," *Intelligence Report,* Winter 1998, 24.

Sproull, L., and S. Kiesler. *Connections: New Ways of Working in the Networked Organization*. Cambridge, MA: MIT Press, 1991.

Steele, Claude. "Twenty-First Century Program and Stereotype Vulnerability." Unpublished study and program, Stanford University, Stanford, CA, 1995.

Strait, George. "Health Care's Racial Divide." Online, March 7, 1999. Available: http://more.abc-news.go.com/sections/living/DailyNews/racial_healthcare990224.html.

Sullivan, D. "Organization Structure in Multinational Corporations," in *International Encyclopedia of Business and Management,* M. Warner (ed.). London: Routledge, 1996, 3573–3597.

Swisher, Kara. "Diversity's Learning Curve," *The Washington Post,* Feb. 5, 1995, H1+.

Swoboda, Frank. "Study: Many in Graying Work Force May Not Have the Green to Retire," *The Washington Post,* Apr. 18, 1997, G3.

Takaki, Ronald. *A Different Mirror: A History of Multicultural America*. Boston: Little, Brown, 1993.

Takata, Susan R. "The Chairs Game—Competition versus Cooperation: The Sociological Uses of Musical Chairs," *Teaching Sociology,* 25(3), July 1997, 200–206.

Tan, Cheryl. "For College Students, Degrees of Ethnicity," *The Washington Post,* Sept. 3, 1996, B1.

Tannen, Deborah. *The Argument Culture: Moving from Debate to Dialogue*. New York: Random House, 1998.

Tannen, Deborah. *Talking from 9 to 5: How Women's and Men's Conversational Styles Affect Who Gets Heard, Who Gets Credit, and What Gets Done at Work*. New York: William Morrow, 1994.

Tannen, Deborah. *That's Not What I Meant*. New York: Ballantine Books, 1992.

Tannen, Deborah. *You Just Don't Understand: Men and Women in Conversation*. New York: William Morrow, 1990.

Tatum, Beverly. *Why Are All the Black Kids Sitting Together in the Cafeteria?* New York: Harper Collins, 1997.

"Team Building 101," [Online]. Available: http://www.eateamz.com/baseball/instruction/psych/article.cfm?article=tb101rl (May 10, 2002).

Temple-Raston, Dina. *A Death in Texas*. New York: Henry Holt, 2002.

Terkel, Studs. *Race: How Blacks and Whites Think and Feel about the American Obsession*. New York: New Press, 1992.

Texeira, Erin. "Young See Race Divide, But Give Reason to Hope," *The Sun,* Aug. 17, 1999, 3A.

Tharp, Roland. "Psychocultural Variables and Constants: Effects on Teaching and Learning in Schools," *American Psychologist,* 44(2), Feb. 1989, 349–359.

Thiederman, Sondra. *Bridging Cultural Barriers for Corporate Success: How to Manage the Multicultural Workforce*. New York: Lexington Books, 1991.

Thomas, Roosevelt. *Beyond Race and Gender: Unleashing the Power of Your Total Work Force by Managing Diversity*. New York: American Management Association, 1991.

Tuchman, B. W. "Developmental Sequences in Small Groups," *Psychological Bulletin,* 63, 1965, 384–399.

Tully, Sharon. "Why to Go for Stretch Targets," *Fortune,* Nov. 14, 1994, 145–158.

Tutu, Desmond Mpilo. *No Future Without Forgiveness.* New York: Doubleday, 1999.

U.S. Bureau of the Census. *Historical Statistics of the United States, Part II.* Washington, DC: U.S. Government Printing Office, 1976.

U.S. Bureau of the Census. *Historical Statistics of the United States, Part II.* Series Z 20–132. Washington, DC: U.S. Government Printing Office, 1993.

U.S. Bureau of the Census. *Statistical Abstract of the United States: 1994.* Washington, DC: U.S. Government Printing Office, 1994.

U.S. Bureau of the Census. *Statistical Abstract of the United States: 1997,* 117th edition. Washington, DC: U.S. Government Printing Office, 1997.

U.S. Bureau of the Census. Census 2000 Questionaire, "Overview of Race and Hispanic Origin: Census 2000 Brief." Washington, DC: U.S. Department of Commerce, 2001. p.1.

U.S. Bureau of the Census. Census 2000 Redistricting (Public Law 94-171) Summary Files, Tables PL1 and PL2, "Overview of Race and Hispanic Origin: Census 2000 Brief." Washington, DC: U.S. Department of Commerce, 2001. p.3.

U.S. Department of Labor Bureau of Labor Statistics, "Labor Force." *Occupational Outlook Quarterly,* Winter 1999/2000.

Van Ausdale, Debra, and Joe R. Feagin. *The First R: How Children Learn Race and Racism.* (Lanham, MD: Rowman and Littlefield, 2001).

Varson, Alex. "U.S. Population Trends." Online, June 19, 2002. Available: http://www.census.gov/mso/www/pres_lib/poptrnd/sld023.html.

Verville, Anne-Lee. "What Business Needs from Higher Education," *Educational Record,* 76(4), Fall 1995, 46–50.

von Oech, Roger. *A Kick in the Seat of the Pants.* New York: Harper & Row, 1986.

Wax, Emily. "The Fabric of Their Faith," *The Washington Post,* May 19, 2002, C1.

West, Cornel. *Race Matters.* New York: Random House, 1993.

Whiting, Robert. "You Gotta Have 'Wa,'" *Sports Illustrated,* Sept. 24, 1979, 60+.

Wilson, Angus. *The Strange Ride of Rudyard Kipling: His Life and Works.* New York: Viking Press, 1978, 290.

Winkler, Karen. "While Concern over Race Relations Has Lessened among Whites, Sociologists Say Racism Is Taking New Forms, Not Disappearing," *Chronicle of Higher Education,* Sept. 11, 1991, A10–A11.

Wood, Donna. *Business and Society,* 2nd ed. New York: HarperCollins, 1994.

Wood, Julia T. (ed.). *Gendered Relationships.* Mountain View, CA: Mayfield Publishing, 1996.

"Working Together Works." Online, World Wide Web, Nov. 28, 1998. Available: http://www.diversitydtg.com/thoughts/thought_mnu.html.

X, Malcolm. *The Autobiography of Malcolm X.* New York: Ballantine Books, 1965.

Yardley, Jonathan. "Coping with History," *The Washington Post: Book World,* July 6, 1997, 3.

Young, Whitney. *To Be Equal.* New York: McGraw-Hill, 1966.

Zangwill, Israel. *The Melting Pot.* New York: The Jewish Publication Society of America, 1909.

Zunikoff, Jennifer Rudick. Conversation with the author, June 4, 2002.

Suggested Readings

Developing our diversity consciousness requires continual learning. Reading is one important means of challenging and expanding our thinking in the area of diversity. The following books, many of which have been recommended by students as well as educators, deal with a wide range of diversity issues.

Alvarez, Julia. *How the Garcia Girls Lost Their Accents.* New York: Plume, 1992.

Alvarez, Julia. *Something to Declare.* Chapel Hill, NC: Algonquin Books, 1998.

Andersen, Margaret, and Patricia Hill Collins. *Race, Class, and Gender: An Anthology.* Belmont, CA: Wadsworth, 1997.

Anderson, Elijah. *Code of the Street.* New York: W. W. Norton & Co., 2000.

Appiah, Kwame Anthony, and Henry Louis, Jr. Gates (ed.). *Africana: The Encyclopedia of the African and African American Experience.* New York: Basic Civitas Books, 1999.

Arana, Marie. *American Chica: Two Worlds, One Childhood.* El Dorado, AR: Delta Press, 2002.

Armor, Jody David. *Negrophobia and Reasonable Racism.* New York: New York University Press, 1997.

Asayesh, Gelareh. *Saffron Sky: A Life Between Iran and America.* Boston: Beacon Press, 2000.

Banks, James A., and Cherry A. McGee Banks (eds.). *Handbook of Research on Multicultural Education.* New York: Macmillan, 1995.

Battle, Stafford, and Rey Harris. *The African-American Resource Guide to the Internet and Online Services.* New York: McGraw-Hill, 1996.

Belenky, Mary, Blythe Clinchy, Nancy Goldberger, and Jill Tarule. *Women's Ways of Knowing.* New York: Basic Books, 1986.

Bellarosa, James M. *A Problem of Plumbing and Other Stories.* Santa Barbara, CA: John Daniel, 1989.

Ben Jalloun, Tahar. *Racism Explained to My Daughter.* New York: New Press, 1999.

Bradley, Bill. *Time Present, Time Past.* New York: Vintage Books, 1996.

Bragg, Rick. *All Over but the Shoutin'.* New York: Vintage Books, 1998.

The Broad Minds Collective (eds.). *Ourselves as Students: Multicultural Voices in the Classroom.* Carbondale, IL: Southern Illinois University Press, 1996.

Brown, Claude. *Manchild in the Promised Land.* New York: Simon & Schuster, 1999.

Bystydzienski, Jill M., and Estelle P. Resnik (eds.). *Women in Cross-Cultural Transitions.* Bloomington, IN: Phi Delta Kappa Educational Foundation, 1994.

Cadet, Jean-Robert. *Restavec: From Haitian Slave Child to Middle-Class American.* Austin, TX: University of Texas Press, 1998.

Campbell, Bebe Moore. *Brothers and Sisters.* New York: Berkley Books, 1994.

Canfield, Jack, Mark Hansen, Jennifer Hawthorne, and Marci Shimoff. *Chicken Soup for the Woman's Soul*. Deerfield Beach, FL: Health Communications, 1996.

Cisneros, S. *House on Mango Street*. New York: Random House, 1994.

Conley, Dalton. *Honky*. New York: Vintage Books, 2001.

Cortés, Carlos. *How the Media Teach About Diversity: Mass Media as Multicultural Education*. New York: Teachers College Press, 2000.

Covey, Stephen. *The Seven Habits of Highly Effective People*. New York: Simon & Schuster, 1990.

Daloz, Laurent A. Parks, Cheryl H. Keen, James P. Keen, and Sharon Daloz Parks. *Common Fire: Lives of Commitment in a Complex World*. Boston: Beacon Press, 1996.

Dees, M., with S. Fiffer. *A Season of Justice: A Lawyer's Own Story of Victory Over America's Hate Groups*. New York: Simon & Schuster, 1992.

Dog, Mary Crow. *Lakota Woman*. New York: HarperCollins, 1991.

Dresser, Norrine. *Multicultural Manners: New Rules of Etiquette for a Changing Society*. New York: Wiley, 1996.

Duneier, Mitchell. *Slim's Table: Race, Respectability, and Masculinity*. Chicago: The University of Chicago Press, 1994.

Edelman, Marian Wright. *Lanterns: A Memoir of Mentors*. Boston: Beacon Press, 1999.

Essed, Philomena. *Understanding Everyday Racism*. Newbury Park, CA: Sage Publications, 1991.

Evans, Sybil, and Sherry Suib Cohen. *Hot Buttons*. New York: HarperCollins, 2001.

Ford, Clyde W. *We Can All Get Along: 50 Steps You Can Take to Help End Racism*. New York: Dell Publishing, 1994.

Freidenberg, Judith. *Growing Old in El Barrio*. New York: New York University Press, 2000.

Galarza, Ernesto. *Barrio Boy: The Story of a Boy's Acculturation*. Minneapolis, MN: Econo-Clad Books, 1999.

Gallagher, Carol, with Susan Golant. *Going to the Top: A Road Map for Success from America's Leading Women Executives*. New York: Viking, 2000.

Gaskins, Pearl Fuyo. *What Are You? Voices of Mixed-Race Young People*. New York: Holt, 1999.

Glusker, Susannah Joel. *Anita Brenner: A Mind of Her Own*. Austin, TX: University of Texas Press, 1998.

Golden, Kristen, and Barbara Findlen. *Making a Difference: 100 Remarkable Women of the Twentieth Century*. New York: Michael Friedman Publishing Group, 1998.

Goleman, Daniel. *Emotional Intelligence: Why It Can Matter More Than IQ*. New York: Bantam Books, 1995.

Gonzales, Juan L., Jr. *The Lives of Ethnic Americans*, 2nd ed. Dubuque, IA: Kendall/Hunt, 1994.

Hampden-Turner, Charles M., and Fons Trompenaars. *Building Cross-Cultural Competence: How to Create Wealth from Conflicting Values*. New Haven, CT: Yale University Press, 2000.

Henderson, George. *Cultural Diversity in the Workplace: Issues and Strategies*. Westport, CT: Greenwood Publishing Group, 1994.

Hockenberry, John. *Moving Violations: War Zones, Wheelchairs and Declarations of Independence*. New York: Hyperion, 1995.

Hull, Gloria, Patricia Bell Scott, and Barbara Smith (eds.). *All the Women Are White, All the Blacks Are Men, but Some of Us Are Brave*. Old Westbury, NY: Feminist Press, 1982.

Immerso, Michael. *Newark's Little Italy*. Piscataway, NJ: Rutgers University Press, 1997.

Jackson, Phil, and Hugh Delehanty. *Sacred Hoops*. New York: Hyperion, 1995.

Jackson, Susan (ed.). *Diversity in Work Teams: Research Paradigms for a Changing Workplace*. Washington, DC: American Psychological Association, 1996.

Jennings, Kevin (ed.). *Becoming Visible: A Reader in Gay and Lesbian History for High School and College Students*. Los Angeles: Alyson Publications, 1994.

Jordan, Judith, Stephen Bergman, Cynthia Garcia Coll, Natalie Eldridge, Julie Mencher, and Jean Baker Miller. *Women's Growth in Diversity*. Wellesley, MA: Wellesley College Center for Research on Women, 1997.

Kaplan, Justin, and Anne Bernays. *The Language of Names: What We Call Ourselves and Why It Matters*. New York: Simon & Schuster, 1997.

Katz, Judith. *White Awareness: Handbook for Anti-racism Training*. Norman, OK: University of Oklahoma Press, 1978.

Katz, Neil H., and John W. Lawyer. *Communication and Conflict Resolution Skills*. Dubuque, IA: Kendall/Hunt, 1992.

Katz, Phyllis. *Towards the Elimination of Racism*. New York: Pergamon Press, 1976.

Kennedy, Randall. *Nigger: The Strange Career of a Troublesome Word*. New York: Pantheon, 2002.

Kim, Elaine H., and Eui-Young Yu. *East to America: Korean American Life Stories*. New York: New Press, 1997.

Landau, Sy, Barbara Landau, and Daryl Landau. *From Conflict to Creativity: How Resolving Workplace Disagreements Can Inspire Innovation and Productivity*. San Francisco: Jossey-Bass, 2001.

Lanker, Brian. *I Dream a World*. New York: Stewart, Tabori and Chang, 1989.

Lewis, John. *Walking With the Wind*. New York: Simon & Schuster, 1998.

Lewis, Reginald, and Blair S. Walker. *Why Should White Guys Have All the Fun?* New York: John Wiley & Sons, 1995.

Linton, Simi. *Claiming Disability: Knowledge and Identity*. New York: New York University Press, 1998.

Liu, Eric. *The Accidental Asian*. New York: Random House, 1998.

Macleod, Jay. *Ain't No Makin' It*. Boulder, CO: Westview, 1995.

McBride, James. *The Color of Water: A Black Man's Tribute to His White Mother*. New York: Berkley Publishing Group, 1996.

McCall, Nathan. *Makes Me Wanna Holler*. New York: Vintage Books, 1995.

McIntosh, Peggy. *White Privilege and Male Privilege: A Personal Account of Coming to See Correspondences through Work in Women's Studies*. Working Paper 189. Wellesley, MA: Wellesley College Center for Research on Women, 1988.

Mfume, K., and R. Stodghill. *No Free Ride*. New York: Ballantine Books, 1996.

Minerbrook, Scott. *Divided to the Vein: A Journey Into Family and Race*. San Diego, CA: Harcourt Brace & Co., 1996.

Mintz, Steven (ed.). *Native American Voices: A History and Anthology*. Saint James, NY: Brandywine Press, 1995.

Morrison, Toni. *The Bluest Eye*. New York: Holt, Rinehart & Winston, 1970.

Nieto, Sonia. *Affirming Diversity: The Sociopolitical Context of Multicultural Education*. White Plains, NY: Longman, 1992.

O'Hearn, Claudine Chiawei (ed.). *Half and Half: Writers On Growing Up Biracial and Bicultural*. New York: Pantheon Books, 1998.

Okwu, Julian C. R. *Face Forward: Young African American Men in a Critical Age*. San Francisco: Chronicle Books, 1997.

Parks, Gordon. *The Learning Tree*. New York: Harper & Row, 1963.

The Project on Campus Community and Diversity of the Accrediting Commission for Senior Colleges and Universities of the Western Association of Schools and Colleges. *Dialogues for Diversity: Community and Ethnicity on Campus*. Phoenix, AZ: Oryx Press, 1994.

Ramos, Jorge. *The Other Face of America: Chronicles of the Immigrants Shaping Our Future*. New York: HarperCollins, 2002.

Roberts, Bari-Ellen (with Jack E. White). *Roberts vs. Texaco: A True Story of Race and Corporate America*. New York: Avon Books, 1998.

Roberts, Ralph. *Genealogy via the Internet*. Alexander, NC: Alexander Books, 1997.

Rodriguez, Richard. *Days of Obligation: An Argument with My Mexican Father*. New York: Viking, 1992.

Santiago, Esmeralda. *Almost a Woman*. Reading, MA: Perseus Books, 1998.

Santiago, Esmeralda. *When I Was Puerto Rican*. New York: Vintage Books, 1994.

Santos, John Phillip. *Places Left Unfinished at the Time of Creation*. New York: Viking, 2000.

Scales-Trent, Judy. *Notes of a White Black Woman*. University Park, PA: Pennsylvania State University Press, 2001.

Senna, Danny. *Caucasia*. New York: Riverhead Books, 1999.

Shinagawa, Larry Hajime, and Michael Jang. *Atlas of American Diversity*. Thousand Oaks, CA: Sage Publications, 1998.

Shorris, Earl. *Latinos: A Biography of the People*. New York: W.W. Norton, 1992.

Sims, Ronald R., and Robert F. Dennehy (eds.). *Diversity and Differences in Organizations: An Agenda for Answers and Questions*. Westport, CT: Quorum Books, 1993.

Slevin, Kathleen, and C. Ray Wingrove. *From Stumbling Blocks to Stepping Stones: The Life Experiences of Fifty Professional African American Women*. New York: New York University Press, 1998.

Sosa, Lionel. *The American Dream: How Latinos Can Achieve Success in Business and in Life*. New York: E.P. Dutton, 1998.

Soukhanov, Anne. *Encarta World English Dictionary*. New York: St. Martin's Press, 1999.

Stalvey, Lois. *The Education of a WASP*. Madison: University of Wisconsin Press, 1989.

Stavans, Ilan. *The Hispanic Condition: Reflections on Culture and Identity in America*. New York: HarperCollins, 1995.

Suro, Robert. *Strangers Among Us: How Latino Immigration Is Transforming America*. New York: Alfred A. Knopf, 1998.

Suskind, Ron. *A Hope in the Unseen*. New York: Broadway Books, 1998.

Takaki, Ronald. *A Different Mirror: A History of Multicultural America*. Boston: Little, Brown, 1993.

Takaki, Ronald. *A Larger Memory: A History of Our Diversity, with Voices*. Boston: Little, Brown, 1998.

Tannen, Deborah. *You Just Don't Understand: Women and Men in Conversation*. New York: William Morrow, 1990.

Tatum, Beverly Daniel. *Why Are All the Black Kids Sitting Together in the Cafeteria? And Other Conversations about Racial Identity.* New York: HarperCollins, 1997.

Terkel, Studs. *Coming of Age: The Story of Our Century by Those Who've Lived It.* New York: New Press, 1995.

Terkel, Studs. *Race.* New York: New Press, 1992.

Thomas, Roosevelt. *Beyond Race and Gender.* New York: American Management Association, 1991.

Verburg, Carol. *Making Contact: Readings from Home and Abroad.* Boston: Bedford Books, 1997.

Walker, Rebecca. *Black, White, and Jewish: Autobiography of a Shifting Self.* New York: Riverhead Books, 2002.

Walters, Mary. *Ethnic Options: Choosing Identities in America.* Berkeley, CA: University of California Press, 1990.

West, Cornel. *Race Matters.* New York: Vintage Books, 1993.

Wiesel, Elie. *Night.* New York: Bantam Books, 1987.

Williams, Gregory. *Life on the Color Line: The True Story of a White Boy Who Discovered He Was Black.* New York: NAL/Dutton, 1996.

Wiseman, Richard, and Robert Shuter (eds.). *Communicating in Multinational Organizations.* Thousand Oaks, CA: Sage Publications, 1994.

Wood, Julia. *Gendered Lives: Communication, Gender, and Culture.* Belmont, CA: Wadsworth, 1998.

Wymard, Ellie. *Conversations with Uncommon Women.* New York: AMACOM, 1999.

X, Malcolm. *The Autobiography of Malcolm X.* New York: Ballantine Books, 1992.

Zuckerman, Amy J., and George Simons. *Sexual Orientation in the Workplace: Gay Men, Lesbians, Bisexuals, and Heterosexuals Working Together.* Thousand Oaks, CA: Sage Publications, 1996.

Index